Tricky Imp Publishers
Old Post Office, Main Road,
South Reston, Louth. Lincolnshire. LN11 8JQ

www.trickyimppublishing.co.uk
www.acertainsummer.co.uk

This Edition Published June 2012.

ISBN 978-0-9572668-0-3

Cover design Peter Gray
Cover artwork John Brookes

Printed and bound in the UK by MPG Books Group Ltd.

Thanks go to everyone who supported the book.

Special thanks go to my parents who helped in many ways.
and to
Barbara Jane Gray
whose tenacity and unfailing belief in the story made Sam's
world a reality.

In Memory of K.B.

A Certain Summer

Peter Gray

Tricky Imp Publishing

INTRODUCTION

What is it about our past that intrigues us? What mental mechanics cause us to remember unremarkable facts in a way that we consider them to be far better than they really were? Were the skies really that blue? Was the sun always out and did the summers really last for ten months? Obviously they didn't but the human mind always looks for a reason to hope, a hope that better days will once again return. A hope that 'our lot' will improve and life is still worth living.

Why is it so, that when we look back into our past, we almost always consider times of hardship and firmly place rose tinted pince-nez on the bridge of our collective noses to view those long expired days? Maybe we wouldn't if life was one long party with every day full of new experiences and happy times. But it is not, so we dream of happy times when things are not going quite so well. We then embellish those thoughts with attributes and emotions that probably were not present at the time, evolving the recollection into a 'soup' of a memory rather than an accurate recall of what actually happened. It's what makes us human and allows us to develop, being so very important that sometimes, they overlap into our dreams.

More importantly, memories are something to warm your hands on during a cold winters morning, as you wonder if summer will ever return. They are scented with the aroma of cut grass and home cooking, packed full of the sounds of a different era. They can make us smile, they can make us cry but without them we are lost.

Inevitably, a great deal of these memories are from our early lives but we all have very different memories of our childhood, for some, they are traumatic and even tragic, to others, they are sweet and innocent. Which ever type of memories you have, they will be firmly lodged in the mind, constantly nudging and sometimes even deciding what we do in our lives,

9

where to go, what we wear and who to spend our time with. These formative years seem to mould our characters as adults and go a great way into making us what we are and who we will become.

Not everyone will see their childhood as special, not everyone will want to be reminded of those years but if you were lucky enough to have any fond memories of those times, then rejoice in the fact that you can smile, and then regret that they can never be returned to you. Or, not in any tangible way at least.

This story concerns a young lad whose name was Sam, or rather it wasn't but for the sake of this story, he shall be known as Sam, as this was his 'nickname' for some of those years. He was born in the nineteen fifties and lived his childhood throughout the sixties in a rural, working class hamlet in a corner of north east Derbyshire, right in the depths of the Midland's coal fields. This hamlet was called Highfields but you will not find it on any map, it was swallowed up years ago by the main village in the parish although to the people that still live there from those times, it is still known as Highfields.

Sam and his friends played out their lives there in that certain summer, not just one summer but many, all of them blending into one long season through the nineteen sixties. Innocence and naiveté are the directors of this play, the script is from life, the players were real and the places, well, the places have almost disappeared as they originally were in those days from long ago but they still survive in another form, as the 'Five Pits Trail'.

For now, this story still lives, for it is written in every mind of each of the people who were there, and when they are gone, it will exist in this simple tome alone. So for now, let us roll back the beats of our hearts, let us slide back the doors to the past and step through into a place where the skylark sings her watery tunes, where dandelion clocks fly though the air thicker than porridge and where children's laughter jingles like some magical wind chime in the distance. Back, to a time of innocence, back to the past, back to 'A Certain Summer'.

P. Gray. Feb 2012

One morning, in a certain summer, a wary eye peeped out from a crumpled heap of linen that was once a bed. The eye scanned the four walls of a bedroom. Not just any bedroom but one that revealed an horizon of pictures and posters, mostly of indigenous bird life and animals with a smattering of the fauna of Africa. Model airplanes festooned the ceiling, hovering above pieces of junk, varying in their state of distastefulness, randomly scattered around the moderately large room. In one corner, sat a toy dog that was made at a time somewhat previous to legislation that stated that 'bits of sharp wire and old straw could not be included in toy manufacture'. This was hinted upon by the way bits of sharp wire and old straw were thrusting their way through the outer skin, like newly budding snowdrops.

From the old sash window, the stark glare of the obscene sun thrust into the room totally uninvited and yet its presence heralded a new day in which much mischief could be conjured, if only the eye that peered from the pile of linen was complete. Soon, it was joined by its twin and then without warning, a nose appeared. A mouth revealed itself, then, as if by magic, a whole face could be seen and growing from the top of this face was a mass of dishevelled hair, the likes of which would make a self respecting comb or brush scream and run for cover. Not that any such equipment could be seen to be tortured in such a horrific manner.

All these fractions drew together to form a head, which unkindly had to face the cruel world. Hung beneath the head, was the body of a boy known to his friends as 'Sam', and to his mother as 'Little Toe Rag,' though neither were his real name. His mother, of course, thought that he was made of pure gold and cherished her only son but Sam saw through a different kaleidoscope and told everyone that he was adopted, that his real parents were very rich and probably royalty, and that they had been killed before he was born, in a strange experiment hushed up by the government.

It was the first day of the summer school holidays, the fun season had just begun; so had the end of the world, as far as the hamlet of 'Highfields' was concerned. How had this tiny settlement brought upon itself such havoc and mayhem? What unwritten law had its people transgressed? Nothing, as far as its inhabitants could see but Sam and his many friends saw the summer holidays as 'Grown-up Baiting Season' and the Hamlet was about to feel their presence. They would have to act smartly though, as all children knew the summer holidays seemed an everlasting six weeks to adults but time passes quickly to a child when it is diluted with mischief. All too soon it is just a memory. But for now there was plenty of time and so, the body, still hung beneath the head of Sam, walked into the bathroom to use the lavatory. The sink was ignored, being a token of parental domination over his childhood rights. Its only recognition being a quick glare as he gave it the contempt it deserved. He dressed quickly, if not tidily, sporting a dark green polo shirt and some very faded and slightly oversized blue jeans, complete with 'grow into' turn-ups. The whole ensemble was finished off with grey socks and black plimsolls. He then descended the stairs slowly, beginning a metamorphosis that would change him from boy, to something that most adults would see as slightly less than human. The head began to grin as the mind entombed within toyed with the idea of being alone and having control over this body for so long, with no teachers and for the most part, no adults to 'brick-in' his animal instincts for adventure and exploration. It would be hours before Sam's parents would return from their place of work to replace the verbal collar and leash he had just cast aside. Breakfast would be quick - an odd mixture of anything he liked coupled with what he could find; such as corn flakes and golden syrup or milk with sugar in, and then he was off outside. The sun was as warm as its promise, golden kissed and as soothing as treacle pudding, and Sam was soon walking in its radiance past his old 'trolley'. Trolleys were the only suitable transport for children, a rough frame of timber with four pram wheels or similar and a doubtful steering mechanism; the kind of vehicle the Americans annoyingly call 'soap box carts'. Sam considered that soap came in a paper wrapping not a box, though soap had very little interest to Sam. The trolley was ignored this morning as he continued down the garden path towards the converted 'out house'- the colloquial name for a brick utility building, at the end of the garden. This was the 'Black Hand Gangs' headquarters. The history of the Serbian Black Hand Gang was irrelevant and unknown to Sam and his friends, as they had chosen the name purely as an identifiable badge of office. If the Serbian branch had ultimately started the First World War, it was no concern of Sam's. He wasn't there, he hadn't even been born. His troubles were more pressing than the assassination of Franz Ferdinand. After all, a note had been delivered some days previously, challenging the Black Hand Gang to a battle. The note had been delivered unseen and it was signed, "The Red Lion Club". When all the members of the Black Hand Gang (Derbyshire Chapter) arrived, the meeting was officially opened. The leader, who was Sam's cousin, known as Chapper, addressed the assembled members: Sam and a chubby lad called Vernon. The boys didn't know how many people constituted a 'Gang' but three seemed the optimum number to them, particularly as it was impossible to get any more into the tiny gang headquarters.

"Shall we fight 'em or not?" asked Chapper.

"Yeah, lets get 'em." cried Vern.

"We'll kill 'em." called Sam.

This kind of short, shock banter was usual, even when not at war, but today, the gang being at DEVCON 3, decided there was little else to say and the meeting was closed. There was nothing more to discuss on the matter, the membership was unanimous; well they all agreed at any rate. A letter was sent to the headquarters of the Red Lion Club.

To the red lion club.
Yes we do want a fight
and if you do too you come
this afternoon with your gang
if you do. Black Hand Gang.

 The letter was signed by drawing a crude but effective black hand in the bottom right hand corner of the reply and then it was deposited into the Red Lion Club's back garden, with the help of a crude form of mail transport, known locally as 'half a brick'. When this had been done and someone had been observed reading the missive, the Black Hand Gang collected their weapons from the recesses of the converted outhouse. Inside, the walls were painted with the white, powdery, lime material that, with the slightest movement when dry, rains down like a freak snowstorm. In one corner stood a stool, in another was an upturned beer crate, long since emptied, skilfully providing the service of a seat. Having just two seats in a gang of three was an excellent way of assuring promptness at meetings, as the last to arrive sat on the cold, snow littered floor.
Most of their weapons lay behind the door. Chapper picked up a short wooden sword and a whip, the whip being his favourite weapon and his trademark. Sam had a sword and a shield, the shield relinquishing its former life as a large saucepan lid. Vern picked up his trusty spear - a cane with a rusty bolt hammered in the end. Their swords were barely more than simple, wooden crosses sharpened on the long end, "exactly the same as the ones used in the crusades and the Battle of Hastings". Sam even told a story that King Harold actually carried a wooden sword like his, probably even the same one, as iron hadn't been invented in 'the olden days'.
        "Do you think they'll turn up?" asked Vern as they stood on the Backs.
The 'Backs' was a rough dirt track that ran behind the houses, parallel to the main road. It was a basic access road to the coalhouses and dustbin areas for service vehicles and also for the only two private motor vehicles on the street, allowing them to enter the only two garages. It had been the domain of the local children since anyone could remember and was to remain so until the motorcar became an essential for every household and thus, altered the neighbourhood out of all proportion. The name 'Backs'

was short for 'backs of the houses' but it became a noun and was commonly pronounced 'bax' rather than 'backs'.

"Naaa, they're probably too scared." replied Chapper, just as several figures appeared at the top of the slight hill on the Backs.

The Red Lion Club usually consisted of the two Shand brothers, Ben and Breen, and from time to time, one other who, due to arguments, constantly changed. Breen was the younger but no one really knew why he was called Breen. The most probable explanation was that his real name was Brian and if you squinted and covered you ears with your hands, 'Brian' sounded like 'Breen'. Breen had a very famous claim to fame, not on the standards of "Henry the Eighth single-handedly tried to ruin the English millinery trade," or "Hitler was the proud owner of just a single testicle," but in the village of Highfields, he was the only boy who tried to catch a cricket ball with his eye. The aforementioned eye had been in such a terrible mess that if he had been an adult he could have 'dined out on it' for months, well probably not, as it would have put the other diners off - but I think the point is made. In Highfields he was famous for it.

On this occasion, however, the Red Lion Club's normal complement of two or three had increased to five. In addition to Ben and Breen, there were three other boys. The first two additions were cousins of the Shand brothers, obviously visiting at exactly the right time. The fifth member was an older boy known as 'Wilbur', he was the ultimate gang member because his maturity gave him a physical, if not mental advantage over everyone else.

Ranged against them were the members of the Black Hand Gang - lithe, eager and ready for anything. Well almost anything: neither Vern nor Sam were tall and Chapper, who was older than they, had come by his nickname due to his diminutive stature. Chapper was a corruption of 'Little Chap', so it was plain for everyone to see the Red Lion Club had a considerable advantage in size, height and numbers. As the five slowly descended the slight hill towards the Black Hand Gang, there was an air of anticipation. There was also a lot of white powder on the heads of the Black Hand Gang and on the trousers of Vern, who had been the last to arrive at HQ that morning! The two gangs stood and faced each other. Sam thought it was like the gunfight at the OK Corral. Doc Chapper with Sam Earp and The Vern Kid, ready to blast their enemies into oblivion.

"The heat of the noon day sun raged down into the old coral at the end of Dodge City, dust clouds swirled in angry phantoms. Sam Earp noticed the leather loop on one of the desperado's holster was casually flicked off the hammer of his gun. Sam peered out from under his Stetson in the blinding light of the dry Kansas sky, sweat rolling slowly down from his brow, tickling his face and stinging as it flowed into his eyes.

Somewhere over by the livery stable, a horse stamped its feet impatiently and above, a buzzard slowly circled, as if waiting for the outcome of the fight. Sam wondered if it would be feasting on his bones that night. The gunman on the right was slowly but perceptively raising his shotgun, Sam Earp saw it but he also noticed the one in the long leather coat twitch his gun hand. They were out numbered and out gunned but Sam weighed the odds, he would draw on the leather coat and then turn to gun down the shotgun, he just hoped the Doc and the Kid could deal with the other two away to the left. Whoever had bullets left would have to deal with the giant in the middle with the Winchester. With a lightning reaction he drew his Colt and fired at the one in the leather coat."

Vern and Chapper looked on in amazement as Sam suddenly thrust out his hand as if he was going to offer a handshake and then, just as quickly returned it to the hilt of his sword that was thrust into his snake belt. The Red Lions saw this as their chance. One large boot stepped forward but Chapper was ready, he pulled back his whip and lashed out at Wilbur. It had fallen short and Wilbur put his large foot on the end of the string. After just one attempt to release it, Chapper looked sheepishly up at the huge frame of Wilbur and admitted.

"Okay, you win." And the battle was over. It certainly wasn't a battle to be listed in 'Cassell's History of Britain' but, the Red Lions left in victory and the defeat was a shattering blow to the Black Hand's morale, it was unlikely that they would be able to recover after this devastating loss.

"I wonder what's for tea?" asked Vern.

"Nothing for me until my Mam comes home." replied Sam, remembering that he had polished off all the good things for breakfast. Chapper rallied his troops.

"Come on, let's attack them at their base."

"There's too many of them." replied Vern. "an' they have probably set traps."

"Well let's go round and see what we can do." insisted Chapper. The gang duly 'went round' to the Backs across the main road, where a similar arrangement existed on the other, the south side of the street. As they approached the Red Lion Club headquarters, Chapper noticed two union flags on large poles.

"Them flags, them Union Jacks," he said quietly. "Let's sneak up and nick 'em." So, with the swiftness and agility of three leopards they began their attack.

"Captain Sam Samuel of the famed Commandos, briefed his squad earlier in the morning about what they had to do. It was risky walking straight into the Russian Camp to steal plans for a new battle tank but someone

had to do it. Now they were close, just through the barbed wire and past the aircraft hanger and there it was, the secret bunker where the plans were kept.

"Sergeant Chapper, you and Private Vern steal one of those flags to show the Ruskies that we have been here, whilst I break into the bunker and take the plans. If I don't make it, take the flag back to HQ." Sergeant Chapper saluted and silently leapt onto the top of the high security bunker followed by Private Vern. Sam soon found the plans, they were disguised as a small, almost pure black, block but he knew what it was, the plans were etched onto that solid block of Antirillium and it would take his eagle eyes to decode it later. He had to make it back to HQ, he just had to...."

Chapper grabbed one of the flags complete with pole, jumped down off the coalbunker and began to run, followed closely by Sam and Vern, Sam, tightly holding a large lump of coal.

As they ran down the Backs with the steamy sun blazing down on them, Chapper's checked shirt was open and blowing in the slight summer breeze, his small arms straining with the flag pole and his face covered with a grin of delight.

They returned to their headquarters with the prize and hid it in the hedge bottom behind their HQ.

"What are we going to do with it?" asked Vern.

"Don't know," replied Chapper with a grin. "but they won't get it back, that's for sure."

"What now then?" asked Sam.

"We have to make plans for defence. We probably need to build a barricade up to the garden gate."

"I don't think me dad will be too pleased about that, 'specially if the dustbins don't get emptied."

"Well traps then, we'll build traps." insisted Chapper.

"How?" asked Vern.

"We need string, lots of it. We can then tie the string to the pole.... er... then we can run the string up there." Chapper pointed above their HQ. "Yeah that's it and then we can put something 'eavy up there so that when they take the pole it all falls on them." Chapper stood with his hands on his hips, as if the job was already complete but he could see the other two had doubts. "Trip wires then."

"What about me da...." began Sam but Chapper interrupted raising his hands. "Yeah, ... what if your dad trips on it." Chapper looked around for inspiration. He held a finger skyward. "Camouflage" he grinned. " that's what we need."

"What?" grinned Vern feeling sure it was a made up word.

"You are so thick Vern, camouflage! It means making something look like what it's not." The two boys just stared at him. He continued. "It's like, if you had something like ...... er... some sweets that you didn't want anyone to find, you could camouflage them to look like something else."

"Why not just eat them?" asked Sam with Vern nodding in agreement.

"Well not sweets then, lets say ...... er...." Chapper thought for a moment and then said with conviction. "Let's imagine you found an air pistol but your mother wouldn't let you keep it, you would have to hide it right?" Chapper paused to see if the two boys were keeping up, he wasn't sure but he continued anyway. "Okay, so if you had to hide it you would camouflage it so that if anyone came across it they would think it was something else." There was a moment's pause and then Vern said.

"Like sweets?" Once the image of sweets entered the lads' head, it took a great deal to dislodge them. Usually, only another food image would do it.

"No, not like sweets." spat Chapper with frustration. "Like a tree, or bush or ... or..." he was looking around for something better. "A .... a .....er.... oh I don't know, let me show you, get some leaves and twigs." The other two boys looked at each other and shrugged but gathered some leaves as Chapper had asked. Chapper then covered the pole and the flag roughly but it wasn't great.

"There, that is camouflage," he said with a smile.

"It's just covered up," Vern pointed out.

"Yes, stupid it's covered up but you call it camouflage."

"Shouldn't it be camoflagged?" sniggered Vern, Sam joined in the laugh, until Chapper clipped them both on the head and went into the HQ to calm down.

Later that evening, the three went home with pride with their days work. Pride that they had lost a battle but not the war. Sam entered his home to the usual ritual at that time of evening.

"Where the hell have you been? Don't you know I have been going daft looking for you? You better have your supper and get off to bed."

"I was here, I was camoflogged." pointed out Sam.

"Don't get cheeky with me my lad." replied his mother with a lengthy tirade of what he should and shouldn't do but Sam heard none of it. On entering the house, his hearing became terribly bad on most occasions. His speech also became dubious, answering all with an "Errrr."

"Go and get a wash before you have your supper." continued his mother. Sam plodded his way up the stairs and across the upstairs landing to the bathroom. There, he ran hot water in the sink, prodded the liquid with his left index finger and picked up a face cloth with the other hand. He then spat on the dry cloth and rubbed his face. The now dirty cloth was cast aside.

"That'll do." he said, looking into the mirror as if he had made a difference. He entered the bedroom and reached into his pocket and pulled out a lump of coal.

"I'll decode that later." he smiled to himself dropping the lump on the bed.

Armed with an old comic from his bedroom, he descended the stairs to the pit of interrogation below. He then ate his supper and waited for the inevitable to happen.

"Bed!" Just one word, that's all. One word from Sam's mother and he began the long drawn out process that happened this time every night.

"Ohh not yet, let me read for a bit."

"Half an hour then and that's all." she replied. Sam settled into the corner of the settee and buried his head inside the comic. The half hour soon grew into a whole one and eventually, Sam's mother took away his comic and he realised he must retire.

"Alright, but can I listen to my radio for a bit?" He didn't really need to ask, it was just rebellion against the fact that he had to go to bed. His radio was stuffed between his pillows and was left on almost every night. Not that he was awake all night. He would sleep just as well even if there had been a motorcycle scramble arranged in his bedroom. As he slept and dreamed of secret missions, a lump of coal was tightly encased in his hand, depositing small dark stains on the bed sheets.

The next morning the routine was exactly the same. He woke to the sound of many excited birds dancing on the guttering, ensuring that any self-respecting boy could not sleep any later than ten o' clock. The washbasin was avoided with his usual determination and he staggered down the stairs into the cold living room. Sam reflected for a moment as to why it was that, no matter how warm it was outside, living rooms were always cold in the morning. As soon as he was dressed, he went out and sat on the lawn in the sunshine and examined the lump of coal, which had accompanied him through his dream-world adventures and through breakfast. When he was bored with that, he cast the coal into the shrubs and sat on the Backs in the sunshine. This pastime had never been very interesting to Sam and after sitting on the pavement in the sunshine as well as other various place including the front wall, the dustbin and the roof of the outside toilet, the boredom forced him to go to the Black Hand Gang HQ, there he decided to have a look at the flag they had recently acquired.

"Mmm, that camoflog works really well; I can't see it at all this morning." thought Sam. He moved his hand around in the dry leaves and

18

dead grass but he couldn't feel the metal pole, or the fabric of the flag. Sam considered that Chapper had a very unusual skill in this 'camoflogging', because no matter how hard he looked, Sam just couldn't find it. He even considered that Chapper had got up earlier that morning and changed it into a tree or a wall but cast that consideration aside when he remembered that Chapper slept even later than Sam. There was only one other explanation, it simply wasn't there.

"The thieving gits." grunted Sam, forgetting the exact circumstances of how the Black Hand Gang had acquired it.

Later in the day, Chapper arrived and informed Sam that Vern had become a traitor and returned the prize to the Red Lion Club. Well that was it, Vern was out of the gang and all remaining members would have their own seat at the meetings. A gang of two had its problems though, particularly when voting was required and so, ultimately, it meant the demise of the Black Hand Gang. The problem now was that Sam needed a gang to affirm his skills as a warrior. He liked to display his adeptness at sword fencing and conkers, the way he could knock a beans tin off a post at twenty feet with one marble or a similar sized stone from his catapult. The way he could make a sound by squeezing his hands together, and especially the way he could spit into a piece of broken drainpipe from the top of old man Herriot's coal house. All these skills had to be used, so he had no choice in what to do next. It was sad but inevitable, he joined the Red Lion Club but was a little disappointed when he found out they had no entry exam. They didn't even want to see how far he could skim a dried cowpat. Nevertheless, he soon settled in and for some reason that he couldn't quite understand, he was christened Corporal Clot.

The Red Lion Club was a little different to the other gangs he had been in. Not renowned for throwing stones at other gangs or playing 'Knock and Run' and other anti-adult games, this gang actually did things *for* grown ups. At the time Sam joined they were putting together a new play, which would be performed for certain invited adults. This was strange to Sam and he had no idea what it was all about but he went along with it for the time being. He was told he was to be the Producer and would be working with Ben, the oldest member of the gang and the Director of the play. The only thing Sam knew about production was the fact that it began with the same letter as pound, and the word pound interested him immensely. So there he began his first job on the stage. Ironically it was not to be his last.

By now, the Red Lion Club had expanded. Besides Ben and Breen, who was a teller of stories, there included, 'Tools', the set designer, the Shand's cousins, who sang, and another brand new recruit, called Norman. He was to be the ventriloquist but his one and only dummy performed its debut in a dustbin.

The show passed off smoothly. It wasn't exactly Chekhov and it wasn't terribly long but the arena was packed to capacity with all four seats taken, though the 40-watt bulb that lit the stage was a mite underpowered. Sam was very good at producing. Although being in charge of the curtains did not seem much like a pound or producing, whatever that was.

"Maybe the pound is what I'll get," he wrongly thought to himself. After the show, the Red Lion Club's shed was quickly turned back into the fortress it had once been. On a wall were hung catapults, on a shelf by the doors, were stacked various stink bombs and mud bombs, on the bench was a milk bottle full of cow dung, which had the precise and technical name of 'Shit Bomb'. This was more like old times to Sam, who now considered that the curtain operation had been worth it, just so he could go back to being in a proper gang. These precautions were necessary though, as a rival gang had set up on this, the south side of the street, just a little further down the road. The gang was called 'The Highwaymen' and it was run by a local rogue, called 'Barmy', backed by his younger brother 'Weeparina' and a giddy and highly strung boy called Byron, who was inevitably nicknamed 'Biro'. Tools had overheard them planning an attack on the Red Lion Club's HQ. Tools, was the Red Lion Club technical advisor, sometimes called Toolman and Sam struck up a friendship with this lad that endured for many years. Tools could repair anything. Split cricket bats were nailed back together, broken trolleys were lashed with rope and punctures in bicycle wheels were repaired by removing the spent inner-tube and stuffing grass into the tyres. He was also the fastest thing on three wheels, having a speedy little tricycle. This annoyed Sam because the previous Christmas, Sam's mother had bought him a new blue tricycle which sported a picture of 'Wee Willie Winky' which had a working rear boot, just like a motorcar and real blow up tyres but still it didn't go as fast as Tools' 'Red Bomber'. Something had to be done, it was, Sam had a terrible crash, only just escaped with his life. Sheer miracle he didn't lose an arm. They shouldn't put concrete posts outside back garden gates. Pity about Tools' bike. Never mind; it could have been worse, it could have been Sam's bike.

Three members of the Red Lion Club, namely Ben, Breen and Sam sat on the Shand's back garden, as bored as a cannibal at a vegetarian's convention. Only after much sighing and throwing of small pebbles at nothing in particular, did Ben put forward a suggestion.

"Let's go on the Tip and see if anyone's there." The other two looked totally expressionless but they stood, walked out of the back gate and off towards the Tip. The 'Tip' was a very old red shale tip covered in many different types of flora, to the extent that the shale could now only be seen where holes had been dug. On its very top, which wasn't particularly high, it sported a small, makeshift football pitch, a makeshift cricket pitch, a makeshift scramble track, makeshift 'dens' of various guises and something that was very makeshift but was referred to as, The Slide. The Slide was the steep northern bank, where fine but sturdy grass grew along with horsetail grass, which allowed the more adventurous children to slide down the bank on makeshift cardboard sleds or a makeshift car bonnet from the scrap yard, sited at the back of the Tip. The whole Tip was makeshift but it was a children's paradise, hardly ever invaded by adults. If anything, most of their world was either makeshift or Heath-Robinson but, as the boys could never remember the phrase Heath-Robinson, they had a makeshift phrase for Heath-Robinson, which was 'makeshift'. It was also a common ritual for the Tip to be set on fire at least once a week in the summer, so it was advisable not to sleep there or you may find yourself being carried away on a makeshift stretcher to a makeshift coffin. The three boys walked down the Tip path, past the locally famous 'Big Tree' and onto the Tip by the main path. As there were no other people around, they decided to try the slide. There was no suitable cardboard around, so they tried to slide down on their backsides but this became somewhat painful and began to dye their clothes pale green. They found a small piece of metal which was equally painful, as it was a horrible shape for sliding. Sam gave up but Breen, being made of sterner stuff, tried to slide down standing up. This was a complete failure and nearly lost him part of his spinal column when he hit the ridge halfway down. Ben said he had an idea.

"Let's see if we can find anything over at the scrap yard at the back of the tip." This scrap yard comprised a tall, makeshift compound made from corrugated tin sheets and was sited on an area of waste ground at the rear of the shale tip. From here, a man, who was rarely seen, seemed to collect parts of vehicles and for no apparent reason, pull them to bits and throw them out on the lower level of the tip near the railway line. The boys, therefore thought that searching the scrap yard was a good idea and making the short trek to it, were soon in possession of an excellent substitute sled. It was an old truck bonnet, the 'bull-nose' type which, when inverted, makes an excellent 'bob sled'. They dragged the bonnet into place at the top of the slide and faced the bull nose part pointing down the slope. Making themselves as comfortable as possible, they pushed it along with their hands until it moved over the ridge of the steep slope and it began the terrible journey down the side of the Tip. Never in their lives had any of the boys undertaken a journey like it. As the sled came to an eventual rest at the bottom of the slope, they sat, blank and quiet, until Breen said.

"Wow! Let's have another go."

"You must be joking; I'm not doing that again." replied Ben.

"Well I want a go." put in Sam. He and Breen began to drag the heavy bonnet to the top of the slope. It took ages but this just made them more excited. Once again, they sat in the vehicle, before Ben leapt in and they pushed off once more to hurtle down the slope. After another twenty or so rides, this too became boring and very hard work, as Ben, it seemed, was sure he wasn't going on it anymore, so wouldn't help pull it back up the steep Tip side. Strange, how he always seemed to ride down though.

They decided to walk down to the railway line as they could hear a train in the distance. They crossed the line and sat on the stile waiting for the train to pass. It was usual for them to bet on whether the loco would be steam or diesel, though in recent years, steam locomotives had become rare and as this one had sounded its air horn, the mystery was over, as they now knew it was diesel powered.

"Let's bet on how many wagons it's pulling instead." suggested Breen.

"Okay." replied Ben and they all plunged their grubby hands into their equally grubby pockets. Each pulled out a statutory penknife. Breen also produced a small catapult and four ha'pennies. Sam presented three marbles, a penny and a ha'penny, a nail and a conker. Sam was always particular about what should be in a boy's pocket – a couple of coins and a penknife were essential but never a pen. Every boy should also have a marble or two, just in case an impromptu game was announced. The conker was an old one but had served well and he hadn't the heart to throw it away. It was called Tommy, though this was not its original name. It was once called Henry, on account of its having destroyed eight other conkers in combat. In the previous season however, it had reached twelve and Sam considered it needed a new name. The problem was, he didn't know any English kings who were 'the twelfth'. He had asked Chapper who, being older, could reasonably be assumed to be better versed in the names of kings than Sam was:

"Well there's Louis the 14th but that's more than twelve and he was French, I think." The reasoning was sound and Sam agreed that the name should be at least British. Chapper, not wanting to be beaten and seen to be without sound historical knowledge, decided to edge his bets.

"Tommy the twelfth, yep, King Tommy the twelfth that will do." Sam had frowned and admitted that he didn't know of that particular monarch but Chapper insisted his historical position came between Richard the Tenth and Queen Erica the Third. So the conker that lived a charmed life and was now called Tommy, had eventually expanded his 'kill count' to twenty but even Chapper thought that King Edward the Twentieth sounded hard to believe and Sam settled down the fact that Tommy the Conker was greater than all the kings and queens of England.

Ben was the most industrious of the three boys and therefore, the wealthiest. His pockets revealed a thre'penny bit, six marbles, a large ball-bearing and a matchbox containing a stink bomb. After Ben regaled them with unbelievable stories of the power of his stink bombs, they agreed on a stake and then each one suggested a number of wagons the train may be pulling. As the loco rounded the corner, slowly, very slowly, Ben stood and called out,

"Well, that had to happen, a loco with no wagons, no one gains anything."

"I can make you some money." said Breen.

"How?" asked Sam.

"If you give me a ha'penny I'll turn it into a penny for you." This seemed a very good profit margin, so Sam quickly handed him a halfpenny. Ben pointed out that he only had the three-penny piece.

"Will it turn into a tanner?" he asked.

"Um... Maybe even a two bob bit." replied Breen. Ben eagerly passed his brother the coin whilst Sam pondered the profit one could make if only one had the money to speculate. To the other boys' surprise, Breen placed both the coins on the railway line, on the top where it was most shiny.

"Why haven't you put your coin on there?" asked Ben in confusion, knowing his younger brother was always short of money.

"Err, well if you try to do too many it never seems to work," replied Breen, with a little reluctance. The loco eventually came closer and rumbled by, the driver shouting some obscenities at the boys, presumably because they were close to the track. These words however, went unheard, partly because of the tremendous noise and partly because the boys' attention was completely captivated by the Magical Money Making Rail. Sam was considering what he might be able to buy if he could turn his entire accumulated wealth of two and six into a five pound note. Immediately the loco had passed and once they were sure the driver wouldn't run back down the line, they ran to the position where the coins had been placed. Sam picked up his coin, it certainly was the same size as a penny but that's where the similarity ended. Firstly; it still said 'halfpenny' on it and secondly; it was only as thick as a gnat's leg. Ben fingered his coin. It felt warm but this two-shilling piece had nine sides and was bronze in colour, rather than silver. Ben and Sam chased Breen for quite a way over the tracks and back up the Tip.

"Can't you two take a joke?" screamed Breen but his protestations were cut short as he disappeared into the ground. Ben and Sam stopped in their tracks, was this another of his jokes? No, he couldn't have foreseen that. It was inconceivable that he could have arranged the whole morning just so he could disappear in front of their eyes, so the two of them scampered over to where he was last seen. There was a small hole that went vertically down, like a small well. The two boys were quite worried as they recalled a story told them by Barmy about the giant worms that live underground and eat people when they run about. Neither totally believed it, simply because Barmy had told the story but they were a little unsure as they closed in on the spot where Breen was last seen. The hole was just near the edge of the Tip, concealed by a large Elder bush. It looked like a long abandoned 'den' that someone must have dug and forgotten about. Dens were part of a long mining culture on the tip. Most boys had dug an underground den or two in their lives but most had fallen in soon after completion. The better-built ones lasted some time and the best ones endured so long, that they acquired names. There was Bottle Hole, so called because of the large amount of old bottles found as it was dug. There was 'Stinky Farts Hole' named after the boy that dug it. Of course, to consider that even the worst parent would name his or her son Stinky Fart is a nonsense - after all 'Stinky' is quite demeaning but he was known as Stinky Fart because of his aroma. Strangely, he was adept at digging underground dens, which was rather surprising, as no one would ever occupy one with him. And there was the most famous den, 'Willows Den', so named because it was concealed in the area where the willow herbs grew on the east side of the tip. It had the advantage of commanding an excellent view over their 'kingdom' and along the approach to the Tip.

The particular hole, in which Breen was now temporarily residing, was probably new though, as none of the three boys knew it was there, but Sam and Ben knelt and peered into the newly found pit. It was dark and cool and smelled of sweet earth and damp shale. In the gloom, they could just make out a dusty lump that looked like Breen's behind. Sam looked over to Ben.

"Is he dead?" he asked.

"Well if he is, his legs don't believe it." replied Ben. They looked back into the hole and sure enough, Breem's legs were moving and they seemed to be pushing him deeper into the hole.

"He's turned into a rabbit." added Sam. Ben sat up and said.

"We'll need a big hutch if he has." Sam leaned further into the hole and shouted to the body below.

"What exactly are you doing down there?"

"Watching." came the muffled reply.

"Watching what?" asked Sam.

"Watching two people through this other hole, but ..... I need .... to get a bit further in." explained the voice, in broken spurts as the legs tried again to push the body further in. Sam pulled his head from the hole and faced Ben, who was still reflecting on where he would put such a large hutch in their garden.

"He says there is another hole and he can see two people." explained Sam. Ben snapped out of his dream and pushed his upper body down the hole.

"Who can you see?" he asked. Breen waited a moment, then said in a muffled voice.

"It's Socky and Fat Debby." Socky was an older boy, a little larger than they. Debby needs no further explanation.

"I don't believe that you, Socky and Fat Debby are down this hole for one minute." said Ben.

"No, they're outside down the banking." replied Breen in a distant and now whispering voice that was difficult to hear. Ben quickly retracted his head from the hole, crawled the eight feet to the edge of the Tip and crouched behind another elder bush that grew there. Then he moved a few branches and peered through. Sam asked.

"What are you doing?"

"Shhhhh!" came Ben's reply with a finger to his lips. Then the same finger was used to beckon Sam over in the time honoured way. Sam didn't fully understand but hurried over to Ben's side and moved a branch, in order to get a better view. Down the steep bank in the bushes, at the rear of the small scrap yard, he saw Socky and Fat Debby. Socky received his name due to the fact that he always wore white plimsolls with white socks and looked like he was walking around with no shoes on. Debby's name seems harsh at first but this wasn't so. Yes, she was fat, but she was also ugly with horrible wiry hair. However, no one called her Fat, Ugly, Mop-Headed Debby. In fact no one called her Fat Debby to her face, unless they wanted to be punched by a big, fat, ugly girl called Deborah with a giant Brillo Pad on her head.

Sam knew what kissing was, even though he hadn't experienced 'that' sort of kiss because it was something adults did, not for the likes of him. Yes kissing held no mysteries, he had seen it on films and he had seen a girl called Dirty Eggy kiss his school mate Henry. Henry had explained the gruesome details to them all. Kissing was something that happened unfortunately and he had to live with it, so it was no surprise to see Socky affixed to the front of Fat Debby's head. The real surprise was why Socky would want to. Why anyone would want to be in the same scrap yard with her or even in the same village was a mystery to Sam, unless he was being held against his will, which didn't seem to be the case. He could understand that the older boys would have to get some training for when they were married and he supposed that kissing would have to be practiced too but Sam considered that practising on Old Man Herriot's Alsatian was preferable to practising on than Fat Debby. He could even understand why they would come to the rear of the scrap yard - it was quiet and it was out of the way- but he just couldn't, for the life of him, understand why Socky had his hand in the girl's blouse. He began to feel quite ill as he watched, but for some reason, he just couldn't look away. Then his gaze was distracted as he noticed something move, just below where they were hiding. It was hairy and round. It was Breem's head trying to relocate slightly for a better view of the proceedings. Covered in soil, shale and dust it may have been, but it was certainly Breen. He was almost half way out of his little hole now, craning his head to see past the young saplings that grew around the scrap yard.

"Look!" said Ben with a wide grin. "What are they?" Sam looked to where Ben was pointing, back to Socky and Fat Debby. Debby's top half was now naked and on view to the world.

"Don't know," replied Sam "but it looks serious." Amazed at the growths on her chest.

"Poor girl," added Ben. "Fat, ugly and horribly deformed." It was at about this point that a loud shout and a muffled scream were heard and something like a young boy went hurtling down the steep slope of the tip into the scrap yard. Breen, it seemed, had leaned out so far, that the edge of the hole had given way and he had landed between the fiercely petting couple. Two more figures bolted from behind a bush and crossed the Tip path with much haste, yahooing like demented Red Indians on the War Path.

Ben and Sam sat on the coal shed at Ben's house, looking out across the fields, wondering if Breen had escaped.

"Do you think he'll catch what Fat Debby has got, it looks bad?" asked Sam looking down his shirt for signs of rapid growth.

"You daft bugger. I was just joking earlier, all women have them, didn't you know?" answered Ben.

"What are they for then?" enquired Sam.

"They're what keeps them bra's on." replied Ben, in a matter of fact way. Sam stuffed his hands under the backs of his knees and swung his feet around in that 'I want to know more' sort of way.

"But....," there was a long pause. "but ... they look swelled. Does it hurt?" Ben looked over to Sam and raised his eyebrows.

"Does what hurt?"

"The swelling. It just looks like it's gonna get pretty sore when that happens to you." frowned Sam.

"They are tits Sam. Girls 'ave them, you must 'ave noticed." laughed Ben, realising that Sam knew little about the subject.

"I know ladies have them but none of the girls at school 'ave 'em." said Sam, still frowning. Ben shook his head and tried to explain.

"Look, girls don't have 'em because they don't have babies. They only grow them when they get older and have to have babies." Ben laid back on the shed roof, secure in the fact that he was worldly wise. There was another long silence.

"So when do they have to start growing them then?" asked Sam.

"Like I said, when they are going to have a baby."

"How do they know?" Asked Sam.

"They get a letter from the doctor telling them they are going to have a baby, so they better start drinking milk." replied Ben.

"Milk?" screamed Sam. "I drink milk. I love it. I drink loads of milk." Ben sat up and smiled at Sam.

"You know nothing you. Have you had a letter from the doctor?" asked Ben. Sam shook his head emphatically. "Then you aren't having a baby. Anyway, only women can have babies, you daft bugger - everybody knows that." Ben reclined again with a big grin on his face. Sam continued to swing his feet over the edge of the shed. At length he said.

"Why do they drink milk?"

"What do you feed babies on?" asked Ben. Sam thought, but he had little or no experience of babies, they smelled too much like vomit for his delicate stomach. As there was no answer, Ben continued. "Milk you idiot, it's milk." Ben sat up once more and stared directly at Sam. "They drink milk so that it fills up their chest and their tits fill up, then when the baby is delivered it drinks the milk, just like those kittens we saw at the farm." Ben shook his head at Sam's look of disbelief.

"So......," there was another long pause. "What was Socky doing then?" Ben suddenly looked rather panicky as Sam's question sunk in.

"He was.... er. ... he was checking to see...... he was er.... looking to....." There was another pause. "Oh I don't know," called out Ben. "he must have been stealing a drink I suppose." Ben collapsed back down. Sam thought about this for a moment.

"But that would mean Fat Debby has had one of them letters from the doctor. That means....." There was the longest pause of the afternoon, as both boys contemplated the conclusion. Socky was certainly interested in Debby one way or another but it was inconceivable that even he would marry her. Sam suddenly started laughing loudly.

"Ha ha, I bet you thought you had me there - milk, bra's and the like. Ha ha." Ben just sighed. Sam jumped down off the shed and said. "Okay. I'm off before Breen comes back 'cos I don't want to be here when he gets home, he might have caught what Fat Debby has." As Sam turned for home, Ben sat up, shook his head and went inside to make up some lies to explain why he didn't know where his brother was.

Sam crossed the road, prodding his chest all the way to make sure there was no change. He also considered what his supper might be.

"Hot Ovaltine." He smiled. "Hot Ovaltine with lots of sugar." He grinned. "Hot Ovaltine with lots of sugar and made with....." The grin fell from his face as the reality penetrated his brain. "Milk!" he concluded with a deep frown. He opened his shirt and examined his chest more closely. He wasn't entirely satisfied with Ben's explanation but to think it was some terrible disease was also strange to him. He had to be careful.

"You're early tonight," frowned his mother as he entered the back room. He just glanced over and said.

"I don't want any supper. Oh, and I'm having a bath." With this, he went quickly upstairs. It was some several minutes before his mother decided not to go and phone for the doctor.

Man has always been fascinated with his own expression - words and sounds for those times when he needs to put across some inner feeling and make it sound utterly dynamic. That's why he invented words that don't mean anything in particular but which somehow, develop into an irreverent sound. Some kind of offence to the ears, which will convey to everyone within audible distance, just how he feels. - 'Swearing an oath' he calls it. An odd label, since this expression can mean something so different. It seems strange that extra words can do so much. It seems even stranger that these words could find their way into everyday use. In these times where almost every sentence heard in the street starts with an "F", it could be considered incredible that there was ever a place or a time where these expletives were used with consideration of their effect on others and used sparingly. It's not that they were not used on a regular basis, or that most people didn't swear, it's just that they were used for effect, humour and sometimes in desperation, but rarely in public. For Sam, swearing was really something that adults did and as he wished to stay well away from that social grouping, he swore quite rarely – well, for a child anyway. Swearing, as a rule, was used only for purposes of experimentation, effect, humour or desperation. Indeed, there was one particular time early in a certain summer when he wished he had never, ever, heard a single swear word.

It had all started out innocently enough. He and Vern had found themselves trapped by boredom and forced indoors by unpleasantly strong winds. Sam's parents were out at work and Sam was left to amuse himself. Now this wasn't usually a problem but that day nothing seemed the right thing to do, so eventually, Vern suggested that they go up to his attic bedroom and play there. Vern's house was about halfway down a short terrace, having a small rear garden and a tiny front garden, these houses were not ideal for anything but the smallest family. Social propriety dictated that Vern's dad had to embark on a series of 'home improvements', the phrase used loosely because none of the so-called improvements were ever finished. As Vern had an elder sister, Vern was packed off into a new room in the attic at the age of about seven and he had made this tiny room his sanctuary, his escape from the septic atmosphere that sometimes permeated the house when his parents were not getting on. To Sam's eyes, that was most, if not all of the time. The tiny capsule of Vern's world held little of interest for Sam but the boys found two old plastic, toy cars and tried to find something to do with them. They were quite large and simply made, mainly from pliable plastic and the two boys found that they would not break no matter how hard they were crashed together.

"Let's send them down the roof." suggested Vern pointing to the tiny window that opened onto the grey, slated house roof.

"Yeah, a race to the death." grinned Sam. The cars selected, the window was opened to its full extent and the two boys squeezed out enough to hold the cars steady for their race.

"Three... Two.... One..... Go!" and the two cars were sent careering down the terrible slope, gravity having the final say as they bounced over the guttering and out of sight. They both grinned but it was short lived. Somewhere out there, they heard the howl of the Highfield Banshee, Vern's mother. Sam thought Vern's mother knew more swear words than anyone else in the world. She seemed to have no trouble thinking of them as they always flowed effortlessly from her mouth. If the Women's Institute had ever found the need to form a paramilitary wing, Vern's mum would have been their first recruit. She was only small but she was fearless, tireless and unable, it seemed, to speak without using as many swear words as Sam could imagine existed.

"You bloody little shit!" was the start of the tirade, closely followed by plenty more, but Vern had already pulled himself and Sam from the window.

"C'mon, quick." With Sam close on his heels, Vern scampered down the steep stairs from the room, almost leaping most of the way. He then led the way down the second flight and charged through the empty front room. Together, the two boys shot out of the front door and down the street, turning right onto the Backs where they hid behind Vern's dad's garage. In the distance could be heard a voice that Sam knew was Vern's mother.

"I can see the cars on the path," whispered Vern peering round the edge of the garage and looking down the rubbish-littered garden. "I'll make a quick dash and get them, she'll be halfway upstairs by now." With this, he set off down the path, picked up the two cars that were still unbroken and raced past Sam to the safety of the garage. Just then, as Sam peered round the garage very carefully, he saw Vern's mother appear at the tiny loft window at the top of the house and look around as if searching for something.

"I know you're bloody well out there you sodding little shit, you bloody well chuffing wait 'till you bloody well come back you sodding little bugger." Sam tried to count the swear words but she was too quick.

"A real champion swearer." thought Sam.

"Come on," whispered Vern. "she'll calm down by tonight." Sam knew that was unlikely but the boys slunk off to continue their game. After trying everything they knew to destroy the old cars, including a terrible accident involving a brick, a large stick and a coal shovel, both cars looked unscathed.

"Let's set fire to 'em." suggested Vern and the two boys headed for Sam's house and a box of matches. It was clearly too windy to burn them outdoors and so Sam suggested the outside toilet. It was well out of the wind and the cars were duly ignited. The boys were sitting on the floor and didn't notice the smoke gathering in the roof area, nor did they realise it was seeping through to the attached toilet next door - that is until a banging was heard on the toilet door. It was Sam's aunt from next door.

"You silly little buggers. You'll burn the house down, bugger off and play. I'll tell yer' mam when she comes 'ome."

"Not in the same league as Vern's mother." thought Sam but it was worrying that his own mother was to be told about the smoke.

"Let's go inside." suggested Sam. It was his great idea to burn the cars in the hearth, which was fine but in their eagerness to see the cars burn in vivid close up they were dragged further into the room on some newspaper. Now, why the two boys didn't realise that the smoke that had engulfed the toilet, would now fill the house, is a mystery. Just like the fact that they didn't comprehend that newspaper, no matter how well it is spelt, will not prevent burning plastic from scorching or melting the carpet beneath it. It cost Sam dear. He was kept in for a whole week; he wasn't allowed to go out on pain of death. It was like death: day after long day sat indoors with nothing to do. On the third day, Vern knocked at the door.

"You allowed out then yet?" he asked.

"No, I have to stay in 'till at least Sunday."

"Shit!" exclaimed Vern. "Just sneak out and get back before they come home."

"Can't," replied Sam in a sulky tone. "she says if anyone says they've seen me out I'm locked in 'till the end of the month." Sam shrugged his heavy shoulders.

"Okay, I'll be off then." replied Vern shoving his hands deep into his pockets as he set off slowly off up the garden path and onto the Backs. Sam closed the door and slumped into the settee but he was seething with frustration at not being able to go out. He went up to his room and looked around but nothing could replace the loss he felt for his freedom. He then returned downstairs and looked over towards the sideboard, where he saw the tape recorder lodged beneath it. This machine warrants a better description. It was one of those old reel-to-reel recorders with four or five inch spools on the top of a machine that was the size of a wardrobe and the weight of a tank mechanic's tool kit. The microphone that plugged into the front looked like one of those pre-war BBC types, the whole ensemble being made of metal and Bakelite. Sam dragged the massive machine out from under the sideboard and plugged it in. The two spools began to turn, the red tape crackled through the pickup and then the sound was heard. Mostly, it contained music that had been recorded from the radio by means of the simple microphone, so needless-to-say the quality was poor. So was the selection: Glen Miller, Frank Sinatra and Ella Fitzgerald. Not that Sam minded the sort of music that he found there, it was just missing some 'Shadows' or 'Beatles' but then again, he could never be bothered to sit and record anything. He soon grew bored of listening to the same old stuff and decided to risk a walk up the garden.

"Who is going to see me in my own garden?" he asked himself. There was no answer but plenty of doubt.

The sunlight seemed like electricity to him and within seconds, feeling better about life, he walked to where a patch of lawn lay in front of a small rockery and sat on the warm grass. It was a small garden and the addition of one of the first garages on the street made it even smaller but to Sam it was like a desert island. Just to be there and to breath in the pure air, to hear the birds and to smell the aroma of the tiny patch of grass and flowers was just pure ecstasy to him. He laid back and rested the back of his head in his cupped hands and feeling the coolness of the lawn, he simply watched the clouds roll by. He had just begun to get comfortable when he heard a sort of 'mumbling' close by. He sat up, looked around and realised that it wasn't mumbling, it was someone talking at a somewhat greater distance, probably on the Backs. He jumped to his feet and wandered casually up the garden path, past the old outhouse, formally known as the HQ of the defunct Black Hand Gang, (Derbyshire Chapter) and through the homemade gate, onto the Backs. There he saw Vern, a little off to the left. Vern was sitting on the bank, which bordered the field and in front of him was Bonzo, the village dog. Bonzo was sitting looking straight at Vern as the lad seemed to be giving him precise instructions. Sam looked about him cautiously to see if anyone was looking and then slowly sauntered to where Vern and the dog were sitting. Vern wasn't giving the dog the secrets to a treasure map, he was just swearing ..... at the dog. Well in truth, he was just saying swear words, deliberately and precisely. Sam considered that Vern's mum was having some kind of effect on the lad and it wasn't pretty but as he got a little closer, the dog turned to look over to Sam. Vern noticed and he turned too.

"What are you doing?" asked Sam with a puzzled frown. Vern looked back at the dog and said.

"Teaching Bonzo to swear." The dog looked up at Sam as much as to say, "Look what I've found."

"Teaching the dog to swear?" asked Sam his face contorted into disbelief.

"Yeah, I was sat here thinking how funny it is that real bad swear words are never said in the house, it's kind of boota."

"What's Boota?" asked Sam patting Bonzo casually on the head.

"It's what old man Jarvis always says, he says if something is not to be talked about it's 'Boota'."

"Never heard of it." admitted Sam.

"Well maybe it's 'taboota' or some 'ink like that." Vern was staring at the dog and Bonzo, realising this, stared back.

"Bastard," said Vern with precision and then repeated it. "Bastard."

"But you said you were teaching him to swear," said Sam, still frowning.

"Yeah that's right," he said and then turned back to the dog. "Shit-A-Brick," he continued.

"But what's the point?" asked Sam with his arms open wide.

"The point is this." Vern now stared at Sam. "I teach Bonzo all the swear words I know and when he goes home, he will have all these dirty words and no one will know where he got them from." Vern laughed maniacally as he finished. Sam thrust his hands into his pockets, looked up at the sky and sighed. He saw many flaws in Vern's plan but, as he was constrained for time, he decided to point out just two - the two he thought Vern might understand.

"Vern, you are forgetting two things, one - Bonzo here can't speak and two - Bonzo may not have a home." Vern wouldn't be put off.

"'Course he's got a home, he's got a collar and everthin'." Certainly, Bonzo had a collar but this 'everything' Vern was talking about eluded Sam's questioning gaze. Vern may have been alluding to four legs, a tail and a head but as far as Sam could see this by no means meant the dog had a home. Sam had seen plenty of dogs that had no homes and yet carried most, if not all, of their doggy bits and pieces. Vern continued. "'an he doesn't have to speak, it's just funny that he knows the words." Sam shook his head.

"Vern," Sam pointed to the dog and Bonzo looked up at Sam. The dog hadn't had this much fun since he buried Chapper's cricket ball under a cowpat. Sam continued as soon as he had Vern's gaze. "This is a non-talking dog. If Bonzo were a parrot or even a budgie, I would say you had invented the 'funny' of the year and I would pee myself laughing. It would be real funny but this is Bonzo. If dogs really could talk, Bonzo would speak like stuttering Stu from school." To reiterate the point, Sam knelt at the side of the dog, who was merrily panting saliva to the floor. "Now Bonzo, old lad," he patted the dog again. Bonzo stared into his eyes. "I want you to go off to the Post Office and fetch me a quarter of Kali." Sam stood and pointed down the Backs. "Off you go then." The dog just sat there, the saliva just brushing the floor.

"That's just bullshit," growled Vern as he stood and walked away a few feet. "Anyway, he knows you haven't got any money."

"Bonzo, lick your nuts." said Sam pointing to the dog. The dog licked up some of it's spittle that was in danger of being repatriated to the floor but continued panting and watching Sam without even glancing at his own prodigious testicles. "Nope, he doesn't know that one either." grinned Sam. Vern was kicking the ground and Sam could see he was very deflated.

"Come on Vern," said Sam. He had a small idea. "I can't go out but she didn't say you couldn't come round to our house." Vern stopped and turned round with a grin.

"What are we gonna do then?"

"Dunno yet, we'll find something." They walked back but Bonzo was following, so Sam turned to the dog and called.

"Scram Bonzo." The dog barked once and then ran off down the Backs. Sam and Vern looked at each other and burst out laughing.

It was more difficult than Sam had thought, finding something to do in the house. Toys were okay but no boy was going to enjoy seeing someone else playing with their best things. Eventually, they both sat in the main room, bored once more.

"What's that?" asked Vern pointing to the tape recorder still where Sam had left it.

"Oh it's the tape recorder. I tried that, there's nothing much on it." insisted Sam.

"So can you record on it?" asked Vern with a slight interest in his eyes.

"Yeah, we just fast forward to where the last song is and then record." explained Sam in a bored tone.

"Let's do it then." grinned Vern.

"There won't be anything on the radio at this time. It's all that stuff that my aunty listens to - it sounds like cotton wool." frowned Sam.

"I mean let's *us* tape somethin'." replied Vern, still grinning. Sam shrugged his shoulders and switched it on; he soon found the last song.

"What do you want to do?" asked Sam getting the mike ready.

"I'll sing a Roy Orbison song, I'm better than me dad." grinned the boy. His father, along with being an expert on unfinished home improvements, was a local entertainer who mimicked certain celebrities. Sam got the machine ready and into the microphone he said.

"One, two, three, testing." as professionally as he could. He then rewound the tape and played it back.

34

"Great," laughed Vern, "I've never heard my voice on tape." He was obviously excited by the prospect and though Sam had heard his voice too many times for it to be a novelty, he continued, for lack of any other ideas. Sam set the machine going and nodded to Vern. Vern picked up the microphone and began to murder some song or other but when he forgot the words, he stopped and said.

"Don't know anymore." the tape still rolled and Sam was about to stop it when Vern shattered the silence by shouting at the top of his voice the worse swear word he could think of. Sam was stunned for a moment, it was like all decency had been thrown away, Vern had shouted the 'F' word, and in Sam's house. Sam looked down at the tape spools, still spinning and quickly turned the tape machine off. He turned to Vern who had a slight grin on his face and not the look of disbelief that Sam's face radiated.

"What you playin' at for Christ's sake?" spat Sam, looking around him as if the word had been indelibly scorched into the fabric of the room. Vern grinned even wider as he said.

"Play it back, go on play it back." Sam was so surprised by the request that he did just that. The spools were turned back a little and the play button was pressed to let the sound find its way from the speakers. Sam was almost as shocked when he heard that word as he had been previously, but he suddenly realised, it sounded more like "FOG!" through the poor speakers. Sam looked once more to Vern but Vern had already wound the tape back and set it playing once more. This time it sounded like "Fug" but Sam's ears knew what it was. They had heard it the first time Vern had shouted it and Sam's ears had a very good memory. This time though, it didn't shock Sam quite as much. The surprise was wearing off and he turned to Vern with a slight impish grin. This time he rewound the tape himself and when they got to that word, both boys fell about laughing. They rewound it several times and added every swear word known to man and dog, until they both laughed so much they felt ill. They were still laughing and wiping tears away as they pushed the great machine back under the sideboard. Swearing, it seemed, could be great fun and Sam hadn't done with the fun swearing could bring - not by a long chalk.

Sam had been given back his freedom and it felt good. For several days now he had been back out with the boys and fun seemed never ending. One evening, he was making his way home and saw a small child out on the Backs - someone he didn't know. Sam wasn't very good at knowing the age of younger children but he did know that this one seemed a little too young to be out of its own garden and alone.

"Hey, what's your name?" he asked the child. The youngster seemed to be a little hesitant and Sam thought he may not even know his own name but the child eventually worked it out.

"Kev... vin." he managed.

"Where do you live, Kevin?" Sam asked, looking down the nearest garden but he could see no one.

"I got a stick." said the boy, holding out a small twig. Sam considered walking on as he wasn't armed with the tools to deal with this situation but then he remembered that a new couple had moved in to the house with the green gate. The woman seeming very young to have a child in Sam's eyes but he considered the young lad must live there. He walked to the green gate and opened it. It was a bit stiff, so the lad may have locked himself out. He turned to the child and called over.

"Do you live here Kevin?" The boy walked over like a drunken man and asked.

"You want stick?" he was holding out the pathetic twig and offering it to Sam.

"Oh sodding hell." said Sam to himself as he sighed. The boy looked up in admiration. Sam sighed again.

"Me live there." the child said as he pointed to the gate.

"Here?" asked Sam, trying to confirm it wasn't a fluke. The boy nodded but looked unimpressed. Obviously he wasn't keen on returning to the garden. "Right, let's have you back in then." Sam insisted, as suddenly, a light came on in his head. "Parrot." he grinned. Sam headed the young boy to the gate and then crouched by his side and looked into his eyes. "Now then Kevin, say this." Sam paused, then continued. "Bugger." The boy made no attempt to copy, so Sam repeated it several times. Eventually he won the prize.

"Bug... ger," stuttered the boy.

"Shit," said Sam several times until Kevin became 'Filthy Mouth Kevin' at Sam's command.

"Bugger, shit, tit." eventually repeated the boy.

"Righto Kevin, in you go and say hello to your mam for me." Smiling, Sam closed the green gate solidly and walked off towards his home, whistling a nonexistent tune, as adults seem to do, thinking what a good turn he had done Kevin's parents by showing the lad home and giving him a start to his education by introducing him to some lesser known English words. By the time he reached his own yard he was laughing about it.

"Swearing is real fun. Wait 'till I tell Vern about this." he grinned. As he entered the house, he could feel it, that tension that is as thick as black pudding. His mother glared at him in the kitchen and hissed.

"We need to have words my lad." She looked furious and her arms remained folded even as she walked, but Sam couldn't understand it. He had been so careful over the last few days, just to keep in her good books. "In here." she growled and led him into the main room. It was there that he saw it and his blood turned to liquid ice. That pile of steel and Bakelite standing motionless in the centre of the room. His mother pointed to the chair and he sat as ordered. She then pressed the play button. Sam knew what it was. He saw it all unfold in a split second. He tried to think of excuses but in his mind he knew there were none. He felt sick and he felt tears building up in his eyes but they wouldn't come at first because he was too disappointed in himself. This was going to cost him very dear, if only they had remembered to record over that swearing.

Sam developed his philosophy on life very early, long before he knew what 'a philosophy' was and previous to him being called 'Sam'. He was born rather a large child, much to his mother's discomfort but full of life, he only ever cried when he hurt himself. He had a cheeky smile from that formative age, with a face that grinned "Hey, it's great to be here." Everything looked fabulous to the young Sam, his innocence and naivety keeping this open, excited expression firmly on his young face. But, life being life, it had some early tricks to play on him and this had a profound effect on his later philosophy.

Sam hated school. From the very first day it seemed to him that he was being held against his will by weird people who tried to teach him about things in which he had no interest. His mother was no help as far as he could see. Wasn't *she* supposed to protect him from these people? He had no idea that she was also concerned for her young son. The first few months of his school life were quite disturbing to all involved but particularly to Sam, who wondered what he would gain from being able to add two apples and three oranges. Who in their right mind had any interest in fruit? The only fruit he was interested in was 'fruit salad' those chewy sweets he could buy from the shop near the school. Anyway, he already knew how to do arithmetic, two swizzle lollies, plus one sherbet fountain equals a good time.

As his first year of this punishment came to an end and the second year began, it seemed the imprisonment was to continue but by now, Sam had settled into the routine and was a little happier with the situation, mainly due to the fact that he realised that a certain amount of fun could be had. Just before the summer break, the six year old Sam had gone to school and everything seemed fine, until without warning, he felt a pain in his stomach. This pain grew and he considered telling the teacher but held out, as, to Sam's mind, she was quite strict. She had made it very plain that she disliked pupils disturbing her lessons with toilet breaks. When it was too much for Sam, he tentatively raised his hand and the teacher came over to him. It was too late, he had gambled and lost, to his cost. His bowels released their grip on the oily light brown fluid, which had previously been contained inside the boy. Needless-to-say, Sam was in a mess and excrement was running down his legs, even as the teacher removed him from the class and took him to the outside toilets. There, another female teacher arrived and told the first, that Sam would have to be taken home.

"Well not in my car," snapped the first teacher. "Look at him."

"You'll have to walk with him then," exclaimed the second.

"He lives up at Highfields, that's miles and I can't walk with him looking like that, he has got poo all over him," explained the first.

"Well there doesn't seem to be any option." pointed out the second teacher.

"I'll have a word with the headmistress; I'm not doing it." added the first and she walked off. All this time, Sam was having trouble keeping his bowels in check, feeling very uncomfortable and to add to his problems, he was beginning to feel sick. As the head mistress arrived, Sam was expelling more fluid and was firmly upset, he could feel tears welling up. He had no idea what was happening to his body and couldn't understand why no one would help him. It was time to make a decision. That decision was to remove the soiled clothes he had on, but he was stopped.

"Don't do that boy," said the headmistress, "we are going to get you home." There was further discussion between the teachers, some quite heated but it was finally decided that the second teacher would have to take Sam home and they were going to walk. Almost three miles, but they *would* walk.

Very little attempt was made by the teachers to clean up Sam and added to the fact that he felt poorly, he knew that not only was he likely to evacuate his bowels again but that he was covered in his own excrement. Sam was now going to have to walk over two miles, mostly up hill, and to be seen by the whole world to have 'crapped' himself. The young lad was in despair. What sort of punishment was this to mete out to him? He had done nothing wrong, he didn't even know why this had happened. By the time he eventually reached home, he was in a real mess and totally confused. To add to his misery there was no one there. Of course there wasn't, if they had asked Sam, he would have told them that his mother had to work in the day.

"Oh great," spat the teacher as she looked around for an option. She heard a noise from the yard next door and with Sam in tow, went to investigate. There she saw a pram in the yard with a small baby inside, taking the sun. A woman came from the house to see who this person was.

"Yes, what can I do for you?" she asked wiping her hands on a tea towel.

"Er, it's....." but before the teacher could explain, the woman noticed Sam and cried out,

"Blood and sawdust, what happened to you?"

"Do you know where his parents are? asked the teacher. "I thought his mother would be in."

"His mother is my sister and she's out at work like you. Come here lad." She took Sam from the teacher and examined him more closely. The teacher shuffled a little and said.

"We tried to clean him up but it got rather worse as we walked here." Sam's aunty snapped her gaze towards the teacher and growled.

"You mean to tell me you have made him walk all that way?"

"Well he was too soiled to put into the car." she began but was cut off by the aunt.

"My god, it would be nice to afford a car to get soiled. To think that you walked him all that way in this state, just to keep your car clean." She glared menacingly at the teacher before continuing. "I'll look after him now, seeing as you can't. You aren't fit to look after people's children." she left the teacher without another word, heading off into the house.

Inside, she washed the young Sam in a baby bath and threw his clothes in the yard to be put into the boiler. Then she dressed Sam in a large nappy, apologising to him for the lack of anything better. Sam didn't mind one bit, he was just glad to be clean, it made him feel a lot better.

This event may have happened long in Sam's past but it made him realise from an early age, that you can't rely on anyone, particularly people who are supposed to help and protect you. He also nurtured a pathological hatred of teachers, which would have consequences throughout his school life. For the moment however, it set him off down a route that would bring him a new-found independence, and gave him a sort of early philosophy.

He applied his philosophy to most things and though most people saw it as just 'being awkward', Sam didn't care what they thought it was. He didn't have a description for it, it was just Sam being Sam.

School remained something Sam had to suffer. He always hated it and constantly rebelled, which did little to endear him to the teachers. He passed his 'Eleven Plus' exams, much to everyone's surprise and went to an all boys secondary school six miles away in Chesterfield. It was like a boarding school with similar ethics and habits, the only difference being that you went home at the end of the day. It was just more of the same for Sam, doing just enough not to get expelled but not enough for the teacher's liking. At lunch, he would go off into the town with an old friend from earlier days who also managed to find himself in a school miles from home. They truanted together, they stole pencils and other bits and bobs from Woolworths together and they drank beer in the only pub in the town that would serve children - but most of this was still to come. For the time being he continued going to school, albeit with a different attitude, and waited with an emphatic longing for the summer holidays. That six weeks of freedom, six weeks of being who he truly was.

It was when he was at his best, even then his philosophy on life remained a constant. His conception of law was well defined. He knew what was wrong and he knew what was right but like most boys, he knew that occasionally you had to step over the line in order, for research purposes only you understand, to see, to experience, to know, what it was like to break the law. For instance, stealing sweets from the Post Office was fairly easy, but it was only a few sweets after all and it wasn't going to bring down the country. 'Nicking' pop from the shop opposite was easy too, if you were careful, as getting into the store yard was simple. Even, on occasions, taking bits and bobs from other places seemed fair game - fruit from other people's gardens, cycle brake blocks from the shop down the road and any bit of moveable wood on bonfire night. One area that would not be tolerated however, was 'pinching' from your friends. Sam was adamant on this ethic. It shouldn't be done under any circumstances. A lad down the road called Martin had a full set of circus toys. There were all manner of vehicles and attractions, even a big top, and Sam so wanted it but stealing was never an option. He had chances but it was off limits. Sam wasn't that keen on Martin but he suffered him so that he could play with his toys, as he seemed to have everything. This was fine to Sam, getting on with someone so that you could play with their toys made you a complete hypocrite. That was fair game, but you could never, ever steal from them. Swaps were the way to go if you wanted something. Sam swapped all manner of things to get what he wanted. Toys defined who you were, most boys said who they were with their model cars and the like. Some had collections on a theme. For instance, as stated, with Martin it was circus items, with Biro, who lived at the shop, it was tractors and farming items. With Sam's cousin, 'Wicker', it was buses - loads of them. Sam was careful not to alienate anyone who had all these things; it was a kind of expansion of his own toy box. Sam's own collection was aircraft. - Those Airfix items, lovingly painted and assembled and then hung from his bedroom ceiling from strands of cotton.

Sam had a philosophy on most areas of life. Modern fashion, particularly in areas of clothing, was something to steer clear of. He considered it made you part of a club and that wasn't for him. Unless the item of clothing had been out of fashion for at least ten years, it was no good to him and items that had never been in fashion were best. As most of the other boys began to covet baseball boots and turn-up jeans, Sam kept a tight hold on his black plimsolls and wanted no turn-up on *his* jeans. Well, as tight a hold as he could. - His jeans, like those of most other boys, were bought a little large so that he would 'grow into them'. Consequently, they always began life with a turn-up and were then let down, notwithstanding the fact that, in most cases, there was a darker blue colour to the let down section and in some cases, a hole where the fold in the turn-up had worn through after dragging on the floor.

When it was time for the school photograph, Sam's mother decided that he would have to have something new to wear, so that Sam would look presentable on the photograph.

41

"But I don't want a new shirt, I love the one I have." complained Sam. The one he had was a blue and white pinstripe item and as pinstripes were not high fashion, Sam loved it, he was even proud of it.

"Well I'm going to get you a new jumper then to put over it. I don't want you looking a scruff for your photo." insisted his mother. So dressed in his usual school clothes, with his old shirt but a shiny new sweater over it, Sam trotted off to have his photograph taken. Two weeks later Sam's mum had a 'dicky-fit'.

"So what in God's name happened to the jumper?" she cried out as she looked down at the photograph. Looking back at her was the trademark cheeky grin with Sam sporting his old striped shirt but no new jumper to be seen.

"Couldn't see the shirt with the jumper on." grinned Sam, biting into an apple. Sam didn't know if green pullovers constituted a fashion item but he wasn't taking any chances.

"But just look at you in the photo; you look like nobody loves you." frowned his mother.

"I think it looks fine." replied Sam, looking at the shot and feigning interest.

"And where did you get that apple? I didn't buy any this week." Sam stopped chewing and looked at the apple as if he had only just noticed he was holding it.

"Er, someone gave it me at school." he announced eventually. His mother raised an eyebrow but Sam was on the ball. "Er, so what is it about the shirt you don't like?" He was good at changing the subject when it mattered.

His mother never understood the philosophy behind Sam's clothing choice. It was simple when he was very young - he had no say in the matter. As Sam was an only child, everything had to be bought new since there were no 'hand-me-downs' from older brothers. Sam's mother had tried that option as her sister lived next door and having two older boys herself, had some clothes that her boys had grown out of. Unfortunately, Sam's mum saw only anguish for her son as he stood there in third-hand clothes which were so large that the saying "Oh he'll grow into it." seemed as worn out as the apparel itself. So, 'new' it had to be but as the working class purse was usually empty, so was Sam's wardrobe. Sam was lucky though that his father wasn't a gambler or a drinker, so the only time the family's little available money was squandered, was when it was used to buy something for Sam. Take for instance, the time Sam needed some new shoes for school. Sam's school shoes were well past the point where the molecules had the strength to bond together to make a whole but Sam saw them as 'just worn in'. His mother saw them as 'just worn out' so, after much threatening and arguments, Sam agreed to a new pair with the proviso that 'he could choose'. His mother was rather surprised as Sam chose well.

"You're not just kidding me, are you? You will wear them?" she asked with more than a little scepticism.

"Yeah, 'course, I like 'em." he replied as he chose a pair from the catalogue. The catalogue seemed the best place to buy them as it spread the cost over several weeks and dispensed with the trauma of taking Sam shopping.

"But they've got tassels on them." she pointed out. Indeed they had, that's why Sam liked them.

"Who in their right mind would wear shoes with tassels on?" thought Sam. They would never become fashion shoes for sure. "Yeah, I like tassels." quipped Sam. He didn't but he didn't like fashion either and tassels were the lesser of two evils. The shoes were ordered and duly arrived, Sam found some perverse pleasure in seeing these truly magnificent horrors of shoes made doubly awful by the fact that his mother liked them. They must be the worst shoes in the world. True, he was going to have to try climbing trees and kicking a rugby ball with them but that was a minor problem to overcome.

His first day at school in the outrageously unfashionable footwear was just like any other as it began full of hatred and resentment from Sam, closely followed by passionate fury and later by ambivalence. Things, however were soon to change. As Sam walked up to the school gates, some of the other children were staring, Sam was used to this but why were some of them whispering behind their hands?

"It's the shoes." he realised. The footwear was so utterly wrong that he was getting stares and this warmed him inside. Sam even considered the likelihood of his becoming a 'trend setter' for unfashionable clothing and ideas. However, the confusion wrought in his brain from such an impossible set of contradictions made him forget this possibility and he decided instead, to concentrate on the latest manifestation of his rebellious nature. As he strode through the gates, he could feel himself smiling and he could feel his feet smiling too.

As he entered the school grounds, a couple of his classmates saw him and quickly walked over, followed by other sundry pupils. This was a bit too much for Sam; notoriety was one thing but idolatry was another.

"The shoes, wow!" said one lad.

"God, where did you get those?" came another voice. Sam was bowled over by the response, if terrible shoes could get this much attention, just think what the Christmas jumper his gran bought him last year could do, or that tee shirt bearing the legend "I hate Speeling." There was just one problem. - some of the reactions were of a kindly nature and what Sam had taken to be cries of, "What horrible shoes." had in fact been compliments. His ears should have recognised the words "What fantastic shoes." and the alarm bells should have rung earlier. Sam considered his ears must have been sleeping late or reading a comic as he walked up to the school, so he shook his head to wake them up. As they woke, they were certainly relaying the fact that there was an amount of praise for the horrific footwear. Sam was dumfounded and he pulled one particular friend aside.

"What is it with my shoes?" he hissed.

"Don't ask me; you bought them." replied the friend.

"Don't these idiots know crap when they see it?" spat Sam. The friend laughed out loud, then put his arm around Sam's neck and pulled him close.

"What you have on your feet," whispered the lad, "are a pair of the latest fashion shoes, so fashionable that they aren't in the shops yet." Sam was speechless. He headed straight to the woodwork room, and used a knife to cut the cords inside the shoes, thus releasing the tassels, which he stuffed in his pockets. It wasn't long before the adoration on the faces of the other boys turned to the shaking of heads; Sam was more comfortable with that.

"I'm not buying any more shoes from that catalogue." Sam informed his mother. She was slightly taken aback by the "*I'm not* buying" but she let it pass.

"Now what?" she enquired. Sam rolled his eyes theatrically and tutted.

"The tassels have dropped off already." he slumped into a chair and cast the shoes from his feet.

"Well I'll get them returned and we'll get them to send another pair. I'm not paying out for rubbish workmanship." declared his mum. Sam coughed.

"No, er, it's okay, I like them better now." His mother bent down and examined the shoes and then placed them in the cupboard. She had a slight look of anger in her eyes.

"I knew you wouldn't wear shoes with tassels." she growled.

Sam needed to rethink things. All this time he had been wearing clothing from catalogues in the stone-built knowledge that it was the least trendy form of shopping in Christendom. To think he'd been conned into buying shoes that were so very fashionable that Sam was in danger of being considered mainstream. Yes, he would have to do that horrible 'S' word from now on.

It wasn't just fashion where Sam was a maverick. His music taste was odd and so was his interest in wildlife. That subject ran much deeper than the boyish habit of egg collecting - he sat and studied what he saw, he knew what it was all called and its habits and habitat, but probably the oddest quirk he had, from the point of view of other children, was language. From an early age he was fascinated by the English spoken word. Every day a new word could be encountered and he deemed it important to expand his vocabulary. The first instance of his love of words came more from 'sayings' than the words themselves. Sam heard the phrase 'in fact' and though it may seem insignificant, Sam thought that the addition of this expression gave his comments greater impact. For instance the phrase "There are loads of good gardens to scrump." could be improved by saying, "*In fact* there are loads of good gardens to scrump." Sam struggled initially as it was difficult to remember some of the longer words and he would sometimes get them wrong. There was the case of the 'Charming' earwig, the problem of the 'Eloquent' chair and the embarrassment of the 'Aesthetic' chicken pox but, with patience and commitment, he managed to conquer the English language, even if a little slowly. He needed to soak up all the information he could. Like most boys of his age, his mind was expanding, the new experiences and new ideas needed somewhere to live. Sam's brain wasn't exactly the Ritz, but for the type of thoughts that were to reside there, it was comfortable enough. They just had to keep squeezing over to allow more in, as there were no boundaries to what he wanted to know.

The day he decided that he wanted to learn how to cook was important to him, but slightly problematic to his parents.

"Can I make some of that, mam?" Sam's mother looked down at the pastry she was making and considered it was a good idea.

"Okay, you can make some pastry."

"I want to make a proper pie." grinned Sam.

"Well you'll have to make the pastry first," insisted his mother. "But first you'll have to scrub your hands, you can't make anything with hands like that." Sam went to the bathroom to make some attempt to clean up his hands. When he returned to the kitchen, his mother had laid out the things he would need on a small table. Sam was shown what to do and put a great deal of vigour into his work, so much so that the pastry landed on the floor several times before he decided it had been tortured enough. It looked more like brown plasticine than pastry, as some of the ground-in dirt from his hands transferred to the 'blob'. It became a sort of Quatermass Experiment, but he was proud of it. He wanted to complete this 'objet d'art', so a filling was added and the whole thing topped with more brown plastic. This gastronomic disaster was duly baked and left to cool under Sam's unfailing gaze but he couldn't help thinking that his pie was somewhat 'different' from the ones produced by his mother. Hers were light golden brown, his was dark brownish blue. Hers were plump and round, his was flat and crinkly. Hers were light and crusty, his was heavy and gluttonous but still it was Sam's first pie, he was proud of his offspring and didn't see the significance of its malformed and twisted countenance.

Teatime was traumatic for Sam's parents. Sam's pie could now possibly be classed as a new life form and Sam's mother was going to try everything possible not to have to eat any of it. Dinner arrived at the table with an ample part of Sam's mum's pie on each plate and sat on the table on its own dish, was 'the thing from outer space'. Sam's parents sat staring at the object as Sam beamed and said.

"Aren't you going to try it?" Sam's mum picked up the thing and passed it to Sam's father saying.

"Here, look what your son has made for you." Sam's father frowned at his wife, replying.

"You will have to share it with me." His mother turned to Sam and added.

"And some for you son." She cut it into three after a struggle to penetrate its armoured exoskeleton. Sam's dad expected it to scream but it didn't and a small part of it was placed on each plate. Now the decision was whether to eat it first and get it over with, or leave it until last. Sam's parents decided on the former, Sam on the latter. Sam's mother had decided that to refuse to try it would be deflating to Sam's ego but by the same token, so would vomiting. It was a dilemma but she reached a compromise by eating a small part of it and saying it was nice but it was a little under- cooked. Sam's father was less diplomatic; he almost retched as he forced a small piece into his mouth. It put him off eating most of his dinner, including the pie his wife had made. That wasn't a problem though because when the plates were cleared away, Sam's mum noticed that Sam had cleared every crumb of her pie from all their plates but had left his portion of his own pie almost untouched. Even the garden birds wouldn't eat the remains and Sam decided there ought to be quite a gap before he cooked anything again.

5   The Expedition.

Occasionally, man reaches out into the unknown and to undiscovered places all over the planet. His reach is very long and has even extended to walking on the Moon. This roving instinct was also strong in the minds of Sam and his friends and so, one day in a certain summer, they all set off to spend a day in the wood. It was known simply as, Bluebell Wood.

Sam, Vern and a slightly younger friend of theirs named Weep, called at the Shand brothers' house and together with Ben and Breen they set off down the path towards the Tip. As they passed the 'Big Tree', Breen and Weep just could not resist a swing on the thick rope that hung beneath - it was traditional and it was good fun. Weep also tried to climb the rope, he was so small and light he was like 'The Human Fly'. He came by his nickname 'Weep' from his elder brother, who decided that the young lad was always crying, mainly it must be said, because of the attentions of the said older brother. 'Weeperina' soon became shortened to 'Weep'.

Walking past the Tip and onto the railway, Weep and Breen caught up with the others and on they all strolled, past the old guard's van. Although the small window remained intact, the van was now blackened here and there by the smoke from 'over adventurous' children's fires, or maybe just vandalism. Halfway along the railway embankment stood an old railway signal, the long-arm, semaphore type, painted yellow with a black chevron decorating the 'Vee' notched end. It stood high on a wooden telegraph pole with a steel ladder fixed to one side, thus giving access to the signal mechanism and the lamps. Even this old relic was to be turned into a game for the children. The idea of this particular game was to climb to the top of the steel ladder and set the counterweight swinging. As if this wasn't enough, the child had to hurl himself back down the ladder before the counterweight stopped or he would have to do it all over again. Sam and Breen were not very keen on going up but they did and made it down before it stopped. The signal arm itself was riddled with small holes which all the boys were sure had been made by German aircraft in the war; yet none could explain why any Second World War Luftwaffe pilot should shoot at an unimportant railway signal on a coal mine branch line in the middle of the Derbyshire countryside. Yet it seemed possible, as a large crater in the next field was reputed to have been caused by a bomb, or depending who told the story, a crashed German bomber. The whole legend was supported by the claim that an RAF pilot had once crashed nearby on the site of an allotment garden, though no one could substantiate the claim with hard facts.

It was Weep's turn to climb the signal. He was like the famous cartoon comic character 'Spiderman', up the pole before you had time to say, 'Achtung Spitfire!' The others noticed he had started the weight swinging but he remained at the top. He was pointing down the railway line, which curved slowly around to the right and he was shouting something.

"Come down." called Ben, and Weep did, even faster than he had gone up.

"Somebody is coming down the line." he said quickly.

"Let's hide." said Sam, with no idea why. The reason could be worked out later, after they had reacted to whoever the person was. It was however, too late to hide, it now being obvious that the approaching wanderer could see them, just as clearly as they could see him. It was Tools.

"Where you lot goin'?" he asked, as soon as he was within hearing distance.

"To the wood, are you coming?" Ben asked.

"Yeah, can do," replied Tools, as if he had other things to do but they could wait a couple of hours. "come on then lets get off." and he turned back the way he had come in the hope that they would not ask him to climb the signal. Tools was good at most things but climbing wasn't one of them and he hated heights.

On they trudged, playing other games as they walked, such as jumping across the sleepers and walking along the top of the steel lines. As they neared the quarry, Weep suggested a walk into the 'far basin'- a term used to describe the deeper of the two small, overgrown quarries that sat at the side of the single track railway line but the others were eager to reach the wood. They had set off rather early but the morning was already wearing thin. Moving away from the quarry, the railway headed into a deep cutting where it merged with another line from the left. The boys carefully continued keeping eyes and ears open for the diesel shunting loco run by the National Coal Board, the owners of the line as they did not take kindly to the boys being there.

The sides of the cutting were very steep, topped by hawthorn hedges and trees, giving the boys a feeling of security within this world of theirs. Half a mile down the line was a brick-built bridge where the boys decided, with little success, to try and make echoes by shouting. They soon tired of this fruitless attempt and continued towards the wood. Further up the line, the cutting opened out and the line found itself atop a large steel bridge, paralleled by another, which carried the old L.N.E.R. double track main line. The two tracks came quite close to each other here and reached out across a chasm over a quiet country lane, then disappeared alongside the wood, the destination for the boys. Sam climbed onto the side of the bridge and looked west to where a farm stood and then down to the road far below.

"That is a long way down." he thought to himself as he spat and watched his spittle fall. Weep was a little less subtle and dropped a rather large rock, which exploded on impact with the hard ground.
One by one they moved on and reaching the other side of the bridge, Ben stopped, held one finger in the air and said.

"Listen!" and so they all did, hearing what could only be described as a rumble; yet they all knew too well what it was.

"There's a train coming." cried out Tools, and all the boys crossed to the main line. As they reached the tracks Tools rest his ear on the steel rails to try and work out what kind of train it was. He couldn't of course, but it looked technical. All the other boys ran across the main line to the opposite bank as Tools stood up and casually joined them, since this was where the train was going to pass through. They found what they considered to be a 'good spot' in the long grass and waited for the loco. Eventually a dark grey, belching beast came forcefully out of the trees, clanging and screaming its terrible cry, thundering through the cutting, pouring smoke and steam into the summer sky, like a mad painter trying to blot out an unspoiled canvas. The noise hit a peak as the loco bolted past the boys, bending the lush grass with a jet of warm air. Eventually, the steam hid the leviathan from view and all that remained were carriages, eager to follow their master along the track. As the last coach hurtled away into the distance, the boys lifted their heads and sniffed that very lovely smell of coal smoke, hot oil and steam.

"A four six two." said Sam, as if it had some inner meaning rather than describing how many wheels the locomotive had. As the train disappeared from view leaving only traces of white steam along the edge of the cutting and a low rumble in the distance, the countryside once again breathed out and all the familiar sounds returned as the boys turned to face the wood and continued towards it. They soon crossed both lines once more and entered the wood, squeezing through a frail wire fence. Their first port of call was the 'Woodpecker Tree', where a small rope swing hung over a bank with a brook at the bottom. It wasn't one of the best rope swings in the shire and they soon tired of it, deciding to become Robin Hood - every one of them. They could never agree on who was to be Robin, so they all played the part. Sam climbed onto his horse and spoke the words.

"I Robin Hood of Loxley and my merry men, swear to take from the rich and give to the poor."

"With this, his fine white stallion reared up and Robin "Sam" Hood galloped deep into Sherwood Forest, twisting through the trees on

the fastest horse that ever put hoof to soil. In a clearing in the centre of the wood was Sherwood village. Here, Robin known as 'Good Robin' to his friends, dismounted and entered the inn. It wasn't a hostelry he used often but it was a good place to get information. To his surprise, it was full of the sheriff's men.

"Kill him!" screamed the sheriff, as Robin ran outside. There he drew his fine gold sword and fought with the sheriff and his men. It was a hard fight, he was outnumbered fifteen to one but he had fought with worse odds. The two big men with spears came at him first but Robin was quick, he ran the first one through and tripped the other as he jumped towards a tree. This protected his back but four of the ruffians came forward together and though Robin dispatched two of them quickly, more came round the sides and things were looking grave for this hero of England. Robin fought well, but he was outnumbered then, from the side, a big burly giant of a man grabbed Robin's arm but still he fought on until another grabbed his leg. As the sheriff's men tried to hold him he still fought for his life."

At about this same time, a certain David Short was poised to enter the life of '*Good Robin*'. Why should it be? Who knows? Mr. Short, at thirty two years of age, had never done any wrong that he knew of. He was married, with a nice house, and was out walking his dog 'Patch'. He had considered that it was such a lovely day that he would have a stroll into Bluebell Wood. Strictly speaking, the wood was private but the owner didn't mind people walking through it, as long as they didn't harm anything. As he entered a clearing in the centre of the wood, his innocent eyes met a terrible sight. A small, scruffy boy was caught up by his clothes in a large bramble bush, waving a long stick furiously about him, shouting.

"Die, die, die you Norman swine, take that, you murderous piece of dog shit."

"Er .... Are you all right son?" The words from Mr. Short instantly stopped the boy who had a look of surprise on his small, excited face.

"Er ....er...... ... I was attacked mister." replied Sam, just before he yanked himself free of the shrub and hurried off deeper into the wood, glancing back more than once over his shoulder. Mr. Short raised his eyebrows and stood for a moment.

"Norman swine?" he puzzled. He glanced about him and then looked down at the dog by his side who seemed even more shocked by what they had seen.

Sam soon realised that he could neither see, nor hear the rest of the plague of Robin Hoods, in fact he felt quite alone. Never mind, this was the life of an adventurer, so he climbed onto his horse and rode off deeper into the forest - faster than Errol Flynn had ever done.

"Good Robin was sure he would find his merry men at the far end of the wood but as he neared Nottingham Castle, he was attacked by a large band of the sheriff's men who knocked him from his horse. One of them, the largest, much larger than Little John or even Friar Tuck, sat on his chest preventing him from getting up.

"Let me up you varlet or you'll feel the edge of my sword," said Robin."

"You what?" asked Vern. "You're mad you are."

"Get off!" screamed Sam but the chubby Vern held him fast.

"You get me off." smiled Vern.

"Fat pig!" insisted Sam. This indeed was a fair epithet for Vern but Vern did not see it that way and flicked Sam's nose several times.

"Shit face." yelled Sam which wasn't quite as accurate but it seemed to have the desired effect, for Vern did release Sam, not before picking up a handful of dirt and depositing it on Sam's face.

"Now who's a shit face?" laughed Vern, as he and the others ran away. Somewhat annoyed, Sam picked up a strong stick and ran after them, not forgetting to mount his white horse of course. So it was, that brave Robin chased after Robin Hood, Robin Hood, Robin Hood, Robin Hood and Fat Robin Hood.

"As they neared the edge of the wood, Robin noticed all the other Robins had fallen to the ground and were hiding in the long grass and the carpet of Bluebells that grew between. He also noticed that they were armed with rifles and machine guns, not swords and spears. Sam hit the deck. Of course only his friends called him Sam, for back at H.Q. they called him Major General Samson V.C. and bar. This was to be his most dangerous mission yet for just ahead of him, hidden in the grass, were five of the toughest soldiers to ever come out of Germany. Adolph Hitler himself had trained them. Sam readied himself after crawling several yards and hiding behind a dead tree. He searched around for grenades and found two lying nearby. Then, without thought for his own safety, he hurled himself thirty or forty feet to the cover of a row of bushes. He laughed as he heard the "Uh - uh - uh - uh – uh" of the Nazi machine guns firing. "They can't get me that easily," he said confidently to himself. He checked their position once more and it was a good job too, for one of the Germans was slowly coming towards him. Sam rolled from behind the bushes and fired his gun.

"Uh - uh -uh - uh - uh - uh - uh – her," said his weapon of death.

"Aahh!" came the reply as the first German fell dead. Another stood and rushed towards him. *"Uh - uh – uh,"* once more cried his gun as a second foe lay still on the forest floor. Sam crawled back behind the bushes and on, towards the old wooden fence. From here, using the skills honed when he was training James Bond, he managed to circle the other Germans and creep up at their rear.

"Uh - uh – uh," cracked his gun, *"Poom poom,"* went the grenade launcher and *"Powmm powm,"* exploded the grenades. Two more Germans were dead but where was the last one?

"Eh - eh - eh - eh – eh," came from behind him but it was too late. In a flurry of twitches and jerks, reminiscent of late fifties popular dancing, Major General Samson V.C. and bar fell lifeless to the floor, blood pouring out of his body and staining the grass deep red."

"Now what are we going to do?" asked Breen as he hauled himself up from his position as a German corpse.

"Lets play spies and go and blow things up." suggested Weep with excitement in his eyes.

"We could blow up the railway to stop the Germans taking all the gold out of France." added Ben.

"Why? Is there gold in France?" asked Weep.

"I don't know, I suppose so." replied Ben.

"There's plenty of toads." added Vern.

"Toads?" asked Breen, smiling to the others.

"Yeah, my dad says France would be okay if it wasn't for all the toads."

"Yer' mean frogs you daft bat." said Ben shaking his head.

"Frogs?" asked Sam. "why are there plenty of frogs there then?" Ben thought for a moment and then concluded,

"Don't know, but there are so many, they eat 'em over there."

"Ughhhhhh," called out the others in unison.

"An' snails, they eat them too." added Ben.

"Ughh, that's disgustin'." frowned Vern sticking out his tongue in a vomiting motion.

"You made that up." laughed Sam.

"Didn't." replied Ben, shaking his head and forming a serious look on his face. "Our Barry went there for his 'olidays and they said that the French eat frogs and snails all the time." He looked to his brother to confirm the story. Breen nodded and added.

"Yeah he said that. He said they eat budgies an' snails an' slugs an' poodles." Ben frowned more as he considered that he could not recall the additional fauna that Breen had listed as being part of the extraordinary bill of fayre but he did recall something about poodles.

"Ughhh." they all said again and several of them began to run about making barking noises as if they were 'throwing up'.

"Why do they do that then, don't they have corn flakes or biscuits then?" asked Tools with a slant-eyed grimace.

"Yeah they have proper food as well 'cos our Barry said he 'ad egg an' chips for most of the time." This little parcel of information did little to quell the song and dance that Sam, Vern and Weep had begun. It was simple but had an effective tune.

"French eat shit-food, French eat shit-food, French eat shit-food." As the song subsided, Sam and Vern slumped down in the grass, slightly out of breath, after their energetic performance but Weep wanted to know more.

"So where is France? Is it a long way off?" To a child who had travelled little further than the largest local town, comprehending how far away other countries were was problematic. "Is it further than Chesterfield?" he added. Ben laughed.

"Yeah, loads further."

"Sheffield?" asked Weep as being a place he had heard of but not visited.

"Yep, further than Sheffield." grinned Ben.

"It took them six weeks to get there." insisted Breen.

"No it didn't," frowned Ben, pushing his brother over. "Have you heard of London?" asked Ben looking directly at Weep.

"Course I 'ave," replied Weep, as if it was an insulting question.

"Well it's nowhere near there." laughed Ben as he stood and threw a handful of grass at Weep. The others laughed and then stood. They joked and danced around Weep until he tried an unsuccessful kick at one of them, only to fall on his backside. Then they left the wood to the wildlife once more. Boredom was beginning to raise its strange and ugly head though.

They tried to get on the horses in the field by the wood but the horses had other ideas about a pack of unruly children trying to entice them to the fence with less appetising items to eat than they had on offer in their own field, so the boys chased them instead. They threw stones at an empty oil drum near the railway. They made pea-shooters out of Hogweed stalks and used Hawthorn berries as ammunition. But still they were bored. In desperation for entertainment, Ben, Tools and Vern pushed Weep in the drainage ditch that ran by the side of the railway then moved with haste further down the track. Weep emerged from the ditch and began to throw stones at them before wiping the greater part of the mud from his jeans. When he caught up with the other five boys up, he noticed that they were staring into the distance with excited faces.

"What you lot lookin' at?" he asked.

"The Pit." replied Breen. Weep looked too. It was the black mass that was Pilsley Colliery.

"It's been closed years, you know." said Tools in a matter of fact way.

"It looks like it too." said Ben, still not taking his gaze from the colliery.

"Me uncle used to work there." replied Tools.

"Shall we go then?" asked Breen, not daring to look away from it.

"No!" said Ben.

"Yeah." contradicted Sam.

"Why not?" asked Tools, not really wanting an answer.

"Yep." coughed Weep.

"I'm not going." announced Vern. Weep, Sam, Tools, Breen and Ben followed the railway track that snaked its way right into the Pit Yard. Vern followed sixty yards behind, trying to prevent further advance by calling out unheard messages like,

"We'll get caught." "Someone will see us." "Our dads will find out." "We could get killed." The other boys were not listening. They were toying with the potential of the structures, gantries and walkways that joined and spanned the various buildings and installations, all except Ben. He knew they didn't ought to be there but the magnetism won and he gave in to inevitable roguishness. The colliery had been closed for a few years and some of it had been pulled down but there was plenty left to play with, it was the ultimate adventure playground. If architects had any intelligence, instead of building adventure areas with a few bits of scaffolding and some half buried concrete pipes with the inevitable but 'samey' sand pit, they would build a disused colliery. That's what children want. If an adult can tire of something in two hours, then a child can tire of it in four and a quarter seconds. They need adventure, excitement and exploration, it's what stops them destroying things and being a nuisance to adults. This colliery had all the things that a child needs and the boys were going to put it to good use. It was a paradise, heaven on earth. All it needed was some willing volunteers to try it out for size. Breen looked up at the mass of steel and brick.

"Wow!" he said as he tried to work out how to get to the various places. Sam thrust his hands into his pockets, as if he was studying the layout and said,

"It's big, where shall we start?" Tools was already sorting through the piles of scrap, looking for bits of useful machinery.

"That's handy." he said, holding up a piece of rusty iron that Sam thought looked like a duck with a propeller on its head. Gradually, the boys made their way forward and found a rusty iron stairway up into the first building. It was dark, apart from the odd places where the tin sheets were missing and it was dusty. It smelled odd, it was creepy and there was no obvious pattern to the interior of the buildings. Perfect in every way.

Deeper into the complex, the boys walked quite slowly as there was much to see and investigate but just like a hungry monkey, the instinct was to climb higher. They went up several stairs, ascending a couple of floors and discovering a new adventure at every turn. Vern still hung around outside, not joining in very much. Weep was becoming bored with the others, who were looking at a large piece of machinery and alleviated his boredom by dropping bricks through a hole in the floor to the ground, some thirty feet below, narrowly missing Vern as he finally decided to enter the building.

"Pratt!" screamed out Vern, thinking the missile had been designed to hit him. As they reached the top floor of the complex, their excitement and pleasure were taken to new heights. Here was a large room that was empty, save for one large machine and two inches of dust everywhere. It was fairly light having perspex-type windows, though everything was so grimy that little light permeated through the gloom. The boys, nonetheless, saw this as their own private headquarters, fitted with every luxury. Ben began making the place feel like home by drawing rude pictures on the floor in the dust. Sam broke open a box of washers and began to roll them down a broken piece of drainpipe lying on the floor. To Tools this was bliss, the aforementioned machine was thoroughly examined but he still didn't know what it was supposed to do. He found a way inside it and climbed in for a closer look. He noticed that there was an opening at the back of the machine and so he climbed out and over the machine, dropping onto the floor in the tight space at the rear. He peered through the dusty opening and saw that a conveyor belt issued from the machine into a long covered gantry hidden by the machinery.

"Hey you lot," he called. The others looked around for the source of the voice but it was a mystery. "over here, look." Tools was frantically waving his hand, rather than make the long journey over the machine. The boys saw the hand and then his face darkened by coal dust smiling from the far side of the machinery.

"What have you found?" asked Sam, peering through the machine trying to trace Tools' route over the mass.

"Come and look." replied Tools, before disappearing. Lacking all the technical jargon needed to describe such a sight, Tools decided that their own eyes would tell them a more accurate story. Gradually, the boys followed the intrepid explorer to the dark side of the machine and one by one, peered into the opening. The conveyor and the long passage stretched well off into the distance. The gantry was suspended high above the ground, protecting the coal-carrying conveyor. The belt was still in place but there was now no coal upon it.

"This is brill'." exclaimed Breen climbing onto the conveyor belt. The boys soon discovered that, if they ran down the belt and fell to their knees, the highly polished surface would allow them to slide for a few feet. The thick dust that lay almost half an inch deep in places also turned their blue jeans into black jeans.

Vern had continued to follow them, it was not difficult, as their trail of destruction, crude, rude drawings and footprints in the dust were clearer than any sign posts. The other four followed Tools along the conveyor belt until he found a piece of wood and began to strike the roof beams of the passageway. This of course, brought down onto the four followers a cloud of coal dust that had been forming for many years. When they could see again, they ran after Tools and caught him where the passageway opened out into another large room, where a similar piece of machinery stood. There was a stair going down and opposite, there was a large double door in faded and peeling blue paint. There were no windows, the light was supplied by clear corrugated plastic sky lights in the roof. The large blue door was interesting, simply because it was locked.

"It's locked." Breen informed the others as he toyed with the padlock and hasp.

"I wonder what's in there?" asked Ben.

"Something good or they wouldn't have locked it up." smiled Sam. Tools looked carefully at the lock and said.

"It's not a treasure lock."

"What?" asked Ben. Tools pointed to the lock with authority.

"It's not a treasure lock. I know a treasure lock when I see one and this ain't one." He was pointing at the lock as if it was offensive to his eyes. "If there was treasure behind that door, the lock would be bigger and stronger." This was watering the issue down. There was a door preventing them from seeing inside and they had to go through.

"But it doesn't have to be treasure, it could be some other kind of secret." added Sam trying to peer through the crack where the two doors met. Breen looked at the lock.

"He's right. There is something in here that they don't want us to find and that means it's got to be worth opening."

"Even if it were secrets, it would still have a treasure lock on it." retorted Tools with his hands on his hips, as all experts do when they know they are right.

"Explosives!" cried Weep.

"There's no explosives in there." laughed Ben.

"No we need explosives to get in there." The others ignored Weep's suggestion and started to look for a better plan. One by one they attempted to break the lock.

"I can't break it." said Ben as he threw down the piece of steel with which he had been striking the padlock. Sam kicked it, Breen hit it with a stick and Weep spat on it but still it would not break. Finally, Tools suggested that they smash the whole door. This suggestion seemed to have the ring of success about it – rather more so than Weep's attempt to split the lock open at least. Tools produced a rather short and worn screwdriver from his pocket and began to remove the screws from the hinges in both doors. As the screwdriver was likely to give up on the job having previously been used as a chisel, a drill, a knife, a tin opener and the point of a spear, it was fortunate that the wood was a little rotten and the screws were not difficult to remove. One by one they were extracted.

"That's it." said Tools, confidently standing back to let one of the lesser technically-minded deal with the rest of the operation. "One kick and it will go."

"I'll do it." said Weep backing up for what looked like a shoulder charge.

"No!" insisted Ben. "We don't want to break anything that might be in there. I'll do it." Ben stood one pace from the door and placed a well-aimed kick at its centre, just below the lock where the two doors met. The doors fell in, well actually, they fell out. They fell eighty feet to the ground below and shattered into a million pieces, though no one was counting. They fell very well for doors, as the doors had no training at falling. Neither had Ben but he almost followed them.

"Shiiit!" called out Ben as he tottered on the edge.

"Bloody 'ell!" said some of the others as they pulled him back and hauled him to the floor where they had all instinctively dropped. The boys carefully peered over the edge, to the ground far below as they lay flat to the decking of the high room.

"Jesus Christ," said Weep, in a slow quiet voice. "That's a very long drop."

"It must be an old loading door." said Tools, seemingly unmoved and the only one still on his feet, as he returned his trusty screwdriver to his deepest pocket.

"Don't know 'bout that," piped up Breen, still looking at the door below, "but it's a soddin' long way down." Weep confirmed this fact by standing and urinating over the edge - a sort of gesture to the world. He was urinating in the face of fate, celebrating the fact that he did not charge the door down and was not lying where he was now peeing. Breen noticed the flood of liquid snaking it's way down to the ground and his eyes followed the jet back to the source in Weeps jeans.

"Have you had that trapped somewhere?" asked Breen.

"Get lost!" was the instant, if not eloquent reply as Weep tucked himself away, just in case it *did* look different to any other boy's private parts.

By now, Vern had caught them up but managed to mingle within their ranks without being noticed. Once again, Tools found a way out of the room. It was another conveyor passage but this time it had a severe gradient. As the boys stood at the top of the sloping conveyor belt, Weep decided to roll a piece of coal down it. The coal lump picked up speed until it bounced and bumped and struck the steel superstructure, disintegrating in a cloud of dust.

"Brilliant!" called out Breen and he was soon sitting on the belt facing down the slope. He was well known for his eagerness to fling himself into danger. His brother Ben, realising the danger explained emphatically.

"If you slide down that, you'll break your neck." Breen looked back as Weep joined him with an enormous grin on his face. Breen copied the grin and launched himself down the belt. Before he was fifteen yards away, Weep was on his way too - down the slippery black belt and heading for the bottom. He was followed by Sam and eventually Tools, though Tools had less conviction about the sanity of such an action. Ben watched Tools leave, then he turned to Vern and said.

"Well I'm not walking back all the way we came." and he leapt onto the belt and began his doubtful ride. Breen was halfway down before the startling reality struck him of "How do I stop?". His cry of "Weeeeeeee," became "Aahhhhhh."

Weep, who followed him was characteristically spitting on the belt behind him so that the next one down would collect it on his jeans. The collector was Sam but he was too busy to notice, letting his hand rub on the corrugated sheeting that formed the sides of the man made tunnel. This caused a dust cloud behind him. The collector of the thick dust cloud was Tools who, in a panic caused by his lack of vision, tried to halt himself by grasping a thick cable overhead as he passed but the cable gave way and he fell back onto the belt. So did a wooden box that the cable had obviously been supporting. It too, slowly, *very* slowly at first, began the descent of the belt. Far too slowly for Ben, who was bearing down upon it with haste, seeing its shape just discernible through the slowly clearing dust. By the time he reached it, the thought of a collision made him instinctively attempt a leap from the belt but his shirt caught on the superstructure and he was thrown back onto the belt, accompanied by tearing sounds, striking the box and adding speed to it. Somehow he was now in front of the box, hurtling downwards, but head first. Vern had decided to walk down the side of the belt on the perfectly good walkway, skillfully provided for the purpose.

Breen was now near the bottom of the belt and saw before him a vast metal chute but before he had time to brace himself, he struck the harsh steel and fell into the blackness below.

At 251 Station Road, Pilsley lived Mr. and Mrs. Beal. Mr. Beal, known as Frank to his mates and Clanger to his brother, had a ten year old son whose name was Kenny. For twelve years Frank had worked for the National Coal Board as a miner until, eight years previously, he had an accident. It wasn't life threatening but he was off work for six months and was told he would be given a steadier job when he restarted. Pilsley Pit was however, to be closed and so, he was told that he would have to move to another pit. He moved to Bolsover Colliery, working on the surface as a sort of 'Fitters Mate', helping with repairs, oiling machinery and performing general maintenance around the pit top. He remained living in Pilsley though and had fond memories of his time at the local pit, which over the next few years, was to be totally demolished. As he lived just six hundred yards from the colliery, he would often walk through the yard for old times sake and before the whole lot vanished forever. He frequently took his son with him on the short walk, telling him tales about the mighty pit in better days. Today was no different. In fact there was nothing at all particularly different about this day except that it was Sunday and Frank did not usually visit his old work place on the Sabbath. Today however, the weather was perfect for a walk before tea. As he and his small son reached the site of the black mass of Pilsley Colliery, Frank instantly sensed something was amiss. His step quickened so much that little Kenny had to positively trot at his side to keep up.

"Daddy? Daddy?" keened Kenny, panting and slightly worried but Frank couldn't hear him. His attention was elsewhere. As they reached the pit yard Frank stopped. For one brief moment, he looked up and saw the pit in full swing, once again brought to life. Had it all been a dream? He shook himself and came back to reality.

"No, the pit is closed; some of it was pulled down years ago." he said with a look of disbelief. "They can't have started it up again, they would have told me. Anyway it's Sunday for God's sake." He inwardly chastised himself for taking the Lord's name in vain, looked skywards and shrugged his shoulders.

He quickly made his way towards the remains of the old screening plant and stared around with amazement. He knew something was wrong. One clue was the earlier sight of coal dust issuing from some of the gantries like black steam. Another was an old, wrecked double loading door by the bunker, seemingly a wooden suicide victim, flung from its normal position high in the building. The final conclusive piece of evidence that all was not well, revealed itself when he reached a pile of fine coal dust under the coal hopper. There had been a clunk and clouds of dust, before a small boy had issued from the chute and deposited himself on top of the coal pile. Before Frank had time to ask the boy if he was hurt, there was another clang and another boy fell from the chute. The two boys sat up in the coal pile, the first had blood on his face, the second a large dirty grinning mouth that said,

"Jesus Christ!" Well it was the Sabbath, but as Frank gathered his reason, another clang heralded yet another issue from the chute and once again, a boy fell from the sky. As this one landed on the other two boys, his quote was heard to be

"Bloody Hell!"

"Not so Christian but just as profane." thought Frank. The three of them saw Mr. Beal and immediately began to look grim, as if they had been told they were never to eat sweets again. They nervously slid down the pile of coal slack and began to dust themselves off. It was a token gesture as they were as black as Satan's riding boots. Before they had time to think of an explanation, yet another clang and yet another small boy breached the chute to the sound of a long drawn out

"Shiiiiiiiiiit."

Mr. Beal and his son stood amazed as the boy landed in the coal and a stream of dust and fine coal was exhaled from the chute, covering him like black icing on a boy shaped cake. He too slid down the coal pile to join the others but saw no point in dusting himself down and gave off a continuous dark cloud as he moved. The man and his son looked up at the chute expecting another boy but none came. Mr. Beal grappled through his shock and pointed at the boys saying.

"Now then!" but his stern words were cut short by another clang, he covered his sons ears and waited for another boy, this one was slightly larger and came out head first calling.

"Holy shit....." The boy pulled his head and shoulders from the coal pile, spitting dust and debris from his mouth, and slid down. Before Frank could reprimand him for blaspheming however, another clang gave warning that the amazing child-producing hopper was to give birth yet again. This time the exhaust from the chute was not a boy but a wooden box, about two feet square. The wooden box slid down the coal pile to Frank's feet. Frank looked down at the box and bent to wipe the coal dust from its lid. It displayed the faded legend, 'NCB 223/K.' He looked up at the chute once more for reassurance and then carefully opened the lid of the box expecting to find a map, or treasure, or something. He didn't know whether he was disappointed or not to find nothing. The box was empty, save for a little coal dust. Even the coal dust looked like any other coal dust. It was black and slightly shiny as the afternoon light reflected on some of the particles here and there but looked just like any other coal dust. It certainly didn't seem the sort of coal dust you would endanger your life for, or try to sneak out in a special wooden box.

Frank was dumfounded, he looked up to the boys for an explanation but they had gone, leaving a barely perceptible dark cloud and black tracks along the railway siding. Just then, another small, not so dirty boy came steadily down the steel stairs by the side of the chute and quite innocently asked,

"Have you seen five boys mister?" Suffering mild shock and still crouched by the empty box, Frank just pointed down the track. "Thanks mister." said Vern as he trundled away. Frank looked down at his son, he too was now covered in coal dust. Frank quickly dusted the lad down, fearful that his son may end up in a coal bunker somewhere only to be spit out, some years later, in the sight of other innocent parties and the cycle would begin all over again. 'The Hopper' mystery they would call it. 'The Strange Mystery of the Coal Children.' He shuddered.

Frank spent the next two days locked in his house with Kenny.

The boys set off on the long trek home, discussing the day and laughing as they went. Near the quarry, they passed a woman walking her dog, she stared at them harshly. The boys looked at themselves and realised they were in quite a state. They looked like Zulu warriors returning from a battle. Breen was cut on his forehead and the blood had mixed with the coal dust to form a ridge down his face. Tools had lost one of his shoes, Ben had ripped his shirt and Sam had torn his jeans. Not that the clothing was a great issue, as it was difficult to say where one item ended and the other began.

" We stopped bank robbers missus." grinned Weep. The boys laughed and looked at each other. They were so black and grubby all they could do was laugh. Even Vern was now covered in dust just by being in close proximity to the others.

"God, I would love to walk into my sister's room like this." he laughed and began to walk like a zombie. The others joined in and they were laughing so much that Sam rubbed his face to stop his cheeks aching. As he took his hand away, the others fell about laughing at the mess he had made. Tears of laughter mingled with the dirt and the whole process began again. They had laughed so much that Ben was holding his ribs. He looked at his brother.

"Hey Breen," he chuckled. "even our mother won't recognise us." The laughing stopped. The smiles quickly faded. Their mothers!

Sam's mother had put his pocket money up to ten shillings after much complaining from Sam about what he was unable to do with his current pittance of spending money. His mother had been very forthright about what he *could* do with the previous allowance but Sam never let optimism get in the way of sheer greed. Now it was ten whole shillings, a 'ten bob note' each week, he was nearly a millionaire. He looked down at the marvelous note, a deep, rich, red-brown colour, the colour of real money and to think the 'powers that be' were about to change that wonderful note into a cold, nondescript coin, harsh and insensitive in the hand. Sam couldn't imagine a world without a 'ten bob note', but whilst he still owned one he decided to call for his friends and spend some of his new found wealth at the 'Wakes'. The Wakes was a local name for the travelling funfair, a name that had been used since medieval times for the great fairs but in this part of Derbyshire the name was still in use for the funfair. Sam loved the fair, it was one of the few places he really felt at home. Most boys of Sam's age wanted to grow up to be firemen, or train drivers or jet pilots, not Sam, he wanted to work on the bigger rides at the fair. Sam, Tools, Breen and Ben set out for the travelling fair that had set up at Holmewood, a village two or three miles further east.

Scanning across the rough field, Sam could see a Whip, Speedway, Ghost Train, Dodgems and his favourite ride, the Waltzer. Sam was eager to be on the field in the thick of the fairground, to embrace the smells and the sounds that were so unique, there was nothing else like them, or could be compared to them. The smell of the onions from the hot dog stall, the sound of the PA systems firing out the latest chart hits, the subtle whiff of diesel fumes drifting over from the generators at the rear of the rides, the loud interruptions of the ride announcers as they tried to get more punters on with promises of speed or excitement. The rasping smell of electric sparks from the dodgem cars, the acrid dart of camphor that always seemed to be present at the coconut shy, that blissful sticky scent that lingered on the air from the toffee apple stall and the intoxicating waft of the general mix of everything at the fair. Over to the left, the 'ping-ting' sound of the air rifle booth, the loud siren of the Ghost Train as it sent another car of unimpressed customers into the void. To the right, the sound of girls' screams as some ride or other careered them into new heights of excited frenzy and straight ahead the very centre of the fair. Sam stood in that hallowed spot and held his arms out straight and wide. He held his head back, closed his eyes and breathed in deep as his ears cuddled everything that came their way. This was Sam's world. This was Sam.

"What are you doing?" asked Breen but Sam just stood there in the same manner and said.

"Being happy."

"Come on you idiot," barked Ben. "before you get us noticed." Ben pulled at his arms and Sam walked on but the silly grin on his face was fixed. The boys went on the Whip first. It was a fast and exciting ride, in some areas known as the Skid, Sam blissfully grinning his joy to the world, and before the ride had come to a full stop they jumped off and went to buy candyfloss.

"What's this stuff made of?" asked Breen.

"Cotton wool." answered Ben.

"It can't be," answered Sam "it's pink, sweet and sticky and anyway you can't eat cotton wool!"

"That's true," confirmed Ben. "It would be as dangerous as swallowing bubblegum!"

"What?" asked Tools.

"Bubblegum, it sticks to your ribs and you die!" explained Breen.

"My gran says that too but why does it?" asked Sam, pressing some of the sticky floss into his mouth.

"Dunno," admitted Ben. "But it tastes good and as long as you spit it out you'll be safe."

"What about Candy Floss then?" frowned Breen, picking some strands of floss from his cheeks.

"What about it?" sighed Sam.

"Well d'you have to spit that out?"

"Daft bugger." laughed Ben and he turned, as did the others, and headed towards the Ghost Train. Breen was left standing alone and wondering what it was he had said. The Ghost Train bore no relation to the modern rides we have today, it was a large trailer that was unfolded to produce a smaller ride than you would expect. The cars seated two so Sam and Tools occupied the first car and Ben and Breen took the second and waited for the ride to begin.

"Keep your 'ands and feet inside the cars at all times." announced the attendant.

"That's odd." exclaimed Breen.

"What?" asked Ben.

"These aren't cars, they're trains." said Breen. "It's a ghost *train*." Ben sighed and Tools turned rearward to explain the situation but his speech was blotted out as the siren sounded and the first car / train / vehicle jolted and the ride began.

It wasn't that the ride was particularly scary, or that it was very dark inside, but the boys made a point of shouting and screaming throughout the journey - it was traditional. After pointing out that one of the monsters looked like a certain teacher, they headed towards the toffee apple stand and then on to the Speedway.

The Speedway was a circular ride that had stylised, carved wooden motorbikes instead of the usual horses, a ride that showmen call an 'Ark'. These wooden bikes leaned in, towards the centre like real speedway bikes but were still painted in the same unfeasible colours as other traditional, travelling fair rides. On every third bay or so, there was a kind of chariot seat. These, it seemed, were designed for the more demure ladies to sit upon. On the outer edge of the rows of motorbikes was a metal fence that was probably there as a safety barrier, just in case anyone slipped from the bike. Ironically though, it was more usually used by the older, nonchalant boys, who thought it looked 'hip' to lean on it rather than sit. The Speedway was also fabled as the fastest ride on the fair, but Sam and his friends wanted it even faster and that would be difficult in the daylight, Sam preferred the fair at night for, as every fair expert knew, the rides were always faster then, but needs must and he was here in the early afternoon. There would be other times when his parents would take him to the fair at night but for now the boys had to improvise. Sam chose his bike, the one on the outer end of the row which was the fastest, Tools to his right and Ben and Breen on the row behind. Immediately in front of them, two pretty girls climbed aboard and sat in the chariot section ahead of the boys and smiled at the lads as they took their places. The boys weren't over-enthusiastic about girls but they made the effort and smiled back. Strangely, Sam felt a tightening in his stomach and wondered if the others felt the same. The youth collecting the fares arrived at their section and held his hand out for the payment. Sam seemed to be struggling to find his money but this was the delaying tactic for a faster ride, it would give him time to talk to the attendant who was trying to collect fares as quickly as he could.

"Was it your fair at North Wingfield last month?" he asked the youth as he found some money and handed it over.

"Nahh, not us." replied the attendant.

"Mmm, I thought not," replied Sam and he turned to Tools to his right and continued. "*they* have the fastest Speedway in the country you know." Tools understood and agreed, nodding his head in an exaggerated way.

"Really fast from what I heard." added Tools. The youth handed Sam his change and stared at him for a second or two and then stepped through to the row behind. Sam looked over to Tools and grinned and then tried to make himself as comfortable as he could on the leaning bike.

When the fare collector arrived back at the booth in the centre of the ride, he seemed to be in discussion with the ride operator. Sam leaned over and tapped Tools on the arm and nodded towards the booth. Tools turned round to look at the booth just in time to see the youth motion back towards Sam with his thumb. The operator nodded grimly and the youth continued collecting the last fares. Tools grinned at Sam and they both turned to the boys behind with their thumbs up and a wide smile.

"Take your seats now!" called the operator over the P.A. system. "The fastest ride at the fair starting in one minute." Sam gripped the handlebars of the bike, this was what he loved, the expectation and the thrill of the fair. The music was loud and the yellow and red roof lights flashed maniacally. Sam had a quick look around to soak up the atmosphere and glanced over to the two girls, one of whom glanced back and smiled. Sam was immune to outside influences for the next few minutes, he was immersed in the ride and nothing could drag him from that. The man on the PA system called out, his voice just audible above the music which was The Monkees' "I'm a Believer".

"Here we go now folks, hold tight, you are riding the Speedway." As the ride began its initial steady movement, Sam looked around at his friends and then back to the two girls who were eagerly chatting to each other. Gradually the ride increased its speed and as it did so, Sam and the others leaned further towards the centre of the ride to compensate for the forces on their bodies. Sam looked forward and noticed that the speed of the ride had pushed the two girls to the edge of their chariot and that their long hair had been whipped over the back of the seat by the breeze. The music was turned up louder, the lights flashed faster and the Speedway picked up more speed. Sam was in ecstasy and he yelled at the top of his voice, the others following suit as the operator called out, "Okay, you want more speed?" Just about everyone on the ride called back, "Yes!"

"Scream if you want more speed!" he called. The reply was predictable and loud. Everyone shouted or screamed and the operator pushed the handle further over and turned out the lights. This was supposed to let the experts know that it was 'flat out' in time-honoured tradition. It felt like it too! Sam wasn't sure what centrifugal force was but this didn't prevent it from trying to pull him off the bike and deposit him in the 'Hook a Duck' stall. They let out another shout - this was life! This was why they had been born! Eventually the ride slowed down and as it came to a steady halt the passengers readied to leave, a few remained seated for another go. As Sam stood and jumped from the slowly revolving ride the fare collector passed by and asked,

"Fast enough for you?"

"Brilliant." replied the smiling Sam and he looked towards the operator's booth and gave the man a 'thumbs up' salute.

The girls had left too and were heading towards the Dodgems.

"C'mon!" instructed Ben, as he followed the girls. Over at the dodgems, a ride was in progress so they stood and watched. It was customary for them to watch for one turn to pick out the fastest cars.

"Green, number fourteen." thought Sam. The ride stopped and the crowd ran for empty cars. Someone reached car fourteen before Sam, so he jumped in black ten, a car he had considered was equal to the task. As he made himself comfortable, he searched out the girls, they were together in a red car. Then he found Tools, Breen and Ben over the other side. The boys had a car each, after all there were girls to show off to. As the music played, there was a cacophony of clicks that came from the pedals within the cars as they were pressed and released. Sam, however, kept his pressed to the floor so that he could move immediately the power was turned on.

A horn blew and the cars came to life, loosing sparks from the top of their contact poles. Sam turned left to reach the two girls but saw Ben bearing down upon him. Sam swerved, a brilliant manoeuvre, and swung around Bob's red twenty one but lack of concentration helped Tools to 'broadside' him and sent the car spinning around, trapping him between two others. A well practiced move of Sam's let him spin the steering wheel 180 degrees and send the car into reverse. In this position, he sought out the girls and headed their way, deftly releasing the wheel and catapulting the car into forward motion. How impressive was that? The girls couldn't fail to like him, if they had been watching, that was! The reason they were not watching was that Breen had bumped into their car and had trapped them into the side of the arena. Sam moved on at full speed but who should he bump - the girls or Breen? It was a big decision. If he bumped the girls, they might take offence. If he bumped Breen, they might think he wasn't interested. Oh what? Which? He decided to bump Breen then smile at the girls. This was it, Breen was in his sight. It wasn't his day though - from his right hand side another car hit him, pushing black ten into an empty car at the side of the arena. His assailant was a middle-aged man with a stupid laugh and a little brat with melted candyfloss instead of a face. Sam reversed and waited for the girls to come around. Here they came, no other cars anywhere near. This was it, victory was his! He booted the pedal to the floor and black ten lurched forward, its mighty metal wheels biting at the steel floor plates as it tried its best to find traction and push Sam headlong into the girls. Then, in an instant it slowed and stopped, the ride was over.

"Shit!" he said to himself. The girls left their car and headed away from where Sam sat. Dejected, he walked away from the mighty black ten, his dead chariot and shuffled towards the goldfish stand, looking for the other boys. He could see Ben and Tools by the air rifle stall, but he couldn't see Breen. Sam looked back over to the dodgems but still couldn't see him.

"Hey Sam," called out a familiar voice. Sam turned, it was Breen behind him. "Listen, those two girls from the Speedway will go on the Waltzer with us."

"When?" asked Sam with a complete morale recovery.

"After they've been for a hot dog." he said confidently.

"Let's get rid of Tools and Ben." said Sam, as subtle as he needed to be. This was all new to Sam, chasing girls. The two boys hatched a plan to be rid of the other two. Ben and Tools joined them.

"Hey," said Ben. "let's go on the Waltzer!"

"Okay," smiled Sam. "I'll buy us some toffee apples, I'll meet you there." Sam looked at Breen and said, "Help me carry them?" Sam paying for something was unusual and they were sure the other two boys wouldn't believe him but it was the best he could do, given the short time available to him. Breen and Sam watched at a safe distance until Tools and Ben became bored with waiting and then eventually walked off towards the coconut shy. It wasn't long before the boys noticed the girls standing by the Waltzer.

"This is it!" insisted Breen.

"No, wait!" pointed Sam. They looked back and watched Tools and Ben leaving the coconut shy and head off towards toffee apple stall. Sam and Breen almost ran towards the girls but Sam could still not understand what force was making him do this. The girls smiled again and stepped into one of the cars. Sam and Breen sat either side of them and rested their feet on the safety bar. It looked more casual than pulling it down over their legs and after all, safety hadn't been invented yet. The Waltzer began its inevitable journey with the cars rocking as they rolled over the apex of the undulating track, as ironically, the Hollies' new single "Riding Along on a Carousel" began. As the machine picked up speed, the occupants were flung into the back of their seats. The girl next to Sam pushed herself against him for security. Her long mousy hair was soft and smelt of soap, slightly scented. He felt sick but strangely good. He wanted to turn away but as her hair lapped across his face again, he breathed in the scent and felt a compulsion to touch it. He resisted and turned away trying to focus on the lights that flashed by as they swirled around. The car spun again and the girl grabbed hold of Sam's arm. His heart pounded; it was the worst feeling he had ever felt but it was so good! Like riding a roller coaster and finding out that the track was missing, only to land in a tank of feathers. "If this is what love is like .... well .... well." thought Sam, he was confused.

As the ride ceased, the girl released her grip on Sam's arm. The four of them jumped out of the car and walked towards the rifle range. Not sure what to do, the boys walked behind the girls. 'Fish out of water' wouldn't apply here, for fish know what to do, they wriggle and move. The girls soon tired of the shy boys and left them near the Whip.

"Where's the toffee apples?" asked Ben when they found the young boys.

"Oh, eaten we couldn't find you!" shrugged Sam. The other two boys frowned as there were no tell-tail red marks around Sam or Breen's mouths. For another hour they walked around the fair and at good intervals, tried most of the rides and eventually ate toffee apples and hot dogs. Soon the money was spent and fairs are not quite as much fun when you have no money left.

As they left the field to the sounds of The Beatles pulsing out from one of the rides the four boys headed home and Sam asked.

"Have you got a girlfriend Ben?"

"No." replied Ben as if he had been asked an insulting question.

"They are trouble." insisted Tools. None of the boys had sisters so it was hard to know how girls thought, they may as well have been an alien race. Sam realised he had to know more. The only friend he had with a sister was Vern. *His* sister, Suzy, was a couple of years older but she was a very good looking girl. Sam went to visit Vern the next day.

"But why do you want to know?" asked Vern.

"Just interested that's all, I just wondered what it's like to have a sister."

"I've told you before, it's horrid!" insisted Vern. Sam thought Vern's answers were getting him nowhere, he would simply have to explore for himself. One week later he had the chance. He was at Vern's house one evening when Vern's parents were out. Suzy was there and Vern suggested she did a strip for the two boys, it seemed she had done this before. At first, she pretended to be embarrassed but soon agreed and put a suitable single on the record player. Sam and Vern were seated on the settee, Sam examining her with glazed blue eyes. Suzy nearly always wore a short skirt but somehow she managed to hoist it up a little higher whilst dancing around the room. Slowly she unbuttoned her blouse, allowing it to drop open to reveal her small white bra. She discarded the blouse onto Sam's lap, he was anxious and slightly afraid at feeling its warmth on his arm. Looking her up and down he could feel his feet twitching - he knew what was coming but tried to resist. Suzy twisted her arms behind her back and pretended to unfasten her bra. Sam covered the 150 yards home from Vern's house in just under twelve seconds, somewhat faster than Black Ten!

The railway that ran through the village of Highfields was a simple, single track affair, that connected a network of local collieries in that part of North East Derbyshire to the main lines. These were the main L.M.S and L.N.E.R. main lines and for the early part of Sam's life, both main lines, following the merger of the 'Big Four' in 1948, belonged to British Railways but they still carried quite a few trains. These two main lines were just a couple of miles apart in that part of Derbyshire and the railway culture was therefore, an important part of life. Sam's father had been a fireman in his early working career, he had worked for British Railways and told may stories of his time on the footplate. Sam knew every anecdote by memory they were so worn. The railway was a large part of Sam's life in many ways, for as many as ten trains a day rumbled over the railway crossing at the bottom of the small hamlet. The little railway ran from the Midland line past Alma Colliery down to Grassmoor colliery and along a spur to Williamthorpe Colliery, continuing to Highfields and over the crossing. It then ran south from the crossing, on past the Tip and eventually to the old quarry and beyond the wood. At the quarry the line divided, one branch going to Pilsley and Morton Collieries, the other to Holmewood Colliery and the coke ovens beside it and then on to the L.N.E.R. main line. All along the route were sidings, where full and empty wagons were deposited. These wagons were usually moved by small diesel shunters ready for larger locos, powered by steam or diesel, to haul them to the main lines. At the turn of the century there had been ten collieries in just a few square miles, all connected by miles and miles of railway, yet the countryside seemed to live in reasonable harmony with it all.

Just half a mile from the crossing at Highfields, heading south, the track curved to the left, past the Tip and then curved to the right along a high bank parallel to a small siding. It was here that Breen, Sam, Vern and Weep decided to go one hot morning in a certain summer. Standing on the siding were fifty or so wagons mostly filled with very small lumps of coal, almost coal dust really. This coal was destined for the Nottinghamshire power stations but for the while, here it sat, waiting to be picked up. Seated in one of the wagons were the four boys - one in each corner, perched on top of the coal with the greater mound of the load piled up in the centre. Breen was poking around in the coal dust in his corner.

"What shall we do then?"

"Well I reckon we should go down to Peggy's Brook and climb the trees." said Weep.

"Nahh," was Vern's instant reaction. "I want to go bird nesting on the Tip." Breen shuffled in the coal and said.

"That's borin', anyway we did that the other day and found nothin'." Sam then spoke.

"Lets go and throw stones at old man Clark's door." Breen shuffled even faster. There was a long silence broken by the sound of an air horn in the distance.

"There's a train coming," said Breen, as he stood and pointed up the line. The others also got to their feet so that they could see over the side of the wagon.

"Yep, I 'spose we oughta get out then." suggested Breen.

"Down!" hissed Sam as he ducked down into the wagon. The others followed his lead and dropped back in the safety of the coal.

"What's up?" whispered Vern.

"Two blokes coming down the line from the other direction," answered Sam, pointing in the opposite direction of the train. "It's probably the shunters."

The four boys ducked further down into the wagon as the noise the big diesel loco became louder and louder until it seemed the loco was going to climb in the wagon with them. It eventually passed and stopped a little way up the line. The engine became quiet as if it was listening for the boys. They lay motionless until they heard what must have been the two men's voices. Breen tried to peer over the wagon side but Vern pulled him back down. The engine note rose again and the loco sounded as if it was moving.

"Good it's going." proffered Vern but suddenly, with a jolt, their wagon began to move.

"Shit, what's happening?" asked Breen, with a startled look on his face. Weep, who had been rather quiet, threw all caution to the wind and peered over the side of the wagon.

"The shunting loco is pulling us towards the quarry." He had a panicky look about him as he ducked back down.

"That's bad news." frowned Sam.

"Why?" asked Weep not sure if he wanted the answer. It was Breen who provided it.

"Well, I reckon the shunter is taking us out of the siding and connecting us to the loco." He looked at Sam as if looking for some ideas but Sam had none. The wagon continued past the standing loco and on towards the quarry. Eventually it stopped and after a short pause began to reverse the way it had just come.

"When it stops to couple up to the loco, we can climb out and run off down the bank. They won't see us if we are quick." suggested Breen, trying to lift their spirits. They all nodded except Weep who looked more than a little worried. Soon the wagon banged to a halt as the train bumped into the big loco.

"Now?" asked Vern looking at the others. Breen just nodded. They stood, but as they did so, they heard the men's voices, quite close, over the sound of the big loco. They ducked back down and Sam and Breen scurried to the rear of the wagon, through the coal dust, and peered over.

"English Electric, and two of 'em." pointed out Breen in a whisper. Sam didn't know what locos they were and didn't care, he was just looking for a way out of this. He turned to the others and in a louder whisper said,

"We can't get out here, there are four of 'em and we'll get caught." There was a clanking of something metallic, like the sound of heavy chains.

"Right Harry, that's it. Lets go." said one of the voices. The engine screamed, there was jolt and the wagon began to move once more.

"They're taking us away," cried Weep.

"Shut up!" said Sam.

"But they're taking us away, we'll end up in Stockport." Weep added.

"Where?" asked Sam. Vern interrupted.

"He said Stockport."

"Why Stockport?" asked Sam.

"He's got relations there, it's the only place he knows of out of Highfields." explained Vern. Weep stopped his crying and said sternly.

"It is not, I've been to Clay Cross, Wingerworth, Grassmoor and ..... and .... er ...... Billsmothers." The three boys looked at each other, very puzzled.

"Never heard of it." said Sam.

"Nor me." added Vern.

"I don't think Weep has either." added Breen.

"I have, I have." shouted Weep.

"Where is it then?" asked Sam. Weep lowered his head and poked around in the coal dust.

"Well I don't know where it is but I've heard people say 'It's raining over Billsmothers.'" The other three boys began throwing the small lumps of coal at Weep, in turn he began crying again. Vern noticed that the train was picking up speed.

"It will have to stop at the main road to open the crossing gates." he pointed out.

"Yes, yes that's right," said Sam, smiling eagerly. "When it stops, we can all jump out to the left and run into the bushes at the top of the bank. Even if they spot us, they'll never follow us in there." They all felt a little calmer but as they neared the crossing in the village the loco did not seem to be slowing.

"Any minute now it will stop." said Vern, trying to cheer himself up. He was wrong. The gates were already open and the train began to increase speed as it proceeded through and over the road, continuing north.

Mr Norman Philip Boyde was sitting in the front seat on the top deck of the 'D1' service bus with his small son.

"Why have we stopped Daddy?"

"Well David, we must stop at these gates to let the train through. Keep watching and you will see the train come between the houses and across the road."

"Where is the train Daddy?" asked the impatient boy.

"You will see it in a moment." replied the father.

"How long will the train be Daddy?"

"I don't know David, but I'm sure it will be here in a moment."

"Will it be steam Daddy?"

"Probably David, or it could be one of the new diesel locomotives."

"Will it take long daddy?"

"No David, in fact, here it is now. Look, it's two diesel engines pulling big wagons."

"What do they put in the wagons daddy?"

"Just coal David, just coal." replied the father reminiscing about his own childhood train set.

"And children?" asked the infant, quite unruffled. Mr Boyde looked up just in time to see a wagon speed past with four dirty, worried faces peering over the top, just as he was about to say no. Mr Boyde's glassy stare continued after the train had passed.

"That's right David, children too."

The train was still at speed as Breen pointed and said.

"Look, it's the Wolfy and Alma Tip." These landmarks were the furthest the boys wandered in normal circumstances. They were beginning to panic as just perceptibly, the train felt as if it was slowing down. Yes it was and within half a mile or so it came to a halt.

"Now what?" asked Breen. The four dirty faces looked at each other questioningly, there were no more words left to say. As one they leapt up and scampered down the side of the wagon quicker than any mountain climber could have achieved it. With relief the four jumped into the long grass on the bank. Waiting for them was a tall, red-faced man in a uniform.

"And what do you think you lot are doing?" Weep began the build up that heralded that he was going to cry.

"Nothing mister, honest." said Breen. "We all fell asleep in the wagon after being chased by a madman."

"Yes," continued Sam. "He chased us for ten miles an' we decided to rest an' hide in that wagon, but it moved away an' brought us 'ere."

"I see, you better come with me." said the man in a very stern voice. He took them across the lines to another siding. There stood a small loco with a guard's van, it was obviously where the man was taking them.

"Please mister," spluttered Weep. "we didn't mean to get in your train, it just 'appened." The man looked down at the lad. His face was black from the coal dust, all except for two lines running down from his eyes and over his cheeks where the tears had run. The man seemed to be biting his lip and then he covered his mouth and coughed. Sam thought that maybe his teeth were coming loose. He had seen that happen to his granny and knew it was a very serious problem.

"Right you lot," said the man, "let's have you in here." They followed the man up the short ladder into the guard's van. Inside it was quite dark, a small fire in a steel box was heating up the water in a tiny kettle. It was like a long, narrow room but tidy and sort of homely. Sam didn't feel too afraid about the situation now, this small room on wheels felt cool and comforting.

"Right, sit down the lot of you." There weren't many places to sit but Sam and Vern sat on a small bench, which was covered with a stuffed pad. Breen sat on a small chair and after wiping more tears from his cheeks, Weep sat in a tiny recess in the middle of the van.

"Now listen to me you four," began the man. "keep out of them wagons and stay off the railway. If I catch you on here agen', I'll fetch the coppers and get 'em to take you to your fathers." The man produced a paper bag and dropped it on the table in the middle of the van.

"Now then, take one each." he said. They were boiled sweets. Sam, Vern and Weep eagerly took a sweet each. Breen took one and pointed out that he had a brother who liked sweets too.

"Okay, you can all take two." he said smiling for the first time at the children. It was when Breen asked if he could take his brother two that the man picked up the sweets and returned them to his jacket pocket. The red faced man asked them how far they had all come and when they had managed to explain, he looked up at the clock on the van wall and said.

"We will have to see about getting you lot back." and he opened the door to leave. "Wait here." As soon as he had left Vern said.

"C'mon let's scarper."

"I'm not, there might be more sweets." explained Sam. Breen nodded in agreement.

"I wanna' go." sobbed Weep barely holding back his tears.

"Well it's up to you but we're staying." said Breen. It didn't take long for Vern and Weep to come up with a purely natural instinct that there was safety in numbers and they sat back down. The man returned.

"We're off back that way so we can drop you off near the Tip, but stay off the line in future." He pointed at them and they nodded sheepishly. It wasn't long before the shunting loco tooted its horn and the red faced man leaned out of the van and waved. The van began to move and was soon on its way back up the track, the way they had come on the coal train. They stopped at the crossing to open and close the gates and then continued towards the tip. When they reached their initial point of departure in the sidings, the loco stopped and the man stood and jumped off.

"Come on lads, here we are."

"Thanks mister." said Vern and the man pulled the bag from his coat once more. Sam and Breen grinned at Vern and Weep.

"Just one this time and if I catch you down here again..." He pushed the now almost empty bag into his pocket and then climbed back up, waved to the shunting loco which revved it's engine, and set off south. The red faced man leaned on the rail at the back of the van, clearly smiling and shaking his head slightly.

"I think he's potty." said Vern as they turned to leave. Potty he may have been for, if the man had examined the situation, or even known any of the boys personally, he would not have bothered telling them keep clear of the railway. Here were four, very cunning lads, who, after having an adventure, were rewarded with three boiled sweets each and then a casual ride in a guard's van. It was certainly worth doing again.

As they walked up the tip path in their coal-covered clothes Vern said,

"I want to be a train driver when I grow up."

"Not me," said Breen, shaking his head. "it must be borin'." Breen turned to Sam. "How about you?" Sam thought for a moment.

"Naaa, not a train driver but I wouldn't mind his job." He pointed his thumb towards the railway.

"What 'im with the red face?" asked Vern.

"Yeah, why not? It's brilliant in that guard's van. It's got every comfort and you get to ride about the country." Vern turned to Weep.

"Where you gonna' work Weep, the water works?" they all laughed except Weep whose bottom lip began to curl down.

"No, 'an I'm not going to work at the bloody pit like you lot." The other three were bemused. It was as if he hadn't listened to the previous conversation.

"What d' you mean Weep?" asked Breen.

"My dad says all the useless bloody kids round here 'ill end up at the pit." he frowned, his lip still curling downwards.

"Well he's bloody wrong then," spat Sam with a frown so deep his nose curled. "I'm not going to the pit, that's for sure."

"Me neither," growled Vern "and I'm not going in the army like me dad wants either."

"Army?" grinned Breen. "Why does he want you to go in the army?"

"He says they're the only ones who can knock some sense into me." The others grinned but Vern didn't see the joke.

"What about you then Breen?" asked Sam.

"Me? Oooh I was thinking about fighter pilot or something but I will probably be a prostitute." There was a silence until Vern asked.

"What's that then?"

"Erm, I'm not really sure but you do it in Chesterfield, and you have to do a lot of walking." The others continued to walk in silence again until Sam stopped and turned to Breen.

"If you don't know what it is, why do you want to do it. It could be eating dog poo or somethin'"

"It's the money." insisted Breen. Sam nodded and they continued to walk. As they passed the Big Tree Sam asked.

"So it's well paid and it's in Chesterfield an' there's a lot of walking. It doesn't sound like you would get lots of money for that, you're making it up."

"Am not," insisted Breen. "you know Sally Walker from down the village?"

"Yeah." nodded Sam.

"Yeah, she's Tommy Walker's sister. So what?" added Weep coming out of his scowl.

"Well that's what she's going to be. I overheard my mam and dad talking about her. Mam told dad that our Ben had to dance with her at the May Pole dancing at school last spring."

"So what, I had to dance with Anne Young and Sally is nicer than Anne." frowned Sam.

"Well let me finish the story then." They had reached the Tip Gate and so the four of them sat on its top rung like large, dirty starlings on a telegraph wire.

"Well," continued Breen. "my dad then says, 'What? Alice Walker's girl? I bet that did Ben no good.'- an' my mam asked what he meant an' he told her that, from what he's heard, she was in advanced training for becoming a prostitute."

"So?" asked Sam, shrugging his shoulders. "Where's the money come into it?"

"Well, me mam said, 'Aww Bert that's not fair.'" Breen had jumped down and was doing a very poor impression of his mother, for comic effect. "Then my dad says," he then tried an equally unconvincing attempt at his father complete with gruff voice. "'It's true though and, I have to say, she'll make twenty times more money than any of the other kids on this street.'"

"Wow! Twenty times more?" gasped the others with disbelief. Weep had the fingers of his dirty hands stretched out try to work out what that meant.

Just outside the grocery shop, at the side of the bottom opening near the Tip Gate, the delivery lad had dropped a dozen cream cakes all over the pavement. He was being chastised for doing so by the owner of the shop, the father of one of Sam's acquaintances with the name of 'Biro'. Biro's dad was explaining to the delivery lad that he couldn't imagine any excuse for his stupidity. The delivery lad, who had only had the job for six weeks, having been forced to leave his window cleaning round when he developed vertigo, was needless-to-say, rather worried. He was desperately trying to find an excuse for dropping the cream cakes from the tray. He had considered earthquake but that was rather poor, flood but it hadn't rained for three weeks, a wild horse riding past and even a fainting fit. When he began to think of 'crocodile attack', he knew he was going to lose his job. After all, who would believe that he had just seen four skipping boys ranging in ages from about nine to eleven, arm in arm singing the repeated line, "We wanna' be prostitutes."

Sam, or any of his friends if asked, would say that the summer school holidays were simply not long enough. They would argue that a child needs freedom and time to develop and for this natural process to happen, they need time away from the restrictions of school and adult guidance. They probably wouldn't put it in quite that manner but the sentiment would be the same. The truth is that the summer holidays went on forever - six weeks of fantastic freedom - but it is a very long time to go without seeing your school mates. So this particular morning, in a certain summer, three boys - Kev, his younger brother Dan and their cousin Neil - walked the three miles up from the village into the little hamlet of Highfields to call on Sam.

"We thought we would come up today." said Kev standing at the door of Sam's house.

"Good." replied Sam locking the door behind him. "What shall we do then? Any ideas?"

"Not really, we're completely bored. We've done all the things we can think of so we thought you would have some suggestions."

"No, nothing special. I was just thinking about going for a walk." concluded Sam, thrusting his hands into his pockets. They all stood by the door leaning against the wall, wondering if a walk was even slightly interesting, when Sam had an idea.

"Let's call on Weep. He's a bit younger than us but he's usually up to something." They set off following Sam to this person's house, as no one but Sam knew him. As they reached the back garden, Weep was leaving the house with his friend Mumble, who was of a similar age, and they were both eating something.

"What you got there then?" asked Sam peering at the food.

"Narna samidge," replied Weep, scoffing at the sandwich.

"Yuk, horrid." scowled Sam.

"So you're eating a banana sandwich?" asked Kev. Weep looked cautiously at the stranger.

"Yeah, why?" Kev didn't answer, he just burst out laughing.

"It's good with sugar on." added Neil. Kev stopped laughing and looked in horror at the comment.

"You eat banana on bread with sugar on top?" he asked with his eyebrows skirting the top of his forehead. Neil just shuffled as Kev and Sam made retching noises.

"It's not exactly dog poo." frowned Weep, as he pushed the last remnants of the meal into his mouth. Mumble had already finished his.

"My cousin Chapper has raw 'tater with salt on." added Sam.

"Ugh." said Kev and began to make more vomiting sounds.

"Bloody hell." added Neil, but the swear word caused Weep to look back to his house quickly and then suggest they move into the opening. This they all did and then Sam asked,

"Where were you two going anyway?"

"We're going to the quarry." replied Weep.

"We could all go together then, it would be more fun." Sam introduced the other three and Weep considered this for a moment. Two of the three strangers were of Sam's age and Weep was just over a year younger - about the same age as Dan, Kev's brother. He considered that it was always the younger ones who bore the brunt of any tomfoolery. Then he considered Mumble. Mumble was always seen as slightly odd and Weep considered that he was probably at the bottom of the food chain on this particular outing.

"Okay," he grinned, "and we could play with the Tiger on the way, if it's there."

"The Tiger?" exclaimed Kev with an amount of alarm in his voice, still recovering from the thought of banana sandwiches and raw salted potato. "What the hell is the Tiger?"

"Oh you'll see." replied Sam nonchalantly, as if Tigers roamed every part of northern Derbyshire. As they walked down the opening between the houses towards the main road, the three boys from the village hung behind the local boys, mumbling incomprehensible phrases such as. 'Tiger!', 'must be barmy' and 'not bloody likely'. Still, they all crossed the main road to the Post Office and shop opposite. Weep noticed the shops and suggested.

"We ought to take something to eat." pointing to the red painted window of the Post Office.

"What are you thinking of buying - raw potato sandwich, or is it salted banana this time?" laughed Kev. Without thinking Mumble burst into speech by announcing.

"I quite like sweetened condensed milk." There was a pause and in a slight whisper he added. "Sweetened condensed milk." There was another pause and then Sam announced.

"Yeah, I like that, the Fussells stuff. Yummy."

"Is there only me here that's normal?" asked Kev.

"It's nice, I like Fussells," began Neil. "an' if you drip some of that Camp Coffee into to it...." he motioned, licking his lips. He stopped though as soon as he realised there was complete silence. Silence because everyone was staring at him with blank expressions. "What?" he asked holding out his arms.

"Coffee is poisonous to children, you realise that?" explained Sam.

"Hey?" exclaimed Neil, with shock in his voice.

"He's right Neil," added Kev. "coffee and coffee flavoured sweets, deadly to anyone under fourteen." Neil just frowned as his gaze passed from one to the other of the unbelieving faces. Eventually the boys turned one by one and walked to the shop.

"I'm worried about you Neil, Camp Coffee? Leave that for your granny." frowned Kev as he turned away too. They stood in front of the Post Office and Kev said,

"I'm not sure I could eat anything after hearing about your weird food habits, give me Kali any day of the week." The others had to agree on that, Kali was fantastic.

"Sherbet fountains." added Weep.

"Crispets - brilliant." insisted Sam.

"Oooo, frozen Jubbly." suggested Dan.

"Definitely Swizzle lollies for me." concluded Neil, as they eagerly thrust their hands into their pockets. Unfortunately, they all came up with the same conclusion.

"None of us has any money." explained Kev, shrugging his shoulders. Weep grinned at Sam and said,

"That shouldn't be a problem, watch and learn."

Inside the shop it was dark and dingy with bits and pieces of everything all over the place. There was a particular smell known to haunt this type of shop – a mixture of timber, glue, rubber, paraffin and sawdust. It was what would now be called a D.I.Y. shop of sorts yet at this time D.I.Y. would probably stand for Don't Injure Yourself or Danger In Yorkshire. It was the kind of shop that can no longer be found now because people prefer to buy from 'Supermarkets', a word for 'Shop that is the same as all the other shops in every other town'. In these far off days, all shops were very different, Aladdin's caves full of things you have never seen before. This shop was no exception. It was like the site where Sinbad's ship had run aground, scattering all manner of treasures from around the world on the beach. To the boys, the only treasures worth taking an interest in were sweets.

Behind the counter was a tall thin man with a large lump of plastic fixed to his ear. Weep walked up to the man and said.

"Two ounces of Crispets please."

"What! speak up." called the man, pointing to the lump of plastic.

"Two - Ounces - Of - Crispets – Please." replied Weep, in a slow but much louder voice, animating the action of eating at the end. Kev's brother Dan, giggled at this seemingly laughable situation which caused some of the other boys to join in. Not Sam and Weep though, they had the hard and serious business of survival to contend with.

"I don't think we have them." said the tall man. "I'll have a look." and he began searching through the bags and boxes of bicycle parts, torches, puncture repair kits, tinned food, and even car spark plugs, but he couldn't find those particular sweets. He eventually went into the back room for further investigation and as soon as he was out of sight, Sam and Weep began filling their pockets with chocolate and sweets closer to hand. The other three did not need an education in this subject and had already seized their own booty.

"No, I'm sorry, we don't have them." said the returning tall man to the five assembled angelic faces.

"Okay," smiled Weep, "Thanks anyway." and they left the shop with the tall man bemused at such precision in child shoppers.

They ran and ran until they came to the Tip. There, they emptied their pockets and laughed about the affair, doling out the goodies in equal rations.

"Where do we go now?" asked Neil munching on a Fry's Five Boys. Sam pointed across the Tip to a far distant clump of trees and explained,

"Over there, that's where the quarry is and that's the railway that we have to follow." He retracted his finger from its former use to place another sherbet lemon into his mouth.

"When do we see the Tiger?" asked Dan, with a mouth full of chocolate. The two other village boys had forgotten completely about the potential child-eating, striped, Indian quadruped. His question brought it all back.

"Later." said Sam, still seeming unconcerned with the beast, in fact more anxious with the wrapper of a Mars Bar.

When they had eaten quite too much they continued down the Tip path until Kev said,

"I wish we'd nicked some pop, I'm right thirsty." Sam stopped and looked up the side of the Tip.

"You been in Willows Hole recently Weep?" he asked, still scanning the tip.

"Naaa, not for a few days." Weep replied.

"C'mon then we'll have a look." Sam led the group up the side of the tip, through tall willow herbs, until they came to a clearing near the top. There were obvious signs of recent activity here and just ahead, they saw a small hole at the top edge of the tip. Sam bent down and had a quick look inside then turned back and said to the others,

"Wait here." He slunk inside into the darkness and Dan bent to follow but before he could enter, he met Sam exiting with a half filled bottle with a dark liquid in it.

"Finest D and B." he smiled. Mumble reached for the bottle but Sam pulled it away handing it to Kev and saying, "Guests first." Kev took the bottle and read the label. Dandelion and Burdock was the legend he read. Kev removed the top and wiped the bottle neck on his jumper in the traditional manner, then smelt the dark drink.

"Smells great." he said, before trying a little. It was obviously to his taste, as he drank greedily. He passed the bottle to Dan who again wiped the neck and guzzled the pop.

"Taste good?" asked Sam to Kev.

"Great, yeah." replied Kev.

"Only the best we can get. We don't nick rubbish round here." smiled Sam. The bottle was passed to Neil, who drank, and then passed it on to Weep. He, in turn, passed the bottle to Mumble, who immediately guzzled at the cool pop. Sam turned to leave but Kev called out.

"You not drinking?"

"Naa. Some people round here think it's funny to top it up with piss." Mumble spit it out and threw the bottle into the hole.

"Uuugh!" called out those who had drunk. "You arsehole." called out Kev, as Dan began to wipe his tongue with a dock leaf. Kev was furious but just caught a tiny wink from Sam.

When they reached the railway, they turned left along it and walked a little more. On the siding by a tree there stood an old disused guard's van that, for some reason that no one knew, had been left there for a couple of summers now.

"Let's go inside." suggested Kev, although there was never any doubt that they would. No matter how many times Sam walked past the van, he could not resist the urge to enter and explore. For Kev and his brother, being inside was not enough. They had to climb high up on the roof. The boy, Mumble, stood outside watching and talking to himself. He was a little odd, to be truthful. In those days, not many boys of that age wore spectacles, not many boys that age talked to themselves, but no boys whatsoever repeated everything they said to themselves in a whisper. Mumble did. That's all he did too. Everything seemed too dangerous to him. So it was at this point that excitable young Dan began to leap up and down on the roof of the van shouting, "Nutty four eyes." to Mumble. It was only natural that Mumble should pick up rocks and throw them at Dan. It was only natural that such a bad shot as Mumble should propel one of the rocks through the van window. It was not so natural that a man walking his dog should chase the "Bloody young vandals" away, but he did.

When they thought they had run far enough, they collapsed at the side of the railway track. Dan was spread-eagled across the sleepers of the track and Sam noticed this. He nudged Weep and pointed to Dan on the track making a strange, spider motion with his hand. Weep knew exactly what the signal meant and they both sat on the bank grinning and waiting for the inevitable. Mumble saw them watching Dan, as he lay watching the wispy clouds slowly pass by. Kev noticed the silence and sat up to see the three local boys sat together watching his brother intently. Before he could ask what they were doing Sam caught his movement in the corner of his eye and put a finger up to his lips, gesticulating to be quiet. Kev joined the three to watch whatever they were waiting to see. Dan too was suspicious of the silence and sat up, resting his bottom on the shiny rail.

"What?" he asked simply, unsure of the sickly grin on three of the boys' faces.

"What?" he asked again. He became bored by the attention and began to look around but the other boys remained intently watching for some unknown reason and Dan became very uneasy.

"You lot are crackers, you know that? What's up?" They said nothing. Weep almost burst out laughing but covered his mouth with his hand. Kev and Neil just sat looking at Dan and then at the three boys, wondering what was in store. Dan stood.

"I'm off home if you don't stop it. Tell 'em Kev." It was then that a change was noticed. The look on Dan's face began to alter from one of 'I'll get my revenge you idiots.' to one of 'I think I'm being possessed'.

"Ow!" he called out. "Ouch! Ouch! Bloody hell." He was now standing and dancing around in a way that his elder brother had never seen. Kev still didn't understand what was happening but the other three were in hysterics and it was infectious, so he joined in.

"Ow! Ouch, oww! Sodding ants! Everywhere," continued Dan, as he began to run up the railway line casting off all his clothes. The others fell about even more at this until tears ran down their faces. Eventually, Dan came back, still naked, carrying his clothes and occasionally beating them against the floor.

"There are ants everywhere and you shit bags knew." said Dan with a frown, the red bite marks clearly seen all over his body.

"There are always ants on railway tracks." explained Sam in between bouts of renewed laughter.

After the laughter subsided and Dan began to hurt less, Sam suggested that they head towards the quarry. Dan insisted on walking on the bank rather than the track even though it was hard going. Most of his clothing had returned to his body but he was still uncomfortable. They walked a little further past the signal gantry until the mighty trees that surrounded the quarry, loomed into view along side the railway track. They crossed the track and slid down the bank through the trees and into the quarry. It was cool in the shade and the lovely smell of the trees and the undergrowth was sweet. In the quarry, a length of rope hung in a tree to make a swing and this held their attention for a good half hour. The quarry was in two parts but it wasn't really a true quarry. It was probably where the rocks had naturally been cut away through pre-history by the little brook that ran in the bottom. To the local boys, however, it was always known as 'The Quarry'. There were two basins, fairly deep escarpments, where trees grew in the bottom and around the edge. It nestled in a 'Vee' shape catchment, which had been created many years ago, when the mining companies had built the railway. This triangle was surrounded by the railway on two sides, the third side was to open fields up on a high bank. Weep suggested going into the other part of the quarry and this took them deeper into the triangle, into the 'Vee' of the actual railway tracks. In there, the trees and undergrowth were thick, making movement slow and here and there, little clearings had been made where other 'rope swings' had been hung. The brook ran in the bottom, coming out of a small tunnel at one end and disappearing into another some 70 yards away. The boys had traversed the low tunnels many times and it was always a good adventure but today, Sam and Weep were looking for something more. The other boys followed them along the quarry floor, leaping the brook and continuing up the steadily rising bank. This was the point of the triangle and they were only thirty or so feet from the railway but it could not be seen through the thick tree line. As they climbed the steep bank out of the far end of the quarry, Weep and Sam stopped and sat on a log which seemed to have been used as a resting place many times. Sam looked at Kev, as he was the leader of their 'pack', and began to explain.

"The Tiger might not come today. We don't really know when it will come but if it does, we will hear it in plenty of time." The visitors sat in wonder. This was getting quite scary and Dan felt more than a little worried. Sam continued, "Now, if either me or Weep shout 'run', you better bloody well run and keep running until we stop. We usually come back into the quarry and run down the drainage tunnels, they never follow us down there." He pointed down the bank to where the stream was trickling into the culvert.

"They?" asked Neil, more than slightly worried. "You said *the* Tiger, not lots of tigers." Sam smiled at this.

"There is only one tiger, you daft bat. There can't be more than one, the Tiger's too big for two of them to come."

"Sod this." said Kev, as he stood. "This sounds like madness. How big is this tiger exactly and why the hell can't it get down the tunnels?" Sam couldn't understand his concern, it wasn't like it was that risky, or even dangerous.

"Kev," began Sam to calm him down. "It's just a ....." He didn't finish, as he had noticed Weep raise his hand and turn his head. Kev crouched back down instinctively and they all listened.

"What is it?" Sam whispered to Weep. One great skill Weep had above all others, except climbing, was his hearing. He was renowned for it.

"It's coming." he grinned. Kev felt his heartbeat quicken and Neil and Dan were already creeping slowly towards the drain tunnel. Sam seemed to be sniffing the air as he listened to a sound coming through the trees. All seemed quiet. Even the birds were quiet. Mumble began to wonder what the long term consequences might be if he filled his jeans in front of the other boys.

"I'm scared." whispered Mumble, then repeated in a lower whisper, "I'm scared."

"Sodding 'ell Mumble, you must have seen the Tiger before." growled Sam but Mumble just shook his head slowly with a look of abject terror. Sam looked up to the top of the bank and said quietly,

"Listen, do you hear that?" The other boys instinctively looked around at the trees. Yes, there was a sound. There were many sounds. The tinkling of the brook trying to get into the tunnel as quick as it could for fear of seeing the Tiger, four heartbeats, as each child strained his ears for some more dangerous sound. The sound of a slight breeze beginning to push through the woodland and the sound of utter silence beyond that. Earlier there had been the sound of thousands of birds, blackbirds, thrushes and even a Jay amongst them but now there was nothing. Then like an audible spectre another sound came creeping round the trees, quietly nudging at the senses. At first, not really a sound you could hear but more a sound you could feel. Then it was more audible, like a rolling roar, but quiet, sort of similar to distant thunder ... but not. A sound nothing like Kev, Dan, Neil or Mumble had ever heard before. It was hard to pinpoint the direction but there was an eerie rumbling moan that sounded some distance away but coming closer. In the darkness of the woodland there was a spooky feel, yet the trees seemed to offer some sanctuary. The sound was becoming louder and another squealing sound occasionally broke through too, but still not from any particular direction. Then a louder sound struck the quiet as Mumble broke wind. Sam and Weep fell over, laughing silently behind their hands, but the others weren't so amused.

"That sound," said Kev almost shaking. "What is it?" There was a look of excitement on the face of Sam and Weep as Sam replied.

"That my friend is the Tiger!" The other boys shuffled nervously and began to look around them into the trees but Sam was crawling slowly up the bank.

"Shouldn't we be going that way?" asked Neil, pointing to the tunnel at the bottom, but Sam and Weep were already heading to the very top of the tree-lined slope. Kev began to wonder about the sense in meeting a tiger face to face but the excited look, carried by Sam and Weep as they climbed, went some way to assuring him that it did not necessarily mean certain death. The rumbling and the roar became louder and louder until it seemed that the sounds were right beside them. Peering up through the trees, however, revealed nothing and the sound became slightly quieter as if it were now moving away but at that moment Sam called back,

"Come on or we'll miss it." Kev doubted his sanity but still followed. As they broke through the edge of the trees at the top of the bank they copied Sam who was lying in the long grass by the side of the railway, then they crawled slowly from the cover of the shrubs, laying as low as they could in the grass. Sam and Weep were looking back down the track in the opposite direction from the way they had originally arrived. In the distance they heard the purring, rather than the roaring, of the Tiger and as they turned to face to same direction as Sam and Weep, they looked, slightly afraid of what they may see. What they actually saw was the back of a large yellow and black striped object - the Tiger no less. There was no fur on its body, no large teeth in its head, in fact it had no head. All was now clear to them, the Tiger was a shunting loco. It had stopped about 100 yards away and the driver had jumped out to change the 'points' so that he could go onto the other track.

"It's a bloody train." hissed Kev.

"It's a shunter actually, what did you expect a real tiger?" Sam said it in such a way that Kev was not likely to admit that he did indeed believe that his end would come at the jaws of an enormous cat.

"Get ready." said Sam, as in their lunacy he and Weep stood up in clear view.

"Get down, he'll see you." insisted Kev but Sam and Weep were already making rude gestures to the man - Weep sticking his tongue out so far that the driver could have oiled it for him. The driver began to run towards the boys shouting and waving his fists. Sam and Weep jumped over the others and ran back into the quarry. It needed no explanation for the others to follow.

"He'll catch us in here." said Neil, as they stopped near the fallen log.

"He won't, even if he comes in, which they never do, just get into the tunnel." explained Weep. They ran into the bottom and stopped at the brook. Dan tossed a large stone into the water as if to test its depth but really to make a splash. Mumble added,

"Down the tunnel? Down the tunnel?" He leaned over to try and work out how long it was but all he saw was darkness. He shuddered and began to tell himself how dangerous it would be to go down there. The boys waited for a short while until the noise of the Tiger rose and then disappeared in to the distance, giving the birds senior authority once more and the chance to make up for some lost singing time.

They then made their way back up the bank to the spot where the Tiger had been and a couple of them stopped to play with the point lever. It proved too heavy for them to move. As they passed it, Weep stopped and turned to Sam.

"Shall we go up to the farm?"

"Can do, we've got plenty of time." replied Sam with an air of 'Well I'm leading this party but I'll allow suggestions.' They walked along the railway - the part that made the 'Vee' into a letter 'Y' shape - and under a bridge into a deep cutting. Ahead, in the distance, the top of the canopy of Bluebell Wood came into view. They left the tracks as the cutting opened out and climbed down the steep banking into the field, heading towards a farm that could be seen to the west. As they approached the farm there was a barn some 200 yards ahead of it and it looked to be full of straw and hay. It was an excellent place to explore and look, someone had left a very long ladder there. How kind of them to consider the boys and to provide such perfect access. They might as well have made a sign that read, 'Small boys this way'. Once on top of the bales in the barn, they built tanks, igloos, racing cars, battle ships and spacecraft out of the straw bales. This culminated in a simple but traditional straw fight with every bodily nook and cranny filled with itchy straw. They rested and began to talk.

"My sisters got a new boyfriend. *My sisters got a new boyfriend.*" began Mumble.

"Anyone we know?" asked Weep.

"No, he's a lot older than us.... *Than us.*"

"I wish I had an older sister." interrupted Kev.

"Why?" asked Weep.

"Well, Mumble here must have some fun sometimes."

"What do you mean? *what do you mean?*" asked both Mumbles.

"Well, you know, you must see something." Mumbles face was blank.

"He means when she gets undressed and you are peeping through the crack in the door." laughed Neil.

"I don't do that. *I don't do that.*" answered and repeated Mumble with certainty. He walked away towards the ladder.

"Well I still wish I had one." reiterated Kev and the others laughed.

"I'm glad I don't have one." admitted Sam.

"Why?" asked Kev.

"Well, less presents at Christmas." he grinned. The boys smiled as they followed Sam's thinking. He was an only child and if he had a sister, or even a brother for that matter, then any spare Christmas money would have to be split two ways.

"Are we supposed to be up here? *up here?*" asked Mumble from over by the ladder.

"Of course not. Why?" asked Sam reclining in a pile of straw.

"Because there are three men looking up here." The boys jumped to their feet and ran to the edge of the stacked hay to have a look.

"Come down, you little sods!" shouted one of the rough looking men. The top of the ladder began to shake which meant one of the men was coming up. Weep and Mumble tried to escape by climbing onto a lower level and jumping down, but it was obvious that this was not a good route. As soon as they touched the floor, one of the men grabbed their collars and began shaking them, swearing and shouting as he did so. Weep was already characteristically crying.

"That's not for me." said Sam, looking down from his high command. The ladder had stopped shaking and so he went for a look, but one of the men was still standing at its base. Sam ran to the back end of the barn and looked down. There were no farmers there, but it was a hell of a way down and he would also have to clear the hedge that ran parallel and close to it. Sam quickly weighed up the odds. If he jumped, he would also have to clear that hedge or he would be trapped between it and the hay of the barn. He knew it was a risky jump and he tried to remember his parachute training, perfected when he had tried jumping off the front porch at home. "Bend your legs and roll." he said to himself, but this was higher than the front porch and also over a hedge that was three feet from the barn. The field also looked like hard ground unlike the soft garden at home. He looked round and saw that the ladder was bouncing again and that there was more shouting. The appearance of a head at the top of the ladder tipped the balance for Sam and he leapt out and down the twenty feet or so into the field. In the air he seemed to have time to think about all sorts of things like breaking a leg or an arm and the story he would have to tell his mother at the hospital. Fortunately, as the ground rose up to hit him, he also thought about bending his legs and rolling.

"As the able paratrooper saw the ground come up to meet him, Wing Commander Sammy Samson looked up at his parachute to check on wind direction. It had been a good jump all the way down from leaving the special Lancaster Bomber which was used only for him and his men. He could see the Germans running for hiding places as he descended, they knew the British would only send Sammy Samson on such a dangerous mission and were therefore, withdrawing to await assistance."

His timing was perfect, a bit of a jar in his ankles, but he was soon up and running towards the hedge at the opposite end of the field, wondering what would happen to Kev, Dan and Neil.

Those very same three people passed him before he reached the hedge and were through it as he arrived. They had taken the same option as Sam, even without parachute training. It seemed that if you did not know about basic physics, then it simply could not harm you. They continued running, even when they were back on the railway and eventually fell onto the ground near the quarry. They were just regaining their breath when they heard dogs in the distance, towards the farm.

"They're setting the dogs on us." cried Neil, as he stood and continued running. They all ran back into the quarry near the tunnels and sat panting, trying to listen for the dogs.

"Do you think Weep will grass on us?" asked Kev.

"No I don't, but Mumble will." replied Sam. "They were both crying when the German officer got them."

"What German officer?" asked Kev. Sam pretended not to hear.

"Oh great, my dad will kill me." said Neil.

"What about us?" implored Kev, "We're still in trouble for burning down the garden shed."

"The garden shed?" queried Sam. "I'm not surprised you're in trouble, how did you manage that?"

"Well ..... Dan said he had mixed a chemical that would put out any fire." Kev glared at Dan, as the younger brother lowered his head. "So we decided to try it out and built a small fire on the garden. Our mother came out, moaning about the smoke on her washing and made us put out the fire, so we moved into the garden shed. We poured some petrol out of my dad's moped into a steel dish and set light to it." Dan began to shuffle his feet as Kev continued, "When it was going nicely, Dan poured the chemical over the fire. It didn't work."

"So now you need a new shed?" laughed Sam.

"Well dad needs a new moped first, oh and a telly," replied Kev.

"Telly? What has your television got to do with the shed?" asked a puzzled Sam.

"The telly was in there, having the switch glued back in place, along with the lawn mower, our bikes and an old pram." Sam shook his head at the mention of the pram. "Terrible waste of perfectly good trolley wheels." he thought to himself. The boys eventually made their way home, wondering if the bad news would get there before them.

Even in the summer months, Britain keeps itself fairly moist and when it rains children generally become hermits. Well some do - Sam wasn't one of these, nor, were most of his friends. Sam decided to put on a coat and call for Weep.

"Come out? It's chucking it down!"

"I know, all the more reason, come on." Sam walked a few steps from the door in an effort to entice Weep out of the house.

"You're mad." called Weep as he followed Sam, pulling his coat on.

"Where are we going anyway?" asked Weep.

"Don't know. Let's try the Tip."

"Why the Tip? There'll be nobody there today, it's raining if you haven't noticed." insisted Weep.

""It's better than sitting in the house. I'm so fed up I could kick the cat of the hearth."

"What?" asked Weep with a grin, trying to adjust his coat so that rain wouldn't drip down his neck.

"I'm bored." sighed Sam

"What was that about the cat?" frowned Weep.

"Oh, it's what me mother says when she's fed up or angry. I don't understand it but then she's old." groaned Sam disinterestedly.

"So does she kick the cat?" asked Weep, intrigued by the thought of a steadily sleeping cat being launched by the impact of a woman's carpet slipper.

"God no, she'd rather kick me than the cat. It's just a saying. Come on let's go." insisted Sam. They crossed the road onto the Tip path and headed for one of the drier dens but even that was leaking. They decided to go to the scrap yard and sit in the remains of an old lorry cab.

"I hate the rain." shrugged Weep as they listened to the pelting of the drops on the metal roof. Sam just screwed his nose up and looked out across the lower part of the Tip. It was just a shell of a lorry cab with no doors, glass or interior, so it wasn't very comfortable to say the least, and the steel felt cold and damp. It was looking more and more as if they would have to abandon their day and retreat indoors. Sam decided however, that the rain was slowing down. It was - there was just a steady drizzle and the sky looked somewhat brighter.

"The sun will be out soon." said Sam as he held his hand out of the lorry cab. "Come on, let's go down Peggy's." Weep shrugged his shoulders and rolled out of the steel shelter.

Peggy's was a brook, a mile or so away, that ran from the quarry weaving its way through fields and along hedgerows. Sam and his friends usually went to a small concrete footbridge that crossed the brook where there were two good climbing trees, a small den in the bank and a rope-swing that hung from one of the trees very close to where the bridge crossed the stream. Sam and Weep trudged across the field until they came to this very bridge. The sky was turning dark again and there was a perceptible increase in the drizzle.

"We're going to get soaked out here." moaned Weep, so Sam suggested they should shelter under the low bridge as the small stream flowed at the northern bank and only occupied a foot or so of the eight feet that the bridge spanned. Sam also had an idea how to make it more comfortable.

"There are some bales of straw under that tree, give me a hand to fetch some." Straw was always useful and the children stashed bales all over the countryside in dens. This one had been re-supplied by Sam himself some days previously and had been tucked away in a small recess, under the large roots of a tree, where it could be accessed from the stream. The den had been excavated slightly into the bank and under the roots. Comfortable in the dry but not so good in the rain, it had however, kept most of the straw dry. They gathered the driest straw from the bottom of the pile and carried it under the bridge. It was really low under there with less than two feet from floor to bridge and as they couldn't sit up straight, a cosy 'nest' was made. It was cramped and low but it was comfortable with the straw and better than getting soaked as the rain increased. It took no time at all to get warm and as they lay there, they both struggled for something to talk about.

"Loz and Vern have got a new den on the Tip." said Weep.

"Where?" enquired Sam.

"I don't know, they won't tell me. I've looked for it but I can't find it. Mumble says it's near the scrap yard but I never believe him anyway."

"Have you looked in the scrap yard? They used to have one on the bank at the far end."

"Yeah I looked there, but I can't find it."

"Breen says he found one at the Big Tree end, near the far slope, but I reckon that's an old one."

"It is. Barmy built that one but it was caved in by Socky and Sloop." There were a few minutes silence as Weep pulled some of the straw around him.

"Do you think there are any spacemen on Mars?" asked Sam, as he tossed a small pebble into the passing stream.

"Dunno," admitted Weep. "Why?"

"I just wondered. Did you see that Quatermass film on the telly?" asked Sam.

"The one where they find the spaceship on the London underground?" replied Weep recalling the film, with a slight grin.

"Yeah, that one."

"I did, yeah. Soddin' scary that one, especially where they showed you all the Martians running about an' that." grinned Weep. He turned to face Sam as he continued, "They were 'orrid, with tentacles and 'orrid eyes, looked just like June Alcott." he laughed.

"Who?" asked Sam, not recalling the name.

"June Alcott, she is in my class at school. She has 'orrible curly hair and goggle eyes." replied Weep, trying to make his eyes bulge. Sam laughed then asked,

"So do you think there really are Martians then?" Weep lay back, looked up at the bottom of the bridge, and began to force his finger into a small hole in the concrete.

"I think there must be 'cos they wouldn't make all the films about them if there weren't, would they?" he said eventually. Sam tried to spread out a little as he said,

"I wouldn't like to go into space in a rocket, it must be ever so scary." Weep immediately turned to Sam.

"You wouldn't want to be a spaceman? Crikey, you must be mad. They pay loads of money for that job."

"What if you met Martians out there though?" asked Sam with concern. Weep lay flat again and thought for a moment.

"Well you would have ray guns and stuff, like Steve Zodiac," he concluded.

"Steve Zodiac is a puppet though. Fireball is all made up, an' do they have ray guns for real?" asked Sam.

"Yeah, course they do. You can't go into space without ray guns." There was a little silence after Weep's reply and then he asked, "Who's best, Steve Zodiac or Troy Tempest?" Sam had no doubt, the answer was immediate.

"Troy Tempest, of course. Stingray is brilliant, better than Supercar and Fireball XL5, and it's like real." Weep began to stick his finger back in the hole. "And it's in colour," added Sam soon after.

"Hey? what do you mean, colour?" enquired Weep, removing his finger and turning to Sam.

"It's all in colour, y' know, not black and white." explained Sam.

"It's not colour on our telly." insisted Weep, with a deep frown.

"Cos you've got a black and white telly." smiled Sam. Weep shuffled in the straw a little and then asked.

"So, have you got a colour telly then?"

"No," replied Sam shaking his head. "but I went to my friend's house from school last month and they must be rich 'cos they had a colour telly. Stingray looks brilliant in colour." Weep lay back in the straw trying to imagine the program in colour. After a short silence, he sat up as much as he could in the limited room and asked,

"So what does it look like?" Sam stared at Weep for a moment and then replied in a sarcastic tone,

"It's the same as black and white, but in colour." Weep slumped back down - he just couldn't imagine it. Sam pulled some straw over his legs as he added. "My mam says you can tell which are colour programmes even on our black an' white telly. She says you can just see colour in the grey." Sam held his hand out beyond the edge of the bridge to see if it was still raining but soon retracted it sopping wet, and then concluded, "I tried to look for colour in Stingray but Marina's dress was still grey."

"So what colour is it for real then?" asked Weep, trying desperately to add colour to his images of the programme.

"Blue, sort or light blue." explained Sam. There was another short silence.

"If I tell you a secret, will you keep it to yourself?" Weep asked quietly. Sam looked over to him.

"Yeah, course." he lied.

"Well Mumble thinks Marina is real and she's his girlfriend." announced Weep, with a slight grin.

"Mumble loves Marina?" laughed Sam.

"Quiet, it's a secret, remember." hissed Weep but Sam was laughing still. "Do you like her Sam?" Sam stopped laughing. He thought for a moment and then he too began to explore the hole in the base of the concrete bridge.

"Yeah, she's alright," he replied quietly before leaning up on his arm and saying, "but she's just a puppet Weep, she ain't real or anythin'." He lay back and, in an effort to change the subject, he said. "We have a new teacher at school who looks just like an Aquaphibian."

"A what? asked Weep.

"You know the fishmen in Stingray." smiled Sam, sticking out his tongue and frowning like the puppets in the show. Weep laughed at this and began making the burbling, gurgling noise that the Aquaphibians made. The conversation continued in this vein for some time, incorporating many of the important issues of the day. Many meetings like this took place on wet days. Small dens were occupied by other boys, plotting and designing at various levels all over the shire. The talk was ended by the approach of running footsteps.

In the mid-1960's the jogger had not been invented. There were still years of development and experimentation, bonding bits of health-fixated individuals on to bored, sedentary people so that they could become the ubiquitous 'Jogger'. These strange people, who ran in the rain, were simply 'runners', or loonies, as most other adults referred to them.

"It sounds like a runner." said Sam.

"Yes it's a runner I'd say." agreed Weep. Unknown to them at this moment, the runner was a lanky older lad by the name of Crabber who was in training for the county sports day. He was soaked to the skin and he decided to stop at the bridge for a rest and some other relaxation.

"Wonder who it is?" whispered Weep.

"I don't know," smiled Sam "but we can have some fun." Sam conjured up his deepest voice, which still sounded like an excited girl and called out sternly.

"Who dares to cross this bridge without paying the toll?" The two boys held back laughs behind their hands, trying to imagine the runner haring off up the field thinking he was being chased by a Troll. The trick did not go quite to plan. There was no sound of retreating footsteps and no answer. To be truthful there was no sound at all except for the constant rain splashing into the brook. The two lads looked at each other, wondering what was going on, but neither was prepared to look out from the bridge.

"He is probably going through his pockets looking for some money to throw down." sniggered Weep.

The rain splashing off the water was soon joined by a stronger fall of liquid and this one was golden yellow. It lasted a short while and then silence returned. The boys waited for something to be dropped into the water. They were not disappointed as a large rock crashed into the brook by their side accompanied by a runner's feet making off into the distance.

"Lets go home." suggested Sam as they stood with drops of water running down their necks, watching their assailant disappear into the distance.

History is bespeckled with small incidents that have changed and shaped the world and because of that, they have stayed with us to the present day. Many of these 'incidents' have become important bridges to our past. Children have no time for the past, it's full of dates, names and places that they can't remember and so they live out these 'incidents' in the present. Robin Hood, Sir Francis Drake, King Arthur, the Second World War and the English Civil War are all very important to children but in a different way to adults. Sometimes the events from other lands also overlap their home heritage, like cowboys and Indians, gangsters and the Zulu wars. They all happened at the same time in history and in the same place, King Charles the first might have been caught up in the trenches of the Somme if he hadn't have been having his head removed about that same time.

In a certain summer, Roarkes Drift came to Derbyshire, mainly due to the fact that a fairly new film that was showing at the cinema. Nevertheless the Zulus spilled out from the silver screen and were seen to be running around the small hamlet of Highfields in a northeast corner of Derbyshire. How it came about was simple, pure boredom.

Sam, Breen and Tools had tired of playing jousting knights on their cycles. After the bikes were put away, they set off with Breen's elder brother, Ben to seek further adventure on the Tip. Once there, they found Weep and his elder brother Barmy, Biro, Loz and Erky playing a relaxed game of football, so relaxed, that two of them were seated.

"Hey up!" said Barmy with his usual cheeky grin.

"Hey up." replied Tools. "What 'yer doin'?"

"Nowt'." was the dull reply. It seemed that 'Nowt' was a popular game just lately. They all moved to the side of the Tip, a part they called, for obvious reasons, 'The Bushes'. Here several 'dens' were hidden and many tracks wound through the undergrowth of tall Willowherb stalks and elder bushes overlooking the path. Dens had an odd fascination for the children. They ranged in style and construction to such an extent that there is no easy way to explain them. Some were well-hidden elaborate 'hides' where all home comforts were supplied, even emergency food rations. Others were no more than a comfortable nest under a bush, or even a hiding place for some contraband of sorts. Some, on the other hand, consisted of full excavations, requiring wood to shore them up. One thing they all shared in common was their need to be secret or hidden. Once a den was discovered, if it wasn't immediately wrecked by the finders, it would certainly be demolished by the owners. There was one exception to this rule. A few dens were allowed to be communal, simply to be used as hiding places from adults or a pleasant place for everyone to congregate. Most of the dens in The Bushes were of this type, simple lounging areas where the children could not be seen by adult eyes.

The boys were seated in Willows Hole den, which although being under a large elder bush, had a flat plateau outside it with a commanding view of the Tip path. As they sat and discussed what to do, an elderly couple walked by on the path just below. Barmy went into offensive mode, a situation well known to all the others. He stood so that he could be seen by the couple and pushed his thumbs deep into his ears, waved his open hands and forced out his tongue so far it seemed his spine would crack.

"Dirty little animal." said the woman. "He should be locked in a mental institution." What the woman did not know was that Barmy wouldn't pass the test to be allowed into such a residency. Barmy was famous for his 'Tongue' act, in fact he found it compulsory whenever a female crossed his path, it was kind of a mild Terrets Syndrome. As for dirty - yes, little - sort of, but animal? No, for animals have instinct and a sense of reasoning. These qualities were absent in Barmy, he was an enigma. He had only cheek, daring, a catapult and a pocket full of stones. The couple were quite lucky if they had only known it, for his 'act' was usually followed by "Get lost you old bag." but they did not escape his ritual of throwing stones when they were out of 'chase' range.

Another traveller walked down the path, it was Mumble, whispering and talking to himself.

"Hey four eyes!" called out Barmy. Mumble saw him and climbed up the side of the Tip. They all retired to better cover within The Bushes to plan what to do next. Between suggestions of cops and robbers, Robin Hood and 'war', which sounded indiscriminate, but was usually English versus Germans, Sam had begun stripping leaves from a Willow stalk to make a kind of primitive spear. Only at the thin end did he leave any leaves, to act as a 'flight' to make the spear fly true. It was a well-known weapon for the boys, experience helping them choose the best stalks for use. After Biro had suggested they play at farmers and Barmy had retorted that they all play 'loonies' and Biro would have a head start, Breen watched Sam throw his spear into the undergrowth and said.

"I know, let's play Zulus". This was agreed by all, as most of the boys had been to the cinema to see the spectacular but wholly inaccurate movie starring Stanley Baker and the new actor Michael Caine and it seemed therefore, to be an excellent idea. The boys began to make their spears and decked themselves out in the discarded leaves and other greenery. Once they were ready and looked 'just like Zulus', after all, it is well known that Zulus stuff leaves into their socks and the tops of their trousers, they searched for their enemies, the problem was, none could be found.

The older boys in the village had decided that a game of football was a good idea, so armed with only their heavy, brown leather 'case' ball, the team headed for the only 'pitch' they knew, the Tip, unfortunately, deep in the heart of Zulu country. As they walked towards the grass covered shale tip they discussed the team. Beetle, Chapper and Socky would play against Crabber, Sloop and Cogger, "rush goalies and no throw-ins". Not exactly the World Cup but it would have to do. They wound their way up the path to the top of the Tip where the very rudimentary pitch was and placed piles of straw or shirts and jumpers to represent the goal posts. The old, heavy case ball was one that had been given to them by someone's father and looking at the thing it probably first saw light of day near the trenches of Ypre, an impromptu Christmas game during the first world war between the Germans and the Allies. Even when dry, it weighed about as much as a small pig and had the aerodynamics of one. 'Headers' were never made in those days unless you wished to be decapitated or have the top half of your spine compressed and even kicking the ugly object required bravery and a good dose of pain killers. If you had the misfortune to kick it where its laces were, you could loose several toes but it was all they had and so the 'casey' was used.

As the game began, the older boys noticed some movement in the bushes and stopped to investigate but before they reached their intended target, Willow stalks came hurtling out of the undergrowth along with a very unusual weapon that the boys called a Sputnik. This was made by forming a ball of soft clay about the size of a fist and then completed by shoving short willow stalks into it all around the surface. A longer stalk was then thrust in and used to propel the object by 'slinging' it through the air. During its flight it slightly resembled the famous Russian satellite but without the distinctive bleeping noise. The only noise this projectile caused was an "ouch" sound when it came into contact with a person. The Sputnik was dreaded by all and it was wise to run whenever you saw one in flight. Sam was convinced that if Adolf Hitler had used Sputniks instead of flying bombs, he would have won the war and the boys would be speaking German and goose-stepping to the Post Office to fetch their 'Imperial Eagle' kali. Lucky for the British then that the Sputnik was invented by some unknown young boy from Derbyshire. After the football team were treated to a deluge of Sputniks, there followed several piles of running vegetation armed with Willow root clubs.

"It's the fourth brigade of the Mansfield market gardeners." quipped one of the older lads. The Zulus struck hard into the football team but the team fought back by hitting the Zulus with the heavy leather football and the Zulus fled into the bushes. The problem now was, they were trapped. The football team attacked the bushes and captured four of the Zulus. The prisoners, Erky, Sam, Breen and Weep were taken at once to Willows Hole den in the bushes and held there by Socky. Erky was a little older than the others, so he changed sides and joined the Football Team.

"Traitor!." cried Sam.

"Shut it!" said Socky as he struck Sam with a Willow stalk. Sam cried out more in laughter than in pain, after all it was just fun and *they* had started it. Still, they had to try and escape, it was in the Geneva Convension, every spy knew that.

"Samuel S. Sams was a spy of the very highest calibre. He had been a spy in every war that had happened in the last 150 years. He had been trained well by every combat expert known. There was only one way out of this, he would have to kill the guard, silently and quickly, or it would be curtains for them all. The large burly guard was holding a sword and a machine gun so Samuel's attack would have to be timed well. Sam reached very slowly and carefully for the hidden knife he always carried in his underwater wristwatch. The guards had failed to find it and now it was time to put it to use. He grasped its trusty hilt and then leapt on the guard and instantly cut his throat."

"Ouch!" called out Sam again as Socky hit him once more with the willow stick. It was his reward for jumping on Socky and trying to rub his throat with a small piece of wood. Weep thought of climbing one of the bushes, his usual method of escape but the branches were too small to hold even his slight weight. Breen tried to run straight out but Socky was too strong for him. Somewhere in the distance, a commotion and a shriek suggested that another of the Zulus had been captured by the seasoned warriors of the Football Team. Weep decided desperate situations demanded desperate measures.

"Let us go and we'll show you some buried treasure." He said.

"Uhh, I bet, if it's still buried why haven't you dug it up yet?" asked Socky. Weep thought for a while and then replied with confidence.

"If we dug it up it wouldn't be buried treasure would it?" Socky gave Weep a taste of the birch. He rubbed the hot part of his arm, just showing a red mark where the willow had caught him.

"Well let us go and we'll show you where some beer is hidden." pleaded Sam. Socky's eyes lit up.

"Beer?" he asked. "Where's that?"

"It's on the flat end of the Tip in a hole." pointed Sam.

"Come on then," said Socky standing. "show me, but if you're lying I'll bring you back and have you tortured." Socky grabbed Sam by the scruff of the neck and motioned the other two to walk ahead of them.

Weep thought about the torture and he knew damn well Sam was lying because if there had been any beer, it would have most certainly been consumed, even if they did not like the taste of it. Weep's mind was ablaze with options, the obvious one was to run, which he did, closely followed by Breen. Apart from a token resistance as Breen and Weep tried to bombard Socky with willow spears from a distance. Sam was alone now as he was still held by Socky and unable to run. So it was, he had to endure the temporary company of the older boy, which meant a quick 'twang' with a willow stalk every time he slowed down. They duly arrived at the back of the Tip and Sam pointed to a hole in the ground, Socky bent over to peer into the hole but could see nothing.

"You must think I'm daft. Get in there." he said pushing Sam to the ground. Sam peered inside and sniffed like a dog examining a foxhole and then very slowly squeezed his body into the perfectly round hole. Socky watched his feet move to the left and disappear into what now looked like a small tunnel.

"Have you found it yet?" he asked still bent over the hole.

"No not yet, it's dark in here y' know." came the muffled reply.

"You little rat I bet you're lyin'." called Socky into the hole, considering going in after Sam. "Come on, get out now."

"I am out." came a clear reply. Socky looked up to see Sam about fifteen feet away at the entrance to another hole, sporting a smug look, like Bugs Bunny after he has outsmarted the farmer.

"See ya', ugly!" he cried as he ran off up the Tip. By the time Socky was back on his feet, he knew he would never catch Sam, so he ambled steadily back with his hands deep in his pockets, thinking up a lie for where he had been and why his prisoners were now free.

All the other Zulus had disbanded and either gone home or moved on to another adventure by the time Sam had returned to the top of the Tip. The thought of the older boys still being around edged him towards considering that the railway line would be a safer way home. When he came to the main road where the railway crossed, he walked up the hill and onto the Backs, the dirt road that ran behind the houses. As he neared his own house, a large piece of wood sailed past his head and someone called out.

"Get lost fatty!" "Drop dead four eyes!" Sam spun around to see two younger boys he did not recognise. The insults puzzled Sam, 'four eyes?' Sam didn't wear glasses and never had done, so it was obvious that Sam had questions about the insult.

"Hey, who are you talking to? I don't wear glasses." The two boys looked dumbfounded, it was likely that these newcomers had a very small vocabulary of insults and that was going to make them second-class citizens in this village. They seemed puzzled by the question, until the elder of the two looked up and shouted.

"Big nose." and threw a large stone which missed Sam by miles. Immediately they ran down their garden path as Sam bent to pick up a small pebble. He cast it with a well-practiced arm, so accurately, that it struck the eldest of the boys square on the head. The boy yelled as he fell, Sam decided it was time to leave and headed towards an area called 'the Garages' for fairly obvious reasons, and there he found a broken pane of glass so he could look at his nose in the reflection. He considered these new children, who could be long-term enemies if the introduction was anything to go by, were probably short sighted. For one thing, they had managed to miss him with the piece of wood and the stone, secondly Sam was well built but not fat, not compared to Vern or Fat Debby anyway, maybe Weep was thinner than him but Weep was made of wet straw. The 'big nose' was a puzzle too. A voice brought him out of his dream.

"Oy! where you goin'?" It was Barmy.

"Nowhere really. Anything 'appening?"

"Nope." said Barmy emphatically. "You got away then?"

"Yeah but no thanks to the rest of you." frowned Sam.

"I was caught by Cogger and Sloop and they threw me down the far side of the Tip." Barmy grinned. "I just made a run for it. Seen anybody else?"

"Nope." said Sam shaking his head. They both sat on the gate to the field near the Garages and stared into space until Sam asked.

"Now what?" Barmy looked up at the sky and then said.

"Let's play liars." Now, when it came to this particular game, Barmy was king as he had a natural propensity for that particular art form. There were two official versions of the game, the long version was to think up an outrageous lie and then go and try to convince someone to believe it. With just two players, the simple version was usually undertaken. This was simply telling lies for comic effect or belittling people you didn't like. Barmy had a long list of the latter. "I'll start ." he said. "Biro eats dog shit." He fell about laughing but Sam just glared at him. "Your turn." Barmy said, still laughing.

"Weep and Vern are crossing the road." said Sam.

"Jesus Sam, that's crap." demanded Barmy. "If we are going to play liars then.." Sam interrupted.

"No really, Weep and Vern are crossing the road, look." Barmy looked round and said.

"Oh yeah." then continued. "Right, my turn. "Fred is taking ballet lessons." Barmy guffawed at this until Vern called out.

"Hey you two, there's been a murder."

"Wait your bloody turn, fatso." frowned Barmy as he spun round to face the approaching boys.

"Turn for what?" asked Vern as he came closer. Weep was still wearing most of his Zulu costume.

"For Liar of course and it has to be a bit believable you pair of idiots." demanded Barmy.

"It's not a lie, tell him Weep." said Vern prodding Weep's arm.

"It's true, there has been a murder." said Weep excitedly.

"A murder? Oh yeah and I suppose it was on this street." laughed Sam. "Barmy is right, it has to be at least slightly real to count you know."

"We're not playing bloody Liar, it's true, there's been a murder." said Vern in a matter-of-fact voice.

"Yeah that's right." replied Weep. Sam stopped his laughing as he noticed the serious look on the other boys' faces.

"So you're tellin' me that someone's been murdered." The boys nodded. "On this street?" continued Sam keeping a small grin on his face just in case they all burst out laughing at having taken him in. The boys nodded again.

"Yeah, exactly. It was last week an' the murderer buried his victim behind the sub station near French's Corner." insisted Weep.

"Yeah there's police an' detectives and blokes in white coats and all sorts of things." Spluttered Vern. Sam laughed again.

"White coats? They only use them when you go nuts and they have to take you away."

"What do you mean?" asked Weep.

"Well," continued Sam. "it's well known, if you go nuts, men in white coats come to take you away in a yellow van."

"He's right." nodded Barmy. There was obviously an inconsistency and the boys began to think it out.

"Maybe the murderer is a nutter?" suggested Weep as the others nodded in agreement.

"They're the worst kind." added Sam with a grim face. "But I still don't believe it."

"Well come and look, they're still at French's Corner." French's Corner was the upper end of the Backs where the house ended and the fields continued, so called because old man French lived in the last house. It was only a three minute walk from where they were, so they set off to confirm that what they had seen was indeed the murder investigation. Sam had a modicum of disbelief as they walked and began to ask questions.

"Who do you think has done it then?"

"Probably the witch." insisted Weep.

"Nah, I reckon Mumble did it, he's mad and that's probably why they brought in the white coat mob." accused Barmy.

"Quiet you lot, let's have a look first." insisted Sam. As they reached French's Corner they hid in the ditch and crawled closer to the site near where the Backs rejoined the main road. Indeed there were lots of police and men in white coats and overalls and the whole area was roped off. From where they were, they could see behind the small electrical sub station where a white screen stood to shield it from the road, but from where they lay they could see everything that was happening. There was a black van on the roadside too, with several official looking men standing by the back doors. As it left, some other men took photographs of the hole before two of the men in overalls began to fill it in.

"Jesus!" said Sam in a harsh whisper. "There really has been a murder." The boys withdrew carefully as they had there was a fear of men in white coats and they headed off towards Sam's house. Here they discussed their next move. Sam suggested that,

"We must catch the murderer before the police, they're not very good you know." He frowned as if it made his argument more convincing. "You only have to watch Sherlock Holmes making a fool of Inspector Lestrade to know that." The others nodded as an idea came to Weep.

"Let's solve it as Sherlock would have done it."

"Good idea, I'll be Holmes." added Sam.

"No, I'll be Holmes, I thought of it." insisted Weep.

"No, I'm Sherlock." interrupted Vern.

"I'm Sherlock!" demanded Barmy as he held out a clenched fist. Indeed, he did look like Sherlock Holmes with his two legs and the same number of arms as the great fictional detective. In reality, the only similarity between Holmes and Barmy was the fact that it was doubtful if either of them were real people. Nevertheless, to the younger, smaller, weaker, less able to fight well boys he was the exact double of Holmes.

"I'll be Watson." suggested Sam.

"And me." added Weep not knowing if there were any other characters involved in the stories.

"Me too." added Vern. Just then, Sam's mother came strolling down the garden path.

"Don't you be late in tonight my lad." she directed at Sam. Barmy had already begun, as soon as he heard her voice, it was useless to try and stop him. His thumbs went into his ears and out came the prehensile tongue. The boys all decided it was time to leave.

"You wait 'til I see your mother." called Sam's Mum.

"Get lost you old hag." was Barmy's reply, showing he was truly on form.

"That was *my* mother." said Sam.

"So what?" retorted Barmy. Sam resigned himself to the fact that Sherlock Holmes probably had the right to call anyone's mum an old hag if he wanted.

On their return to the Garages, they met Tools and Breen.

"There's been a murder." was the obvious greeting.

"We know." was the not so obvious reply. "It's been on the tele', Wilbur told us." explained Breen with a touch of excitement in his voice.

"Have they caught the murderer yet?" asked Sam, not wanting an affirmative answer.

"No they can't have 'cos the cops are knocking on doors an' askin' questions."

"Good!" said Sam. "We're going to find out who's done it, Barmy is Sherlock Holmes and us three are Doctor Watsons."

"I'll be P.C. Wilkes the marksman." insisted Tools pretending to shoot something in the distance.

"I'll be the Hound of the Baskervilles." growled Breen.

"We're trying to solve a murder not form a circus." frowned Sam.

"Shurrup' all of yer', lets go an' find some clues." demanded Barmy. They crossed the road and read all the advertisements in the Post Office window, they listened to a conversation at the bus stop, they even looked for strange footprints in Tools' back garden, until his dad shouted at them for walking in his flowerbeds. They searched for fingerprints on the Tip gate, they found a selection of murder weapons including a rusty tin opener and a broken umbrella handle but still the identity of the killer remained a mystery. Their instincts lead them to the only true suspect, 'The Witch'. There were two witches on the street, one was just an old mad woman who chased them with a stick but the other, well, she was a 'true' witch. The kind of witch the likes of old Matthew Hopkins, the infamous 'Witch Finder General' of the 17th century would have given a pocket full of marbles, a penknife and a 'hundreder' conker to have found. No one had ever seen her come out of the house. It was said she had a tunnel to the Co-op next door because she couldn't come out in daylight to do her shopping. Boys proved their worth by daring to walk down her garden path, not that it was much of a garden and the path had been overgrown for at least a hundred years. It just had to be her. Slowly, the boys fought their way through the undergrowth towards the house until they, very carefully, reached the 'zone of terror', which was her back door. They looked at the grim, green door flaking away for lack of paint and whispered in fear of the witch's wrath.

"You do it Barmy." they all said.

"Why me?" asked Barmy in a rare fit of sense.

"Cos' you're Sherlock." came the whispered reply. Barmy looked once more at the door and agreed that the boys had a point, it was no good being Sherlock Holmes if you couldn't even knock on an old woman's door. When he had just about plucked up courage to knock, he noticed the others were slowly moving away.

"Oy!" he whispered harshly. "Come back here, I'm not doing it on my own." As the boys very slowly returned, Barmy turned back to the door in time to see the scruffy curtains at the window open and an ugly, wrinkled face appeared there.

"Aaaaaaaagghh!!!" screamed all the boys as they fled up the garden taking off skin as they plummeted through brambles. Barmy must have been very afraid as the witch did not get to see his famous tongue act.

When they were safely back at the Garages, they decided that the witch couldn't possibly have done it, owing to the fact that Sherlock and the Dr. Watsons did not have the right interview techniques for someone who has the backing of the black arts. There was only one real course of action left to them, they would have to beat a confession out of someone. That 'someone', was to be Dunny. Rupert Dunn was the eldest of two odd brothers who were rarely seen to leave their garden, due to their mother not wishing them to play with other boys. They were both weak, frail and nervous, Rupert was the worst being nick named 'Dunny the Bunny'. His frailty mattered not to the boys, so whilst Barmy and Weep hid behind the wall at the top of Dunny's garden, Sam stood at the closed gate and called to him.

"Hey Dunny, is this your Batmobile here?" he was pointing to the floor a few feet away. He knew Dunny had a treasured collection of model cars that he was very possessive about.

"Where?" asked Dunny walking towards Sam.

"Just here, on the Backs." Sam drew away from the gate as Dunny came closer.

"I don't think I've had that out today and I'm sure I haven't been through the gate." he puzzled as he neared the wooden defence to his world. Dunny was very wary of crossing that boundary, it was more than a boundary, it was a portal to another dimension as far as he was concerned. As he opened and came through the gate, he closely examined the frame as if he would have trouble remembering it on his way back. It wasn't his lucky day, a sack went over his head before he had time to say 'Dinky' and he was bundled across the Backs and into the allotment gardens accompanied by his own muffled screams. When the sack was removed Dunny was already in tears.

"Now then you big girl," demanded Barmy. "who's done the murder?"

"What murder?" sobbed Dunny.

"Don't give me that!" snapped Barmy. "We know you've dunnit', you 'it him over the 'ed with a shuvill an' buried 'im in a shaller grave." Dunny tried to speak but the words sounded strange.

"I didn't ooooit. I don't wee mee know anyeeeeeee wee meee." He had a very unusual cry, it was a mix of weees, meees and eeees, but the worst was still to come.

"You'll go to prison for a hundred years." grinned Weep, who was apt to cry himself, but enjoyed watching others initiating tear duct floods.

"Yeah, an' they'll smash up all your cars." added Sam, a little jealous of the many toys he had. The mee wee noise developed into a long drawn out eeeeeeeee until it became an almighty wailing banshee sound that was so loud the boys made a quick exit. They ran faster than a burning burglar with dysentery from the allotment gardens leaving Dunny to stumble home with his hands tied behind his back, frightening the birds away with his integral siren. The noise continued until he reached the safety of his gate, which he found easier than he thought but the wailing banshee sound brought his mother out. The old couple who lived next door were convinced it was an air raid siren and so they closed the curtains, searched out their old ARP helmets and stood waiting for the "Damned Luftwaffe, up to their old tricks again."

Dunny survived drowning in his own tears but the encounter had a profound effect on the boy, never daring to venture from the garden unless a rope was tied around his waist and the other end tied to the dining room table legs.

"Now what?" asked Tools as they crossed the road once again.

"We have to identify the murder weapon." suggested Breen pointing his finger skyward.

"Hey, I'm Sherlock." said an indignant Barmy pushing Breen out of his place. "Now then, my dear Watsons, we have to identify the actual murder weapon." also pointing skyward, for no other reason than it was what Breen had done.

"And how do we do that?" asked Tools. "We don't even know where the murder took place."

"Elementary, my dear Watsons." replied Barmy pretending to smoke a pipe. "We ask someone who knows everything." Barmy stopped for a moment and grinned at the others. "Moriarty." he concluded in a rare fit of literary knowledge.

"Who?" said the others in unison.

"Moriarty of course." Barmy did not have any idea who Moriarty was in the stories of Conan-Doyle but he remembered the name from somewhere or other. It was enough for Sam to wonder if Barmy had been possessed by a human. Breen put it down to sunstroke and Tools nearly feinted from the shock of Barmy knowing something about anything.

"Moriarty," continued Barmy once again pointing skyward. "or, as he is known in these parts, Wilbur the Wise."

"Wilbur?" questioned Sam.

"He's clever Wilbur is." added Breen. " 'an it was 'im that told us he'd seen it on the tele'."

"He doesn't look clever." frowned Sam.

"No, but he knows lots." insisted Breen in an, 'and I should know 'cos I live next door to him.' voice. Wilbur wasn't really that clever, he was certainly no sage but he was older and he was taller and he did wear glasses, and he was useless at anything useful. It certainly seemed he was made to know things, because he had no other purpose. Armed with this questionable knowledge, the boys reasoned that he must be clever and as they arrived near his house, Breen, as his neighbour, had the responsibility of fetching him out of the house and onto the Backs. He wasn't very happy about being dragged out halfway through a particularly tense moment in a Thursday afternoon edition of "The Woodentops."

"What do you lot want?" he asked gruffly.

"Have you heard about the murder?" Asked Sam.

"Yes." replied Wilbur with a deep frown on his face. "It was on the television."

"Well," began tools holding out the fingers of his left hand and pointing to one of them with the index of his right as he continued with his demands. "we want to know where and when the actual killing took place."

"It was on the pavement, opposite the sub station." replied Wilbur looking at Tools' left hand.

"You see, I told you he'd know." said Barmy with a smile. "What was the murder weapon?" he asked hoping to confirm that Wilbur was a full-blown mage.

"A piece of wood." replied Wilbur with some confidence. "He hit him with a piece of wood, went home to fetch a shovel and buried him behind the sub station." The boys were now in awe at Wilbur's powers of deduction.

"Right then, Watsons, let's away and find the murderer." said Barmy thrusting his chest out with the knowledge of a job well done.

"His name is Ben Smedley," interrupted Wilbur before the boys could move off. "He lives in Holmewood. Oh and he did it last Friday night." The boys could not believe their ears, here stood a way to make lots of money. 'Wilbur the Wise', 'The Eye to Mystery'.

"Well Wilbur, I have to admit that you are fantastic," said Barmy. "but how does it all come to you?"

"It doesn't," frowned Wilbur unsure what Barmy meant. "I told you, it was on the television. The man gave himself up, then showed the police where the body was. I told Breen about it." Barmy turned to Breen and enquired,

"So why didn't you tell us that bit?"

"I must have missed that part." he frowned. The great detective Sherlock Holmes and his assistants Dr. Watsons chased Breen for almost a mile but Breen was used to being chased, for his elder brother did not take kindly to having his bed sheets stapled together whilst he was still asleep in them.

Sam and Weep shuffled home, content in the knowledge that Breen would have to walk home very carefully, watching all the gateways as he did in case someone ambushed him.

"What are you doing tomorrow?" asked Weep.

"Dunno, probably nowt." replied Sam dolefully. "How 'bout you?"

"The same, nowt." mumbled Weep.

"Always the same isn't it?" continued Sam. "nothin' to do an' nowhere to go and there's never anyone out. Not much chance of anybody writin' a book about us."

"Na, yer' right there. See ya'." said Weep as he turned for home.

"See ya'." replied Sam as he crossed the road towards his house. For about an hour Sam had the ritual of accounting for his actions that day.

Sam, like most boys tried to keep away from religion and politics, mainly because the preadolescent male doesn't understand or have any interest in either subject.   Although there were certainly many discussions on whether God existed, Sam didn't know if any discussions had ever taken place on 'Do politicians exist?' He had considered it at least once, he just wasn't sure.   Sam could remember that he had been in churches many times in his short life; cousin's weddings, some distant relative fourteen-times-removed's christening and even one funeral.   That was a mistake though, when Sam's parents had gone the wrong church but were too embarrassed to admit it. What the congregation thought of the three of them appearing in best finery, his mother wearing a big pink hat and his father with a carnation in his buttonhole at some poor souls funeral one can only imagine.   Yes, churches he had been in but the Houses Parliament? No, he had never been there. It may all have been made up for all he knew.   Sam was always objective, from a very early age he had wondered if there really was a God, he was more reticent to let go of Father Christmas than he was God. He considered that the existence of the many priests and churches did not necessarily mean there was an omnipotent being but neither did it fly in the face of some 'Almighty God' being completely made up.   He had asked his parents and his friends but no one had a comprehensive answer that Sam could get his teeth into and believe in. After a time, he decided that to non-believers he was probably agnostic, to agnostics he was definitely religious and to believers he was an out and out atheist. Still, having no real conviction left him with a mistrust of both churches and atheists, this did not however, stop religion coming to call for tea.

Biro started it, he had told Tools and Sam that he was going on a trip to the Trebor sweet factory in Chesterfield and soon after he was going karting, all completely free with a 'youth club' he had joined in the next village.

"How do you join? Can anyone go?" asked Sam considering the trip to the sweet factory sounded like a great deal of what Sam liked about the world.

"Yes anyone can go, but you have to enrol and attend every Thursday night." instructed Biro.

"What's enrol?" asked Sam never far behind a new word.

"Er, you sort of sign on, put your name in a book sort of thing." That seemed painless to Sam, yep he could do that easily enough. 'Enrol', that seemed like a word he would need to use at some time.

"What do you do every Thursday night?" asked Tools.

"Oh just sing, play games and eat sweets." explained Biro.

"Sounds good to me!" agreed Sam, this Youth Club was becoming pretty damn interesting to him, that was for sure and his mouth began to salivate at the thought of kali and Refreshers. Tools nodded a confirmation that it seemed good to him too.

The following Thursday night, the three boys, plus another recruit called Martin met at Sam's house and then walked the two miles into the next village where the Youth Club was supposed to be. They eventually arrived at the place, ready to 'enrol' for a life of fun and sweets.

"It's some sort of a church!" insisted Sam giving it the look of a vampire at a garlic growers convention.

"No, it's okay," interrupted Biro "the youth club's down the drive behind the church." They walked past the very new red brick church, all sighing with relief that they were not to enter the house of God and pass under the large wooden cross on the front. The building at the rear was a small wooden affair, plain but substantial. Inside it looked far removed from what Sam considered a "Youth Club" would look like. There was formal seating in rows facing a small stage at the far end of the hall. The room was full of thin men in suits and motherly females that looked like they all presented Watch With Mother. Children were very few and were dressed as small versions of the adults, with almost identical clothing. Sam inspected his own clothing, tee shirt, jeans and plimsolls. Excellent clothing for singing, particularly excellent clothes for playing games and eating sweets in, he thought. They had been rigorously tested, he had eaten lots of sweets in these clothes so he knew they worked well. The three boys were ushered to the front seats and told to sit. Soon, a pale, bald man appeared and began to talk. Sam couldn't understand what he said but the word 'God' appeared quite a bit. The most unnerving part was when the whole crowd cried out "Hallelujah!" Sam almost leapt from his seat. They continued to do it after almost every sentence too and after Sam and Tools' heartbeats settled down from the initial shock, they began to snigger behind their hands. When the man had finally completed his mush of words, the whole crowd began to sing songs. Not about sweets or games, but about God and Jesus. Sam wanted to point out that the church was next door and this was the Youth Club and they better leave before the sweets were handed out. He wanted to point this out to Biro too but he was too busy singing with the others. When the singing ceased, another man began to talk. Sam leaned over to Tools and whispered.

"They must move all the seats to the walls when the games start." Tools nodded then sat upright in case God was watching. Sam looked over to Biro who was listening to the man intently and suddenly thought,

"We have been conned". Well, to an extent they had but although there were no games or sweets, there *had* been a promise of visiting the Trebor sweet factory. Biro had to endure complaints all the way home.

The boys suffered the 'Youth Club' until the day of the trip to the sweet factory, then, armed with bags of free sweets and having enjoyed a worthwhile tour, Sam and Tools resigned from the youth club forever.

As they sat and ate some of their sweets in the long autumn grass of the back field, they discussed their religious misfortune.

"Does God exist then?" asked Sam. It was that eternal question again, since no one had ever answered him properly. If anyone could come up with a definitive answer though, it was Tools.

"He must do."

"Why?" asked Sam

"Because we are here. If God wasn't up there." explained Tools pointing skywards with a Sherbet Fountain. "We couldn't be down here"

"Why?" was Sam's obvious question.

"Because he couldn't have made us could he?" answered Tools. Sam thought for a moment trying to remember a story.

"Well what if we came from the monkeys?" he spluttered. Tools sucked hard on the liquorice of the sherbet fountain and said.

"It's obvious the monkeys came from us, they were people that did wrong and God turned them into monkeys."

"What did they do wrong?" Tools looked for a way out of this conversation.

"They did sex more than once a day." he replied. Sam laughed.

"Well where do dogs come into it then?"

"They were people who swore."

"Well I've sworn and I haven't turned into a dog" Sam insisted.

"Well you wait till God hears you, then you'll find yourself eating dog food, running round making a lot of noise, you won't be able to go to school and get clever, you'll have to cock your leg up to pee and you won't care who is looking!" Apart from eating dog food, it didn't seem to be a bad life, added to this, the thought of Old Man Cain's dog getting a whole bar of chocolate every Saturday just for carrying a newspaper, it seemed positively idyllic to Sam. There was a brief silence as the boys polished off more sweets until Tools continued.

"Anyway," he insisted. "If there were no God, who is it that answers all the prayers?" Tools ended by placing two boiled sweets in his mouth at the same time. Sam thought for a moment and asked.

"What prayers?" Sam wasn't sure what he meant but Sam really wasn't an expert when it came to prayers.

"The ones who say..." Tools stopped for a moment as he removed the two sweets to speak as he nearly choked. "The ones who say 'my prayers have been answered' and that." He replaced the sweets only to quickly take them out again to continue. "An' what about them people who say they hear God's voice?" The sweets were thrown back into his mouth. Sam pulled a lemon bon bon from the bag and thought about this point. He still wasn't sure what it was but he tentatively offered an idea.

"Aliens?" asked Sam with a shrug.

"Aiioons?" said Tools and then spit out the sweets for the final time. "Aliens? What do you mean?" He looked down at the two saliva-covered sweets in his hand and then casually threw them away and wiped the mess on his shirt.

"Well it must be, they live near God up there so it must be them that talk to everybody." announced Sam with some conviction as he unwrapped something in his hand.

"Can't be." Demanded Tools. "They can understand us but we can't understand their language, stands to reason." Sam thought this was a compulsive answer and it had no argument but something was about to change the subject.

"Aaauuughh." screamed Sam. Tools looked up from his bag thinking a particularly ugly alien had just joined them but he saw Sam spitting something out of his mouth.

" Liquorish Yuk!" he announced wiping his tongue with grass. "I hate it." he concluded.

"Everyone likes liquorish." laughed Tools.

"I don't." scowled Sam, still spitting out the taste which seemed to linger on his tongue. "When we were at Trebor and we were watching the molten liquorish come out of that machine and I said that it was purple and brown, well Biro said it looked like a cows arse having a poo. I won't eat the stuff ever again." Tools was rolling about laughing.

"Well," he eventually managed. "if God had heard you swearing and turned you into a dog, you would probably want to roll in it." He began laughing all over again. Sam had another question.

"So, do you think that cats are like dogs then? Were they people who swore?"

"Yes, but they were people who swore all the time and then God turned them into cats and now they have to eat cat food and all they can do all day is lie down on the rug and sleep." It was a longwinded explanation but Sam thought that was an even better life than being a dog, after all, that was pretty much all Sam's cat did. Okay, the cat food thing was a bit off putting but even that was better than liquorish. Then again, he considered that his mother's saying about 'kicking the cat off the hearth' injected a certain amount of risk into any such transformation. There was also the regulation mouse eating competition that his cat seemed to enrol in with a sickening regularity. Maybe a dog's life was better after all.

"An' that's for swearing all the time?" asked Sam for confirmation. Tools just nodded, he was busy taking all of the liquorish out of Sam's bag, omitting to replace it with anything *he* wasn't keen on. As the boys parted company, Sam could be heard muttering the words "Shit, shat and tit" all the way up to his garden gate.

During a certain summer the weather seemed to be constantly hot, just as the grass seemed to be constantly green and adults were constantly unfriendly. When it was hot, Sam and his friends found shade in one of their many dens drinking pop freshly 'liberated' from the yard of the local shop. Food came even more easily, it was hanging in the trees and bushes. Blackberries, raspberries, wild strawberries and even crab apples but nothing tastes as sweet as the fruit that belongs to someone else. To this end, the children participated in an age-old custom called 'scrumping', which simply means, the theft of fruit from people's gardens. Sam and his friends were experts at this type of theft, developing it into a fine art. The mainstay of all scrumping was done after the hours of darkness but as you will see, this is not always the case. All good scrumpers, to be successful, have to stick rigidly to this code of practice.

A.   Never Eat All The Apples That You Scrump.
Sam found out that this rule needs to be remembered at all times. One warm evening, in a certain summer Sam, Barmy, Weep, Vern and Mumble began a reign of terror along the south side of the street raiding French's, Webbley's and three other gardens, including the back of the Post Office. Sam must have eaten twelve apples by the time they had reached the Tip Gate.

"Let's go further down." suggested Barmy. 'Further down' towards the railway line was not an area often attacked and the layout of the gardens not too well known to them but there were three perfectly good apple trees to be molested, plus a small but elegant pear tree. Another eight apples later, Sam found himself at the bottom garden, near to the railway line. A tall fence protected the base of the tree but it was no match for the boys. Weep and Sam scaled the fence, whilst Mumble climbed onto a close by shed. Vern and Barmy collected the apples that the others threw down. All except one. Sam found the biggest apple he had ever seen. He felt ill from all the apples already consumed but this apple was asking to be eaten. They exited the garden and ran to a local street lamp at the front of the houses to examine their treasure. Sam showed his prize and polished the skin into a deep lustre, then gently bit into it. The trophy was handed round for all to taste and then was finished off by Sam, the core being casually tossed into the nearest front garden. That night, Sam was so ill, he swore he would never eat another apple and resigned himself to the fact that scrumping was about stealth and the thrill of the kill, not eating.

B.   *Never Trust Girls.*

Another evening in a certain summer, Barmy set his sights on French's pear tree, which stood by the kitchen window of Mr. and Mrs. French. A girl called Trish, daughter of the owner of the tree, assured Barmy that her parents always went out on Tuesday nights and all would be well, as she was babysitting her younger brother. Barmy called together the finest scrumping team in the village, namely his younger brother Weep, Sam, Mumble and Breen, to do his bidding and assist in the rape of the pear tree. The garden was well defended by walls, hedges and locked gates, so the only way in was through the unlocked garage and out through a convenient window into the garden. All went well and the boys were busy loading their pockets with pears. Weep was high in the tree and the others picked from the lower branches.

"Oy! Get out of there you little sods!" came a gruff voice. Sam ran the wrong way and hid under a spruce tree, Barmy climbed a wall and escaped by a neighbouring garden, Mumble froze and began to talk to himself and Weep leapt out of the tree and landed on Breen. Weep then ran for the garage and escaped but Breen and Mumble were caught. Sam waited for all this to happen and then launched himself through the garden towards the front of the house, where he escaped out into the main road. Once he reached home, he crept into the kitchen, removed his muddy shoes and entered the lounge.

"Oh hello," he said to his parents as though he didn't expect to see them there. "I think I'll go straight to bed." Sam left the room and ascended the stairs.

"I'm taking him to the doctors tomorrow. He's never volunteered for bed before." his mother said without breaking her gaze from the television. Sam lay on his bed eating pears, hoping that Mr. French had not recognised him.

"Girls!" he snapped. "You can't trust 'em."

C.   *Never Say Die.*

Sometimes life can be hard and the odds may be stacked against you, so high sometimes that you feel like giving in. One particular evening, after the usual trees had been relieved of their fruit, Sam, Vern, Weep, Barmy and Loz stood under one of only three street lights on the whole road. The light was not particularly bright but it was sighted at one of the opening to the Backs and so it became a regular meeting place. The boys bathed in its meagre but comforting light and tried to think of something exciting to do.

"Shall we raid the bottom allotments?" suggested Weep. The 'bottom allotments' was a 'Dig for Victory' war allotment garden made on the site where a young R.A.F. pilot was said to have crashed whilst training. This place had always been a little taboo for scrumpers, for it seemed that every time they tried to enter, there was someone there.

"No, I'm not goin' it's haunted that place." demanded Vern.

"It's not." contradicted Loz. "It's not haunted 'cos there's no such thing as ghosts."

"There is then, I've seen one." snapped Vern.

"Where?" asked Sam.

"In our house, when I was on my own."

"That would be your sister in her night gown." laughed Barmy.

"No it wasn't, anyway she wasn't in. I know it was a ghost 'cos the room went cold and the tele' went off."

"You're daft." said Sam not wanting to hear more.

"You wouldn't say that if you saw one." said Vern, with a rather serious expression.

"No I'd probably say AAAAhhhh!" howled Sam trying to make light of a very uncomfortable situation. The boys went quiet until Loz suggested,

"Let's raid the back of the shop then." They all agreed and crossed the road to the south side of the street were the shop stood. Again, on this side of the road was another wide opening as access to the Backs. On one side was the Post Office, on the other, was the grocery shop. They walked through the opening and onto the Backs at the rear of the shop, once there, Sam, Weep and Barmy climbed over the high wall and onto the lean-to roof of the scant building that held all the pop. It was dark, so they picked bottles at random and passed them under the large double gates to the waiting hands of Loz and Vern. They had to remain very quiet as the shop owner kept a large Labrador dog that sometimes slept in a kennel in the garden. This done, the three climbed out over the wall and joined the others by the Tip Gate to drink their spoils. It was always the case that a large bottle of pop was too much for one boy, so the remains were hidden for future needs. From the Tip Gate, Weep and Sam noticed, even though it was dark, that the Post Office tree was overflowing with apples. They just had to take some. Vern volunteered to keep watch, whilst the others climbed the wall and then the Post Office out building, to reach the apples. They had barely reached the apples when the shop owner came out of the side door where Vern stood. Vern being the good 'watcher' he was, ran off and left the others to their fate. The boys kept silent and hoped that the man wouldn't enter the garden but the man knew something was wrong when the small boy had scarpered for no apparent reason. He walked round to the back garden to peer through the darkness and there, in the gloom, he saw several small boys hung motionless, like decorations on a large, unlit Christmas tree. There was no fairy or twinkling lights, so the man could see no faces but he could see shapes.

Without a word, he leapt over the gate and lunged towards the tree. Barmy and Loz saw him and smashed through a frail fence to escape into the next garden, whilst Sam and Weep ran up the garden and jumped over a small gate, into a field. The man was close but he failed in his attempt to catch any of them, they were too good for him, even without a decent 'watcher'. In his frustration he called out to them.

"You little buggers, don't you dare take any more apples off my tree." As Sam ran across the field in the dark, those words echoed in his head. That night in bed, he hatched a plan.

The next day was very hot and some of the boys spent the day on the Tip, which was where Sam found Weep throwing stones at an empty pop bottle and not having much luck at hitting it.

"What you up to?" Sam asked as he sat at the side of Weep.

"Not much, it's too hot to do much." scowled Weep.

"Fancy doing some scrumping tonight?" asked Sam.

"Not bloody likely after last night. Vern is rubbish at everything." Sam had to agree and shrugged as he picked up a couple of stones and tried to hit the bottle.

"Tonight it will be different." A slight smile broke on Sam's face. "I have a plan."

"A plan? I hate it when anybody says that." scowled Weep. "It's like when Barmy says; 'Hey Weep, I have a great plan, let's go and torment old man Herriot's dog, he can't get out of the garden if we put bricks behind the gate first', so off we went. We put four bricks behind the gate and then popped up behind the wall and barked at the dog. Trouble was, the damn dog can jump the wall. I got my arse bit for my trouble." Weep had a look of, 'if you laugh, I'll kill you' on his face but Sam couldn't suppress a smirk of sorts.

"This is a much better plan," he explained. "I want to go back to the Post Office."

"What?" spluttered Weep. "We only just got away last night."

"Listen Weep," explained Sam, standing up. He then began to outline his idea in scant detail and concluded by saying. "I have it all planned and this way we can get the apples and have a laugh." explained Sam.

"Yeah it's great but he will be waiting for us."

"That's why we shall go late, very late." grinned Sam. Weep thought for a moment and grinned back. They had done this many times, waiting for their parents to go to bed and then getting up and dressed to meet in the bottom opening at two o'clock in the morning. That night, they did exactly this, crossing the road once more and returning to the Post Office apple tree in the dead of night.

The following morning, the man from the Post Office woke to another warm and sunny day, smiling at the fact that he had received no more trouble from scrumpers, since scaring them off. Children, did they think they could get the better of him? He was adult and adults made the rules. Four million years of evolution had brought man to the position where he was eventually master of his own apple tree, no undersize, half humans were going to get their filthy hands on his apples. He walked to the corner so that he could go and see his tree with its lush, heavy fruit shinning in the sun, true he wasn't going to pick them, and he would only ever eat a couple of them but they were *his* apples and they looked so beau...... As he turned the corner he almost feinted in horror. Hanging from the tree were just apple cores, nothing but apple cores. Every apple had been eaten where it hung, there wasn't a single apple unmolested.

Indeed, as the man had told them when he chased them, Sam and Weep had not taken any apples from the tree and Sam was pleased with the exercise, for he had even followed the first rule of scrumping, "Never eat all the apples you scrump". They had simply bitten off chunks of the apples putting the pieces into bags. This half chewed mess was given to his pet rabbit.

"Scrumping's good fun." thought Sam.

"Scrumping's good fun." thought the rabbit.

D.   Never go scrumping during daylight hours.

It was always thought of as reckless, even suicidal but when boys become bored, they tend to resort to 'Kamikaze' pastimes. So it was, on one particular day in a certain summer, that Sam and Vern met a lad from down the road called Norman. Norman was a bit of an enigma and there was always the smell of failure about him. Nevertheless they decided to attack a well-known gooseberry bush, just inside the top allotment gardens, where a convenient hole in the hedge gave easy access.

It was pretty easy to crawl in, scrump and crawl out and after lying in the barley field eating not quite ripe gooseberries, the boys decided that a few strawberries would go down well too. The problem being that the strawberry patch was in the centre of the allotment. Through the hole, they crawled and hid behind a small shed, looking to see if anyone was working on the garden. They could see no one, so off they tramped to the strawberry patch and began to look for ripe strawberries. With very few picked, Sam and Vern noticed a large man bearing down on them at a vast rate of knots, so they ran for the nearest hedge, Norman did not have the scrumpers instinct and consequently, was the last to get moving. Vern being a chubby lad, was not one to move fast under normal circumstances but Sam had long since noticed that whenever they were chased, Vern always beat Sam to the exit point. This time was no exception and Vern was over the fence and the hedge just as Sam arrived but Norman had also caught up. Sam scrambled over as quickly as he could but Norman, lacking that scrumpers ability, hesitated, this gave him time to panic and he simply cowered under the hedge and was, of course, caught. The other two boys ran over the field until they were sure they were not being followed and then made their way towards the Tip, discussing what to do next.

"Did you see him?" screamed Sam. "the idiot just sat there and ...... and did nothing."

"We should never have taken him, what shall we do now? He's bound to grass on us." exclaimed Vern. Sam thought for a minute and came up with what he thought was the only reasonable thing to do.

"We'll have to run away, there's nothing else for it. We'll just leave home and run away" Vern thought that this was a drastic measure but soon agreed that Sam was right, there was nothing else to do. The two of them headed down the railway and down a steep bank to a large Sycamore, which supported a tree house they knew of. It wasn't so much a tree house, as a tree shelf but it was high up and comfortable, due to having lots of straw laid on its high floor. The boys were confused, it was the first time they had run away from home.

"Where shall we go?" asked Vern.

"We'll join the merchant navy and sail to Australia." replied Sam thoughtfully.

"Why Australia?"

"Well that's where all the criminals go."

"Oh." said Vern. There was a short silence, then Sam asked.

"Have you got any money?"

"No."

"We'll have to get jobs then."

"I wonder if Norman has taken that man over to our house yet?" asked Vern not listening to Sam.

"Oh, I bet he has, "It was them mister, them two made me do it." he'll be saying."

"I'm scared." said Vern. Sam looked at Vern's face and realised there was no need for false heroics.

"Me too." he replied. He lay on his stomach and peered down to the ground below. "After this, I'm never ever going to do anything wrong ever again."

"Me neither, in fact, I'll write a letter to my parents saying unless they forgive me, I'll kill myself." replied Vern with a little stutter in his voice. Sam sat back up, leaned on the tree and looked out across the field and said.

"That's not a good idea, knowing your folks, they would probably say 'Good'."

"We'll both go to hell for this." insisted Vern.

"Do you think so?"

"Bound to."

"Do you believe in God?" asked Sam from nowhere.

"Yes, why, don't you?"

"I don't know, I always say I don't but when I get in to trouble, I end up praying. I asked Tools about it once but he doesn't really know either."

"What do you think God looks like?" asked Vern with interest.

"Probably like ...." Sam drew out the last word whilst he thought of God's features. "Basil Rathbone." he concluded.

"Barmy told me that God was dead, he was killed in a car crash along with St. Christopher and Santa Claus on their way to a party." groaned Vern.

"God hasn't got a car." frowned Sam.

"Oh it was St. Peter's car, Barmy said."

"Jesus has got a racing car." insisted Sam.

"How do you know that?"

"Because God told him to go forth, but he came fifth and won a tea service." laughed Sam. Vern had heard the joke several times and he was not in a humorous mood anyway, so Sam dropped the grin and returned to the problem. "Barmy is Barmy, there are no roads in heaven, just clouds." he explained after some thought.

"Do you think God's alive then?" asked Vern for reassurance. Sam thought about the present situation for a moment and then said.

"Barmy's probably right about him being dead."

"But can God die?" asked Vern.

"Everything dies, I suppose God can die too. The problem is, who would find him?" frowned Sam.

"Hey? What do you mean?" asked Vern staring across at Sam.

"Well, he lives on his own in heaven, so there is nobody to find him dead in his rocking chair, like old Mister Collins last year. He was there for days they said, before his cleaner found him." Sam shrugged and raised his eyebrows. Vern shuffled a little and then said.

"Well I expect God has a cleaner, he's not likely to do the dusting himself is he, not with all the work he has to do?" Sam scratched his ear as Vern continued. "What about the angels up there then? Wouldn't they find him dead?"

"I forgot about the angels." admitted Sam. "Maybe they found him then but how would they bury him without any soil"? Silence overcame them and Sam lay on his back looking at the clouds in a beautiful blue sky.

"What will your dad do if he finds out?" asked Sam after some minutes.

"He'll give me the strap after throwing me about and then I'll get sent to my room without anything to eat. If I'm lucky, he'll get over it by next week."

"I only had the strap once." added Sam.

"You're lucky, I get it most times. What did you get the strap for then?" asked Vern as he lay down too.

"I can't remember, funny thing is, I do remember my dad saying he was going to make sure I never forgot what I'd done but I can't remember." shrugged Sam.

"I bet you will get it this time." insisted Vern.

"I won't, 'cos we've run away, remember." Sam sat up as he prodded Vern on the arm and began to play with the strands of straw.

"So what's Merchant Navy then?" asked Vern, as he too sat up and dangled his feet over the high perch. Sam considered this, he had heard a man in the shop say it but he had no idea what it meant. "I sailed all around the world in the Merchant Navy." he had said. Sam just sighed and said.

"Don't you know?" to give himself time to think. "Well ......" There was a short silence. "The Merchant Navy is..." More silence. "It's sort of like the Royal Navy but instead of guns they have shops."

"Hey?" asked Vern wrinkling his nose up at the slow answer.

"Well.... you know the ships of the Royal Navy 'ave to sail round the world? .... Well, they have to have somewhere to shop and the Merchant Navy take all the shops."

"What, on the ships?" asked Vern not sure about Sam's answer.

"Yeah, well they have shops on the ships anyway." Sam felt more confident by the second and his answers were coming quicker. Sam found lying was like that, it's like sledging down the side of the Tip, it takes some getting started but when you're moving it's difficult to stop.

"So how will we get work then?" asked Vern. "I don't know how to run a shop."

"Well lads of our age start off simple, it's like on land, you start with a paper round." insisted Sam.

"What, on a ship?" asked Vern, his voice getting higher in pitch with his disbelief. This threw Sam a little and he stuttered the answer.

"Well,.... it's easy,..... you get your own rowing boat to deliver the papers in." Sam opened his arms as much as to say, 'isn't it obvious?'. They went quiet once more and laid back down, watching the sky. It was getting late, they could feel the sun's warmth fading. Sam said.

"I'm hungry."

"So am I, I'm starving." replied Vern feeling his not too thin tummy.

"Lets go home for tea." suggested Sam.

There is a tradition in Britain that began in the Dark Ages of naming a large body of water, this is because it was considered that water held many powerful spirits and this made them special places. Most lakes and lochs have names, some famous but what isn't widely known is that nearly all pools of a reasonable size were also named. Probably known only by the very local people and with names that mirror our past. Just over a mile to the north of the hamlet of Highfields was a body of water that had a circumference of about half a mile and was probably formed due to water collecting at the banking of two shunting railways that were built by the local mining companies. It was really two ponds, as the branch railway that came from Holmewood bisected its northern half curving to meet the main branch line. It was said there were once three small ponds but Sam had no recollection of a third pond. He had asked questions but no one could say for sure why it was there, and what ever the reason it is lost in time, as are the reasons for its name for no one Sam ever knew had any explanation of how it came by its odd title. It was known locally as The Wolfie. It wasn't particularly deep and had very few fish in it but as the trees and bushes grew around it, the place became a retreat for peaceful solitude. Many types of waterfowl used it as home as did thousands of insects and water based plant life but it was also a magnet for young boys. It was the best type of adventure playground, it was King Arthur's lake, it was the seven seas and it was home to vagabonds and pirates. There was a very small island of sorts near the middle and a legend sprung up that a pirate had buried his treasure there, although it was never found. What a pirate would have been doing about as far from the sea as you can get in England, is beyond reckoning but it didn't stop the boys playing out the fantasy. Of course, every body of water needs two things, a legend and a craft. The latter requisite was provided by a raft, known simply as 'The Wolfie Raft' which it seemed had floated on the pond since anyone could remember but the truth is, that many such rafts had come and gone using very similar components. Old empty oil barrels, parts of disused railway sleepers, several assorted spars and many lengths of rope all went into making the raft and so, when it fell apart, the whole thing was rebuilt with a certain amount of 'improvements'. The biggest problem with the raft was stowing it away so that not just any Tom, Dick or Blackbeard could get at it. It was too obvious moored at the side of the bank, so various ways were found to try and conceal it from prying eyes, including making it look like a small island, camouflaged within the trees and bushes and anchoring it to the small island near the centre of the Wolfie but none of these options really worked.

There was much discussion on how deep the Wolfie actually was too, its southern shore was shallow and floored with pebbles, with a gentle slope out to fifteen or so feet where the depth was up to a boys waist but it was well known that a few feet further the floor fell away. One day, in a certain summer, several of the boys decided to work out exactly how deep it was and set off to do their own research.

"We could build our own submarine." suggested Vern and even though most of the boys were apt to have flights of fancy, everyone realised that a homemade submarine was beyond their capabilities.

"Oh right," laughed Breen. "and you can be the test pilot."

"Pilots fly planes." insisted Tools who was carrying a length of old rope. In truth it was several lengths of old bailing twine tied together.

"Hey?" asked Sam.

"You don't get pilots in sub's, you get pilots in planes." explained Tools.

"So who drives a sub then?" questioned Breen. Tools thought for a moment and with a grin he pointed and said.

"Vern." The others laughed as they walked north along the railway. Breen covered his brow with his outstretched hand and looked towards the Wolfie, he wiped his face with his sleeve in the heat and said.

"So how are we going to find out how deep it is then?" It was only ten thirty but the day was already showing some of the heat to come.

"We're gonna' use this rope with a weight on it and send it to the bottom an' then measure how much rope it took." explained Tools. Weep was the only one who hadn't added anything but that was soon to change.

"How d' you know we've got enough rope?" he asked.

"There's twenty feet of the stuff here." pointed out Tools patting the twine on his shoulder.

"Well that's not enough then, 'cos Socky and Loz reckon it's a hundred feet deep at least." insisted the young Weep.

"Rubbish," spat Tools. "by my calculations it can only be ten feet." Sam liked that word 'calculations', it was a word you could use to baffle, indeed just as Tools had done as no one asked what the calculations actually were.

"How the hell are we gonna get to the deep part then?" asked Weep.

"The raft." said Sam.

"Chapper and Erky have hidden it somewhere." Weep was shaking his head as if everything but magic spells had been used to find it.

"It's not that small Weep," began Sam. "It shouldn't take long to find it."

"I know exactly where it is." grinned Tools. There was a long pause. Sam couldn't help it, it was his natural need for information.

"So? Do we have to beg to know where it is?" he glared at Tools.

"I'll show you." Grinned Tools. "I bought the information off Barmy, he was with 'em when they hid it." There was more silence as the boys wondered what price Tools had paid but everyone forgot it as they reached the field that contained the main pond. They jumped down the low bank from the railway line and through the fence into the field but as they approached the waters edge Breen asked.

"So where is it?" Tools stopped and looked over the pond.

"This way." he said as he walked off towards the trees on the western bank below the railway embankment. In that area there was a great deal of flora to conceal a raft and so it was the best, but most obvious place to hide something so large. Sam knew Tools well enough though to know that his friend may not have a clue where the raft was and all this may be a complete ruse just for the sake of something to do. As they pushed into the bushes and shrubs by the water's edge, the going was a little difficult but there was still a well-worn path for the boys to follow. Suddenly, Tools stopped, dropped his rope and turned right as if to head towards the water's edge. The boys followed but it was becoming a little boggy under foot and when Tools swung across to the left there was shallow water under the long grass and reeds. Sam, Vern and Breen stopped and watched to see if Tools would find it and Weep had already turned back. Tools went from view into the dense undergrowth and reappeared off to the right walking towards them.

"It's been moved." frowned Tools.

"I hope you didn't pay too much for that information." smiled Sam.

"You can't trust Barmy anyway." admitted Vern. Tools simply shrugged his shoulders and waded back to the dry land, mud and water covering his jeans to the knee.

As they reached the spot where they had dropped the rope, Sam realised Weep had vanished, so he picked up the rope coil and headed off in the same direction through the trees in the hope that the raft had been hidden further around. Sam did consider that, to be fair to Tools, it was the case that when someone came to the Wolfie and found the raft, they would have their fun with it and then hide it somewhere different. It was all part of the game. Sometimes it would be set adrift so that someone would have to swim out to it and that wasn't easy in the dark waters of the Wolfie. On several occasions, the bindings had been cut and the raft broke into pieces but it was usually rebuilt soon after. Sam was just wondering once more if Tools had been truthful about his information, when Weep came hurtling through the trees.

"I found it." he yelled. "It's just at the edge of the trees, it's been covered over." Weep guided them to the spot further around and there it was, just at the water's edge and covered, if not very well, by twigs and leaves to conceal it. Weep and Breen uncovered the raft and set about checking it for sea worthiness whilst Sam, Vern and Tools found a suitable weight and tied it to the rope. They found a railway 'chair', a large lump of steel that was used to keep the rails in place on the sleepers, it looked like one that had been changed and dumped over the embankment in the smaller pond to the north. They dragged it over to the raft that was still tied up.

"What's wrong?" asked Sam.

"Whoever put it here pulled it into the bank and now it's grounded. We can't budge it." explained Breen.

"Okay, lets all give it a go." The five boys put their combined might into pushing the craft from the land, after a struggle it moved. They then realised it was sitting much deeper in the water than normal and that's why it had grounded. They tested it but it seemed fine, so they climbed aboard, one at a time, until Tools passed the rope and heaved up the weight, then he too climbed on. The raft was sitting really low and water washed over its deck but it just about floated.

"I'll walk round." said Vern. "No point in over loading it." and he disappeared into the bushes. They pushed off but it was just about now that they realised they had no means of propulsion and they had to paddle with their hands until they crossed to the shallow side of the pond where there was a gently shoaling beach. Here they tied up the craft and sat on the grassy bank. It was really hot now and Weep had removed his jeans and shirt and stood in his underpants. Sam did the same and bundled his clothes under a small bush by the waters edge. Breen was the last to add his clothes to the hide under the bush but Tools remained dressed, apart from his shoes and socks, which were wet through anyway.

"Are we gonna play pirates?" asked Weep.

"Yeah, if you want." smiled Breen.

"I want to explore the island, I don't think I've ever been on there." interrupted Sam.

"We have some adjustments to make first." demanded Tools as he fussed around the raft. This sounded boring to Weep and as was usual, he strolled off, Sam thought it sounded boring too but he passed the time skimming stones over the water. Weep walked off around the side of the shore to the eastern half of the pond where he saw someone sitting at the edge of the water. Sam saw him too and decided to join Weep who was now crouched about fifteen feet from the man, watching him intently. The man smiled slightly but looked unnerved. Sam sat too and as he did, Weep asked Sam without taking his gaze off the man.

"What's he doin'?" It was obvious the man would be able to hear them.

"He's fishin' stupid." replied Sam also watching the fisherman.

"You don't fish like that."

"Some people do." replied Sam emphatically.

"Why?" asked Weep. Sam shrugged and said.

"Dunno, I s'pose they like all the bits and bobs."

"Looks daft to me." replied Weep resting his chin on his knees. The man looked quite perturbed. Weep looked down into the water and then back up to the man.

"Do you want a fish mister?" he asked in a louder voice. The man tried his best not to answer but he couldn't stand the idea of being impolite to the two young lads.

"Yes, that's why I'm fishing lads." he smiled and shuffled slightly, his rod and line wavering with the effort.

"He's never gonna get one like that is he?" said Weep, turning briefly to Sam. Sam shrugged and replied.

"I've seen it done." The man visibly sighed and Weep stood moving a little closer to the man and then sat a few feet from him.

"What's that?" he asked pointing to the waters edge.

"It's a keep net son."

"What's it for?" he asked.

"It's what I put all the fish in that I've caught." explained the man.

"Can I look at it mister?" asked Weep with an eager face. The man sighed again and nodded saying.

"Yeah, I suppose so, just lift it out of the water but don't make a splash." Weep bent down and lifted the net and looked into it. He then gently placed it back into the water and turned and called over to Sam.

"I told you, not a sausage." The man coughed and pointed out that,

"I haven't been here long and anyway there aren't many decent size fish in here."

"There's a few trout though 'cos you can see 'em in the shallows under the trees over there." He was pointing to roughly where they had found the raft.

"Yes, well," shrugged the man. "there aren't any over this side, and they're more likely bream." he shuffled and straightened up the keep net to no particular benefit. Weep looked at his other equipment and then asked.

"What's that?"

"Look!" snapped the man but he regained his composure. "Look." he repeated. "It's a tricky business fishing, so if you wouldn't mind, I would like to concentrate on the job at hand." He flashed the lad a quick smile and continued staring across the water. Weep had one last look at the equipment, shrugged and turned on his heels and walked back to where Sam sat.

"Yeah, like you said, loads of bits and bobs." Weep said as he pointed his thumb over his shoulder back towards the man. He then lay down facing the water's edge and stuck his arm in the water. The man looked over, rolled his eyes and tutted then made some other pointless adjustment to the rod and line. Weep lay there for some time, Sam still watching the man in silence until the man became so uncomfortable he sighed again and said.

"What exactly are you two doing?" Sam looked around his immediate area and then back to the man with a look of, "Isn't it obvious?"

"I'm watching you with your bits and bobs and Weep here is tickling fish." The man was visibly grinning.

"He's tickling fish is he?" Sam just nodded. "I suppose he's tickling their toes?" Sam frowned a little, then slowly stood. He looked down at Weep and then up at the man before wiping his nose with the back of his hand and saying.

"Fish don't 'ave feet mister, you probably need to know a bit more about them a'for you try an' catch 'em." and he turned and walked away saying to Weep. "C'mon, it looks like Tools is ready." Weep was still laid down with his arm in the water and was totally motionless. The man shook his head and whispered.

"Cheeky young buggers." to himself. He put down his rod and decided to open his corned beef sandwiches and his flask and have a moment, as it was obvious he wasn't going to catch anything now, when suddenly, to his left, there was a sudden splash and commotion. He first thought the young boy had fallen in the pond but as he looked around he saw the boy was standing and holding a small but wriggling trout. The lad struggled for a while to keep hold of it but eventually the fish settled down and Weep walked towards the man. He said nothing but with one hand securely on the fish, he picked up the keep net with the other and dropped the fish inside it, he then replaced the net in the water, wiped his hands on the grass and walked off without looking back. The man sat with his mouth wide open and perfectly still until he looked down at the net to see the brown trout swimming about seemingly none the worse for wear.

"Well bugger me." he said after a few minutes.

Sam was sitting on the raft with the great lump of the railway chair between it and his backside.

"About here do you think?" asked Tools as they reached a point they all considered to be the deepest. They had paddled the raft out using flat bits of timber and a board that they had found and Breen had even sourced an old rusting shovel that worked well. Sam looked down into the inky depths and nodded. There was not much breeze on that hot day, so the raft sat almost motionless in the pool as the boys manoeuvred the lump of steel with the rope attached to the edge of the raft. As it was put on the very edge, Breen and Sam moved to the opposite side to balance the raft as Tools tied the free end of the rope to the raft main decking and Weep sat ready to heave the lump of steel over the side. Weep looked over to the shore where Vern was sitting, waiting for their return.

"Why won't Vern come on the raft?" asked Weep.

"He can't swim." answered Sam.

"He can't swim? What a girl." laughed Weep.

"Shut it Weep." spat Tools checking the final bindings on the rope. "I can't either."

"So what are you doin' on here then?" frowned Breen.

"Well I can't leave you set of idiots to do somethin' so technical now, can I?" grinned Tools, then he called out.

"Now! Weep." Weep heaved with all his might and the steel plummeted through the surface of the water with a strange sucking noise and the rope followed in a flash making the water boil as the rest of the twine shot overboard with lightning speed. Breen and Sam struggled to stay on the raft as it righted itself but just as suddenly, the raft lurched back as the rope went tight and the side of the craft was pulled into the water.

"The rope's not long enough!" called out Tools as he reached for his knife but the raft was now under water on his side and he began to panic slightly, gripping the deck with both hands.

"Tools, the knife." called Sam. Weep was still clinging to the raft and tried to take the knife from Tools but Tools was rigid. Fortunately the rope was so weak that it gave up the ghost quite quickly, the weight sank and the raft righted itself once more. As it bobbed on the water, Sam and Breen sighed heavily and they all lay on the wet deck, exhausted.

"Shit, that was scary." exclaimed Weep after some minutes.

"I told you it was deeper than that." spat Breen.

"Now we'll never know." frowned Weep as he shrugged and sat looking over the edge to where the weight had plummeted to the depths. Tools eventually recovered, sat up and said.

"Well, I think we can assume that was a failure." Sam looked over to the island, which was quite close now and he suggested they paddle over there and tie up with the remains of the rope caught on the planking.

Sam stepped onto the little island for the first time; the others joined him and searched around. There was nothing at all to be seen except a very old Moorhen nest and another long length of old rope, not much better than the remains of the one they already had, so they returned to the meagre comfort of the raft.

"Why do pirates always bury treasure?" asked Weep as he paddled with a small bit of wood.

"So that people can't find it." answered Tools, checking the quantity of rope and adding pieces making them into one long length.

"Why don't they just spend it then, not much point in 'avin' it if you don't spend it." questioned Weep.

"He's got a point." added Sam.

"They probably have so much money they bury what they can't spend." said Tools. "It's not like they can take it to the bank is it?"

"Well why don't they just put it under the mattress like my Aunty Betty?" asked Breen.

"You can't sleep on a pile of treasure." laughed Tools.

"Dragons can." frowned Weep.

"Dragons aren't real." giggled Sam not absolutely sure he believed that.

"What's dragons got to do with it?" asked Tools.

"They collect all the treasure they can find and store it in a cave and sleep on it to protect it." insisted Breen.

"Hey?" grinned Tools.

"He's right," nodded Weep. "there are loads of stories about it, like Saint George."

"That's a myth." frowned Sam. There was a long silence.

"There isn't a myth in Saint George and the Dragon." pointed out Weep with a look of disbelief.

"Not in it, it *is* a myth." pointed out Sam enjoying the use of a word that wasn't easy to place in just any sentence.

"Don't be daft they only come out at night." laughed Weep. Sam frowned then tutted.

"That's a moth you daft bat, a myth is a story that's not true." replied Sam shaking his head.

"I think it is true." put in Breen.

"Why do you think that then?" asked Tools as he jumped off the raft at the shore and threw the rope to Vern who was waiting for them.

"Well it stands to reason," said Breen as he jumped off too. "The pirates buried their treasure to stop the dragons nickin' it, that means that dragons must be real." Weep nodded but Sam wasn't convinced. Tools just laughed. He decided to change the subject.

"What shall we do with the raft?"

"We could put it back where we got it from." shrugged Breen.

"Just set it loose." suggested Weep. Sam thought for a moment and said.

"Chapper and Erky tied it to the island once and it took ages until anybody swam out to fetch it." No one seemed to be volunteering to take it out and swim back, so Tools put in a suggestion.

"What if we had a rope to pull it out there but only we, knew where the rope was?"

"How do we do that?" asked Sam unsure what he meant. Tools began to explain that if they had some way of getting the rope to the island and fixing it there, they could tow the raft out on the rope from the shore.

"No, I didn't get any of that." frowned Breen shaking his head. The others looked just as dumbfounded.

"What about an anchor?" suggested Sam.

"Good idea." agreed Tools then he added, "Problem is, someone would have to swim back from it after throwing the anchor over the side."

"I'll do it." grinned Weep.

"We need an anchor though, something really heavy." said Tools looking around.

"There's a big lump of concrete over there." pointed Vern. "I passed it when I was walking around." The boys went to have a look, it was the remains of an old railway sign or similar, a broken off metal pole with a large lump of concrete at its base.

"We'll never get that on the raft." laughed Breen.

"Course we will." said Tools. "Weep, fetch the raft around here." Weep went off and Sam went with him to help, as it was a heavy thing to pull close to the shore.

It took them a good half an hour to get the lump even close to the raft and an age more to get it up and onto the craft using bits of wood to roll it along. In the heat they were all tired but after a rest and another great effort, the great lump of concrete was on the deck, which was just under the water from the weight. The two mooring ropes had held the raft secure but now they were needed to lash the lump to stop it moving, so Sam and Weep stood in the shallows, waist deep to hold the raft secure.

"Do you know what to do?" asked Tools. It had been decided that the best swimmers would take the raft out, as Weep alone would never get the lump into the water.

"Course we do." smiled Sam. "Me, Weep and Breen paddle the raft out until it's deep enough to anchor, then we cut the bindings and roll the concrete over the side." Sam thought for a moment and then added. "Making sure the rope is fixed to the anchor."

"Yeah but remember to tighten the anchor rope once the anchor hits the bottom or it will move about." Tools was insistent, trying to explain something with his hands but Sam had the situation under control.

"What if the rope isn't long enough?" asked Breen.

"There's over fifteen feet of rope there, I told you it's only about ten feet deep." insisted Tools.

With the three boys on board, along with the concrete lump, the raft was very unhappy and the deck was well under water as they slowly paddled off into the centre of the pond. When Sam thought they were at the right place, he motioned to Weep to cut the binding whilst he secured the other end of the anchor rope to the pole in the concrete lump. Once this was done the three of them pushed and pulled the lump to the edge of the raft, the raft itself tilted and swayed and became very difficult to stay on. Without warning, the lump moved of its own accord and as it did the raft tilted more which began a cycle with only one inevitable ending.

"Jump!" shouted Sam as the raft seemed to leap into the air and Sam knew nothing, only the brief sound of a splash and cold murky water. As he looked around, he could see Weep to his right swimming for the shore and to his left, Breen grinning as he swam to Sam.

"Come on." Sam called and they swam for the bank.

"It's not pretty." frowned Tools with his arms folded. Sam, Breen and Weep were getting dressed as the others looked out to the raft. The anchor line had snagged on the decking and the craft was now half sunk with its rear end stuck inelegantly pointing to the sky, bobbing, sickly with the vast weight of the concrete lump slung unhappily beneath it. Just then, a man walked past them carrying lots of fishing equipment. He stopped when he reached the boys and looked out to where their gaze seemed to be.

"What's that?" he asked seeing what looked to be a black shape sticking out of the water with several brownish yellow circular bits protruding from it, the whole unsightly apparition bobbing slowly and drifting towards the bushes.

"Don't know." said Vern instantly, his instincts kicking in, to deny everything and anything just in case he may be in trouble.

"It's the Wolfie dragon mister." grinned Weep. The man stared for a moment and whispered.

"Well bugger me." before he continued on his way shaking his head and looking back across the water every now and then. Tools was still at the waters edge, arms folded, frowning inwardly.

"What we need is someone to go over with my knife and free the rope so the anchor can fall free." He didn't see the other boys as one of them, silently stuck two fingers up behind his back, neither did he hear them leave. Not until he turned to them with another suggestion, did he see them over on the railway line heading home.

"If only I had the quality of men." he thought to himself as he ran to catch up.

North Derbyshire has its foundations literally in coal, a vast tract of subterranean wealth that the people who hewed it from the earth called, 'Black Diamonds'. Coal was the heartbeat of the industrial revolution and anywhere that coal was found was exploited for everything the industrialists could get their hands on. Once sleepy, little picturesque villages became steam- belching factories in a not very well oiled machine, producing profits for the mighty, new offspring to carry on the toil, tragedy and grief for those who lived there and an unsightly mess for future generations. As work came, a way of life changed and new people from other areas brought differing ideas and morals to what had become a static society. Nowhere was this so true as Grassmoor. Even its name evokes thoughts of a rural idyll, Grass-moor, rolling fields and moor land covered in bleating sheep and young children with rosy cheeks flying kites and eating ripe, red apples. Not scarred landscapes with black-grey spoil tips producing clouds of toxic fumes, a pervading stench of sulphur and petroleum in an environment of cock fighting and bare-knuckle boxing matches. Grass-moor.

Sam's mother was born in Grassmoor, in the lee of the mighty colliery that dominated the landscape of the once tiny village. Sam used to visit the village once every week to see his grandparents, which he didn't mind, as they bought him his Beano and Dandy comics and often gave him a little bit of extra pocket money. Luckily, by the time Sam spent his time there, the great coke ovens that were once a famous landmark, had gone, their towers pumping endless clouds of fumes into the air, the burning torch at the top of a gantry pulsing a bright flaming light for miles around, bringing eternal daytime to the place. Grassmoor had been the village that never knew darkness for many years. With the coke ovens closed, Grassmoor could sleep in darkness again and the air was slightly easier to breath. Still it would take the closing of the mine before the women of the village would be able to hang their washing on the line to dry without it becoming grey and speckled with dirt.

Grassmoor was a village of two parts, the pit and the coke ovens had been at the lower end, where the old pit houses formed a warren of streets, spreading away from the pit yard and the ditches full of benzene, to the well supplied shops on the high street. Along that street, up the gently sloping hill, was the other part of the village, where the school and the public park stood, where, every Sunday the cricket team would glow in their 'whites' and the ladies would wear their finery and parade in the park under their best hats. The men would watch the game and then stroll off home to tend their racing pigeons. On the opposite side of the road, new council houses had been built in the prefabricated style, modern houses with space and room to grow and gardens to front and rear. An area of land had been put aside for allotment gardens which were bulging with vegetables and other food stuffs, all of it edible too since the closing of the coke ovens. The only blight being a new coke ovens plant, built a couple of miles away over the Midland Railway main line, scenting the air with sulphur once more when the wind was blowing from the north west.

Sam's grandparents had moved to a new council house, but not at the top end of the village, after leaving their old pit house they had actually moved closer to the pit because, after all, that was where the work was. True, it was a new spacious house with modern conveniences like indoor toilet and bath but it was situated right at the side of the old spoil tip. And what a spoil tip. It had once caught fire, not from someone irresponsibly setting it alight but a fire from within. Chemical reactions from the coal spoil, the petroleum spillage and other natural warming from under the surface, a fire that burned with an intensity that over-rides anything a fire tender is equipped to deal with, with a determination that the whole of the Derbyshire Fire Service fought for days to overpower. Its core was never put out, it smouldered and burned for years, even after the mine was closed, it would suddenly erupt like a south sea volcano, a vivid reminder in the dark, glowing cherry red, here and there.

Once the colliery closed, the air cleared a little, the dust settled and everyone was left to wonder how they would get work, but they need not have worried for the mine left its legacy on the people like it had done on the land. Most old miners like Sam's grandad dropped dead of a heart attack at an early age, or for some, a lingering death awaited in the form of some lung disease or other. It was to this village, with its background of toil and depravation that Sam would come every Friday and some Saturdays to see his grandparents. During the summer school holidays he would visit for slightly longer periods whilst his mother was at work.

Sam could remember when he was younger and his grandfather was still living, the old man would take him to the colliery when he went to pick up his wages. Sam remembered the smells and sounds that the great colliery made, he was always aware of its presence. It was right in front to him, only a field separating the house from the spoil tip and although the tip was covered on that side by some vegetation, it was intriguing enough for Sam to want a closer investigation. The colliery was now closed and in the year since closure, a great deal of the surface structures had been removed. Next door to his grandmothers house lived a boy just about the same age as Sam, his name was Pip and the two boys got on rather well and spent some time together. So it was, when Sam decided that a trip to the pit tip was in order, Pip was the one to accompany him. The boys knew they would have to approach the tip from the opposite side to the houses, in order that no one would see them climb the grassy slope and so, off they set into the main pit yard. There were very few buildings left, just the old pit baths and some offices with many piles of rubble here and there, it was fully closed and fenced off, but when did a fence stop small boys? They were in the grounds with no trouble and climbed a bank at the rear of the buildings. From here they began a steady climb up a rough track that seemed to lead to the top. It wasn't the highest spoil tip in Derbyshire but it had some excellent views as they climbed and soon they were looking down onto the houses. From here, the track curved to the right, away from the side of the tip and into a slight cutting that opened up into a great bowl, the sides of which were some thirty or so feet above them. The diameter of the bowl looked to be some six or seven hundred yards across and as they reached the peak of the track, they saw a sight that made them shudder. In the base of the bowl was a lake, a light-green lake and it was steaming, or at least it seemed to be steaming. As the boys walked closer to the lake, they found that any sound from outside the bowl vanished, it was sound-proofed due to the height of the walls. There was a strong smell too, like rotten eggs but thicker and more acrid, just like one of Sam's extra strength stink bombs, only much worse. Sam stopped as they reached the shore of the lake and scanned the vicinity and although they had been chatting all the way up the tip, since reaching the lake area, they hadn't uttered a sound. Pip was the first to break the silence and in a whisper.

"What is it?" Sam looked at him and then back towards the lake.

"I don't know." Probably for the first time in his life he was completely stuck for words. It was like being on another planet, quiet, strangely oppressive, smelly and slightly scary. He noticed that no birds or wildlife could be seen, no plants, not even dandelions grew anywhere in the bowl and the odd steam rose steadily off the surface of the strange liquid. The boys stood in awe for several minutes and though Sam was very unsure about this place, there was something he had to do, he just couldn't help it. He looked around for a large stone and soon found one. As he approached the liquid he stared into it for a moment. It seemed like the surface few inches were sort of a lime-green but below there was another level, a sort of brownish-cream colour, or so it seemed. He wondered if that was the bottom and it was all very flat with just a few inches of this liquid on the top.

"It's like a secret world where monsters and dinosaurs live." suggested Pip still in total amazement of the place. Sam drew back the large stone and threw it into the liquid.

"Well let's see what it is." he announced as the projectile fell into the mire. There was a splash of sorts, accompanied by a slight sucking sound but the eruption that lifted from the surface was of a dark brown colour and gave off more steam. Sam considered himself an expert at throwing large stones into water and he knew enough of the sound it made to consider that although this was not just water, if indeed any of it was water, it was certainly deep. The ripples that emanated from the splash were thick and greasy, not at all like water and as it lapped at the edge the boys took a step back. It seemed that their instincts told them that to touch this stuff may not be a great idea. As the ripples calmed, there was a noise and a few bubbles broke the surface where the stone had landed. The boys looked on but then there was silence once more. Sam considered throwing something larger but as he turned, more bubbles struck the surface, this time they were quite big and made a sort of "Blu, blu, blu blub" noise, then more bubbles and the liquid was turning reddish brown around the area as more and larger bubbles broke the surface to an even louder and deeper sound. As several incredibly sizable bubbles exploded at the surface, Sam and Pip turned and ran.

"Something is coming from out of the liquid." called out Pip but Sam didn't wait to see what it might be, he just ran as quickly as he could and he knew Pip was there as he could hear him shouting. They didn't stop until they reached the buildings at the foot of the tip and only then did they look back to see if they were being pursued.

"What was all that?" asked the panting Pip. Sam was leaning forward, his hands just above his knees, trying to get his breath back.

"I have no.... idea but I'm..... not going back." he gasped. They rested in silence keeping their gaze on the track they had just run down but as soon as they had regained their breath they ran across the pit yard and looked for the hole in the fence they had come through, only then would they feel safe. Just as they bent down towards the hole a voice spoke firmly but quietly.

"So what are you two rum buggers at then?" Sam turned to see a tall slim man carrying two small hessian sacks. Pip released the piece of fence he was bending back and it sprung back in place.

"We're not nicking owt mister." explained Pip standing up. Sam examined the man more closely, he knew this man, not personally but by type. He looked like his own grandad just before his early death. He noticed the way he was dressed, the well-presented clothes, even though they were a little shabby, they were worn with a pride. The flat cap, the spotless white shirt, the moleskin trousers, the heavy boots, the waistcoat with the watch chain across the front and the neatly cut hair and moustache. He was a miner, or at least had been before the colliery closed. Heaven knew what he was doing now, though Sam saw the two sacks, one with small bulges here and there showed it contained lumps of coal, and the other sack was more obvious, four rear feet which once belonged to two adult rabbits, could just be seen at the neck of the sack. Sam realised immediately this man was scratching a living where he could.

"'A din't say tha' were did a?" smiled the man. The two boys felt a little easier about the situation as the man continued. "Yer' shunt be in 'ere tha knows, it's dangerous f' two young scamps like yo' rum buggers."

"You're in here though." pointed out Sam with a similar smile. "Av' got special pe'mission," replied the man glancing down at the two sacks, trying briefly to hide the rabbits feet. "an tharl b't leader then will tha'?" The man looked them both over then crouched down to their height before continuing. He stared at Sam. "Any road, tek my advice, it's not t' place for young 'uns like you. Play someweer else lads." He ended with a wink, then stood and pulled back the fence so they could climb through. He followed them through and nodded to them as he said,

"Good day." and he walked off up into the village. Sam thought for a minute about the two dead rabbits in the bag, the idea that the two animals had died some horrible death bothered him, though he used to happily eat his gran's pigeon pie, knowing the pigeons came from his grandad's pigeon loft.

"Does he know about the dinosaur pool do you think?" asked Pip still watching the man walk away.

"Don't know." replied Sam as he turned and walked towards his grandmothers.

"Should we tell anybody about it?" asked Pip. Sam shook his head.

"No, we shouldn't have been up there and I don't think I want anyone to know that we have." Sam could feel all sorts of theories brewing but he said no more about it and he never went near the tip again.

Not all Sam's experiences of Grassmoor were so foreboding. At the other end of the village lived quite a few of his other relatives, his Aunt Beattie and her daughter, his cousin Emma lived in the council estate down Mill Lane, just behind the Miners Welfare and oddly, Emma, who Sam knew was his cousin, was almost his mother's age. He found this very confusing and always called her 'Aunty Emma' as he couldn't bring himself to be so disrespectful as to call her by just her first name. Adults were adults and that was it. 'Aunty' Emma's house was next door to her mother's and their side doors faced each other which made it feel, if you were visiting one, you were visiting both, even the large gardens were combined into one. Sam liked this 'family' feel, it was something quite new to him. Emma's husband Henry was a genial man who had a liking for rough cider and something unique in Sam's world, tropical fish. In the sixties, keeping tropical fish was rare, it was expensive and time consuming so this was the first time Sam had come across it, and he was fascinated. Whenever he found himself visiting, he went to see Henrys fish, with his face pressed up to the warm glass of the small tank he studied these fabulously coloured piscine life forms as if his life depended upon it. There was just one kind of fish in the tank, called 'Neon Tetras', with unfeasible colouring of metallic turquoise blue with a neon red flash down their flanks. Sam thought they had come from another planet. He had seen fish before, in the Wolfie, he had seen sticklebacks and even brown trout, and at Hardwick Hall lakes a pike had been brought out when Sam was there but nothing had prepared him for the neon tetra. Henry had convinced him they all had names and he could tell every one of them from the others. Sam didn't know if he really could or not, he just wanted to watch them. The fish were intrigued by Sam too, whenever he was there, they spent time studying him from their fish perspective, for indeed, they had never seen anything quite like Sam before either.

His Aunt Beattie's husband, Sam's uncle, was known as Chick. Sam liked his uncle Chick, for starters he had a nickname, for his real name was Joseph, and Uncle Chick had nicknames for nearly everyone else too. Even Sam's mother had a nickname when she visited Chick. He called her 'Percy' or 'Perce' for some unknown reason, so to Sam, Chick was special. The whole experience was good for Sam, from the very large, well planted garden that was excellent for play, to the fact that he received a good selection of birthday presents when that time of year eventually came around. It also gave him the 'bigger family' feel which he didn't have at home and this worked well for Sam, for when he left Grassmoor, he was his own master again.

Quite nearby was another aunt and uncle, about five hundred yards away, further down the lane. It was still part of the same estate and the houses were almost identical but there was a difference. For one thing there was another cousin called 'Wicker'. Wicker lived on a row of these houses at the end of Mill Lane, just at the point that the dead-end lane drifted off into the fields and towards the main line railway. Sam liked this part of Grassmoor, it was similar to Highfields in the respect that there was plenty to do. Sam also liked visiting Wicker because of the toys he had. Wicker had an elder sister but as she had left to marry some years previous Wicker was treated as an only child by his doting mother, that meant he had loads of great toys that Sam was always happy to help play with. One of Wicker's collections was a set of buses, loads of them, all different liveries and styles. Sam tried to push one of them around but the pile in the carpet prevented this.

"Where's the lino?" asked Sam looking around the room.

"Lino? What's tha' want lino foh?" replied Wicker looking a little puzzled. Most of the boys had a Derbyshire accent of varying degrees but when Wicker spoke it was almost like a pantomime accent, as if just sounding Derbyshire wasn't ever enough. This very much seemed a feature of Grassmoor, they had a language all of their own. Sam loved language but his sojourns into Grassmoor reminded him that English, particularly when it is let loose in the toy box of dialect, can be very difficult to understand. One particular part of the Grassmoor dialect was the use of something that could hardly be described as a word, but more of a sound, a habit not unknown in other parts of Derbyshire and Yorkshire but the theme was expanded upon to a certain degree. In Grassmoor, it seemed that every sentence began with the sound "Eeeeee." Sometimes drawn out longer than others. It could be prefixed on sentences that announced good things, as well as those not so good. Such as "Eeeeee, what a grand day it is." or "Eeeeee, is it that time already?" or "Eeeeee, what a lovely babby she is." or even "Eeeeee, our Vera's pregnant again." The only time the sound seemed effected by outside influences was when the severity of the subject required some addition to the length and depth of the sound. If Aunty Beattie wanted to mention something that was reasonably common place, she would probably announce, "Eeeeee, he come 'ome steamin' drunk ag'in last nayt." but if the subject had an edge of the unusual or was a mite 'risqué' she would say something like, "Eeeeeeeeee, Mary Wright's daughter has run off with a black man." It really depended on how the speaker saw the incident in question. The sound could even be used as a sort of exclamation, or it could be expanded by the addition of stock words such as the phrase, "Eeeeee, a' say." It took Sam quite some time in his early life to fully understand 'Grassmoorian' until eventually he could almost speak it himself. The 'Eeeeee' sound though was only ever made by adults and Sam considered that young Grassmoorians didn't have the toughened larynx needed for the constant repetition of the sound.

"We don't have lino, we've never 'ad lino."

"So where do you play with these then?" asked Sam with a slight frown, pointing to the buses. No lino indeed. What sort of a house has no linoleum flooring? It wasn't right. If progress meant getting rid of the lino then he didn't want any part of it.

"A play 'ere in 't' bedroom." replied Wicker not quite understanding Sam's question.

"Well it's rubbish, you can't play with cars an' buses and lorries on carpet, specially this sort of carpet." Sam brushed his hand along it, he considered it would be fine in a girl's room but boys needed a more level, flatter work surface.

"Well it's all we got anyroad." shrugged Wicker, standing up and moving to sit on the bed. Sam explored the room and examined anything he could find of interest, it was always fun to look what other boys had. The buses were played with along with a new James Bond car that had machine guns and a pop up screen at the rear; other choice items had their

137

turn too until 'Cobber' called around and they decided to go out and find something to do. Cobber lived a few doors away but as his mother had known Sam's mother since they were Sam's age, Sam also knew Cobber very well and the three of them got on swimmingly. Cobber had suggested going down the lane but as they walked off down the path from the house, two other boys came towards them. They greeted Cobber and Wicker as friends and asked what they were doing.

"We're going down the bridge." replied Cobber. The bridge was a sort of tunnel where the road ended and became a footpath under the main four-tracked railway. There was also a stream that ran through another tunnel close by, making it an ideal place for the boys to spend their time. "So who's this?" asked the elder of the two boys, he looked a year or so older than the others and it seemed his name was Tang. Sam was glad to see that the tradition of nicknames was still in force, even here in Grassmoor.

"This is Sam, Wicker's cousin." explained Cobber.

"Hey up." nodded the older lad. "This is Waz." he continued pointing to the other boy who was with him. Waz looked like he was about the same age as the others but he seemed a little more on the shy side, even more so than Wicker, his cousin who was well known for his shyness, particularly where adults were concerned.

"So are you coming with us or what then?" asked Cobber. Cobber was more open than most boys Sam knew, he was laid back too, not normally so decisive but the three of them knew they had to be back for six thirty, as all their parents were going out and they were going to be trusted to stay at Wicker's house on their own.

"Yeah why not?" replied Tang shrugging his shoulders as if it didn't matter one way or the other. The five of them set off down the lane, which fell away into the valley as it left the main village but they had to wait for Waz to catch up after having a pee in the hedge bottom. To the right was the bank of the hillside and to the left the hillside fell away into the valley, showing the railway line in the base about half a mile away. The road turned off to the right, parallel to the valley side and the single-track road fell more steeply as it went. The sun was fully up and the day was glorious; off to the left, in the field just below, was a large horse.

"Can you ride horses Sam?" asked Tang. Sam thought about the many times he had tried to get on horses in fields and considered this may be Tang's way of testing Sam's mettle.

"Yeah course." he lied. "We ride them all the time back 'ome."

"I bet you couldn't ride that one, it's wild as hell." pointed Tang as they walked. Sam felt slightly apprehensive as he expected Tang to dare him to ride the animal but fortunately he was saved as they heard the hoot of a diesel loco in the distance.

"C'mon, let's see wor it is." called out Wicker, as he began trotting down the hill. Sam saw all the trains he wanted at home but he saw this as an excellent way out of dealing with the horse issue and scampered after him. Near the bottom of the hill, the road turned left towards the line and the dark tunnel beneath the tracks was seen easily but Wicker and Cobber lead the way up the side, through a fence and on to the railway embankment. On the top, there was a small wall where it crossed the footpath below and the three boys took a seat. As Sam looked around, he saw Tang walking steadily down the road and Waz seemingly having another pee, it seemed they had no interest in trains. The great leviathan diesel engine rumbled past, pulling what seemed like hundreds of coal trucks.

"It's a shame all't steamers have gone." announced Wicker.

"Yeah, shame." frowned Sam.

"They just don't seem the same." added Cobber.

"So what we gonna do then?" came a voice from off the path, it was Tang, looking up towards them. The three boys looked at each other and shrugged, Wicker replied.

"Well what's tha' wanna do?" he grinned. Tang shrugged his shoulder too and looked over to Waz who was yet again, standing in the hedgerow.

"I can see why he got that name." whispered Sam to Cobber. Cobber laughed.

"Oh Waz? Yeah, he wazzes all the time, it's some sort o' disease he's got." he chuckled. Sam's grin subsided and there was alarm on his face. The word 'disease' was a word he didn't like. It showed too, as Cobber continued, after a slight pause seeing alarm in Sam's face. "Oh it ain't catchin' or anything." Sam sighed and then looked back at Waz. He was zipping his fly as he walked towards them.

"We could go to the park." suggested Waz.

"The park is miles away an' we've got to be back for half six." explained Cobber with a frown.

"Back for half six, you been naughty you bad boys?" laughed Tang.

"No," grinned Cobber. "all our parents are going out together and me and Sam have to be back to baby sit Wicker."

"Piss off." replied Wicker as he stood and walked off down to the path. Sam and Cobber followed and once on the path Sam explored the tunnel and went through it to the other side. There the path turned back into a single-track road and ran up to the other side of the valley, to a village called Wingerworth. To the right, about a mile down the track, stood what was locally called the Carbonisation Plant, or 'The Carbo' which was the newer coke oven plant. There, they took perfectly good coal, extracted all

139

the finest combustible properties from it, along with some petroleum derivatives and out the other end came 'Sunbright' smokeless fuel. That is, smokeless fuel which will not pollute the air. Sam's young head couldn't work out why anyone could consider pollution from coal when coke ovens made the air for miles around unbreathable, that probably occurred to the people of Wingerworth too but this wasn't Sam's concern, what was, was the fact that everyone was bored and there were still a few hours to find something to do.

"Let's go back through the brook tunnel." suggested Waz, weeing on a small bush.

"Naaaa," exclaimed Cobber shaking his head. "We all got wet through last time we did that."

"What's that?" Everyone looked over to Sam who was pointing down the railway line as he spoke. One by one, the other boys followed his questioning finger.

"Oh it's some kind o' tool shed that the railway men use, there's nowt in it." explained Wicker. They still had to go and check though and as Sam peered inside he saw something.

"I thought you said there was nowt in it." he grinned, holding up an old cycle wheel."

"A did an' a was reyt." replied Wicker. Indeed the wheel was well past its useful life, being connected to a bike was in its history. It was buckled, missing some spokes and there was no tyre or inner tube but Sam saw potential.

"There's a train coming." interrupted Tang. They all looked around but there seemed nowhere to go to get to safety. Sam and Wicker squeezed into the tool shed that was only about three feet square, soon to be joined by Tang who ejected Sam's wheel to make more space but Cobber and Waz had to remain outside but hidden behind the box. Sam was used to trains rumbling past at close quarters but this was an express diesel and it took him by surprise. The air seemed to be taken away as the locomotive screamed by and a shockwave of sound followed it almost unable to keep up with the great machine that had created it. The little cabin shook and at least one of the boys screamed. Its following carriages flew past and then it was gone leaving silence and an electricity in the atmosphere. A slight smell of diesel and hot oil in the air brought a sense of realism back into the world, a skylark singing in the distance put some mettle into Sam, he picked up his wheel and headed back off down the line.

"Bollocks, that were close." said Wicker. Swearing was another talent, of course not in the same league as Vern's mother but Wicker could probably get a place in the All Derbyshire Synchronized Swearing team. Sam headed back down the tunnel as Cobber caught him up.

"So what's the plan with the wheel?" he asked.

"Nothin' much, I just thought we could send it flying down the road when we get to the top of the hill." Cobber shrugged as if it was probably better than not doing it but there was a moment when he considered that Highfields must be a really boring place to live. It was just then that Waz called out, he was of course peeing into the hedge bottom.

"Look what's here." Sam probably wasn't the only one of the boys that wasn't even slightly interested in seeing warm pee but he was the only one who ignored him.

"Hey Sam," called Tang. "the rest of your bike." Sam turned to see Tang pointing close to where Waz was just zipping up; Wicker and Cobber were going to investigate. By the time Sam got there the remains of a scabby old bike had been pulled from the undergrowth. It seemed it used to be red, the paint could be seen where the rust hadn't taken over, it had a back wheel similar to the one Sam still held and the remains of a seat, albeit just a row of small springs. There were no handlebars present but every one of the boys knew they would have to try and rebuild it, for at least one last run. Sam did his best to attach the front wheel back into the twisted forks with the help of Wicker and a rusty nail. The pedals had long since gone, as had the chain, so Tang set about tying a stick through the frame to support the boy's feet. Waz gave advice between bouts of weeing in the hedge bottom.

"Does he do that all the time?" asked Sam as Waz strolled over the road one more time.

"Who, Waz?" asked Cobber. Sam nodded. "Yeah," nodded Cobber. "It's a nervous thing." he added making a circular motion with a finger at the side of his own head.

"The doc says he'll grow out of it." added Tang. "He saw his younger brother get knocked down last year, he's been the same ever since."

"Jesus." exclaimed Sam. "Poor sod, no wonder he's got problems."

"Yeah but what Tang has forgot t' tell thee is that 'is brother owny broke 'is arm an' was up an' abart next day." explained Wicker. "An' even he teks the piss out o' 'im nar." There was a brief moment of silence and then they all burst out laughing at what Wicker had said.

"Teks the piss outer 'im." laughed Cobber. "Very funny." and he barked out his particular laugh.

"What's funny?" asked Waz as he returned.

"Nuthin'" replied Tang. "Wicker just told us a joke."

"That's it then." said Sam in an effort to change the subject. "Who's going to be first then?"

"You're the guest Sam, it's your job." insisted Cobber with a broad grin. For some time it kept the boys entertained as the crazy bike with no steering and buckled wheels gave its final bow before being consigned to oblivion. They laughed and fell about finally as the front wheel totally gave up and collapsed with Wicker on it, he falling to the ground and the bike rolling into the hedge bottom. It was helped into a new grave by the boys, at the side of the road, under a large tree.

"What time is it?" asked Sam wiping tears from his eyes, his cheeks aching at the laughing they had done. Everyone seemed to be looking at everyone else with a vagueness in their faces. Here and there shrugging could be seen. "So who's got a watch?" asked Sam looking at each one in turn. Nothing. "So none of us have a watch or any other means to tell the time?" asked Sam more as a criticism than a question.

"I thought you had one." said Cobber. Sam shook his head.

"So we have to be back at half six but none of us can possibly know when half six is?" he asked in the same tone. He looked at the sky as some of the others looked at the floor.

"What about a dandelion clock?" asked Waz. Sam stared at him blankly, not knowing if the boy was being sarcastic. He looked back the sky and shielded his eyes with his hand. He then looked at the ground to where the fence cast shadows.

"What you doing?" asked Cobber with some interest.

"Trying to work out the time." replied Sam. "I don't think we're late but we better get off back."

"You're bullshitting us aren't you?" laughed Cobber.

"No, can't you do that?" Cobber shook his head.

"What time is it then?" asked Tang, sounding as if he had nearly added 'smart arse' to the question, unfamiliarity preventing him.

"I can't tell the exact time this way, it's not a bloody clock." frowned Sam.

"So ars tha' do it then?" asked Wicker. Sam felt the power of knowledge brewing up inside him. He liked that feeling and he felt the spotlight shine suddenly bright on his face, he was on stage.

"Well," he began as he pointed to the fence. "you have to know what the time is first. Let's say we knew it was half past five, what you do is look at the length of that shadow on that fence post." He looked at the others to see if they were following his logic. Sam was unsure but he continued anyway. "So, at half five we know the shadow of that post is about that long on the road, so if you have to know it's half five on another day you just see what length the shadows are and you can sort of guess the time." Sam folded his arms and then remembered something, he went into his best 'technical voice. "Course, if it's before mid summers eve, then the shadow will be getting shorter every day and if after, it will get longer." All the boys looked at Sam with blank faces.

"Sounds daft to me." admitted Tang.

142

"It seems complicated but it's not daft." insisted Sam.

"So," began Waz. "if I'm out somewhere an' I need to know the time, I just look at the shadow," He pointed casually at the line the post was drawing on the road. "an if I wanted to know it was half five I can tell it is 'cos the shadow will be that long?"

"You got it," smiled Sam. "Simple ain't it?" Waz smiled and nodded.

"Yeah I got it." beamed the lad with pride. There was a moment while he basked in his knowledge but then a frown came to his face and he asked. "But." there was a pause and then he held up a single finger. "But, it's not much use 'cos there is no way that I'm gonna come walking down here to this post just to tell the time." Sam just burst out with hysterical laughter at this but realised he was laughing alone. He stopped and looked at their questioning faces.

"He's got a point." insisted Cobber. Sam shrugged and his shoulders dropped, the spotlight dimmed and the audience left, some of them wanting their money back.

"So what time is it exactly?" asked Tang with a questioning look. "Is it half five or what?" Sam shook his head and he wanted to explain but he gave up and said lamely.

"No, it's seventeen minutes to six." he turned and began his walk up the hill. Tang and Waz were not going back, they considered going over to the park, so they parted company and Cobber and Wicker caught Sam up on the walk up the hill. Sam could hear the two boys discussing time behind him. He didn't care anymore.

"Yeah but it's a bit accurate, seventeen minutes to six." said Cobber.

"He's a clever bastard though." came Wickers reply.

"Yeah but, seventeen minutes?" Cobber was accentuating the number. "It's got to be bullshit." he concluded.

Back at Wickers house his mum had some pop ready for them and a plate of biscuits, which she took outside as they removed their grubby shoes.

"What time is it Mam?" asked Wicker. She had a quick glance at her watch and said.

"Ten to six me duck. Meks a change for you to be on time." Wicker and Cobber looked at each other and raised their eyebrows then Wicker said.

"Well we know how t' tell time from shadders." he replied with a wink to Sam. Even Sam was surprised at the accuracy of his ambivalent prediction but he wasn't going to tell them that. Cobber reassessed his opinion of what Highfields might be like.

143

By half past seven, all the parents had left and the boys were alone in Wickers house watching the television, complete with full stomachs from a hearty tea and becoming just ever so slightly bored.

"Anybody want more shitty pop?" asked Wicker. Two shaking heads were the reply. Cobber looked up as if he had just thought of some great idea.

"What about the.. you-know-what?" he asked Wicker. Wicker looked at him and then to Sam and said.

"Let's do it." Turning back to Sam he asked. "Fancy a drink Sam?" complete with a devilish grin.

"Naaa, I'm all popped up." frowned Sam thinking there was something he had missed.

"We mean a real drink." There was enough emphasis on the 'real' to allow Sam to guess what he meant.

"Beer?" he smiled.

"Better than beer." Cobber insisted. "C'mon." he laughed as he stood. They all left the room and went outside, Wicker locking the door and taking a key with him. Sam wondered where they were going but it wasn't to be far, just a few doors up the road to Cobber's house and into the main living room. It was a very similar room to Wicker's house with much the same furniture. Wicker and Sam sat and Cobber left the room saying.

"Shant be long." He wasn't, within the minute he returned and he was carrying a large bottle. He handed it to Sam and went off to get some glasses. Wicker was visibly eager to get at the contents of the brown bottle. Sam read the label. 'Barchester Cream Sherry.'

"Sherry?" he called out, the label might as well have read: 'Out of date Poison'.

"Yep." grinned Wicker. "Nowt but the finest fur us." and he took the bottle from Sam as Cobber returned with the glasses.

"Bloody 'ell, it's a grannies drink, that." frowned Sam.

"It's great man, gerrit darn yer." laughed Wicker as he lifted the glass and drank deeply. Cobber passed Sam a glass and then retired to an easy chair to drink. Sam smelled the contents of the glass and sipped a little, he had drunk the stuff before but he wasn't a fan.

"Won't your dad get on at you for drinking his sherry?" asked Sam toying with the idea of the trouble that could come your way from a few glasses of alcohol.

"Nope, doesn't know about it, this is mine and Wicker's sherry." smiled Cobber as he wolfed down the brown liquid. Sam considered that this kind of evening must happen quite a lot with these two and decided not to ask how they got hold of the stuff.

"Another?" asked Cobber holding out the bottle. Sam looked into his glass, he had barely wet his lips but he joined in and downed the lot for a refill. After two more, Sam decided he was drunk, it wasn't subtle, it was like a switch being thrown and he knew his eyes were doing their own thing, so he stopped trying to control them to see what they would do. They began to dance and there wasn't even any music playing. He stopped them and looked at the other two boys who were giggling furiously at the curtains, he didn't know why so he asked.

"What's funny?"

"Mundry." said Cobber and both he and Wicker fell about laughing at this seemingly hilarious answer.

"What? asked Sam.

"Mundry," repeated Cobber and yet again he rocked with laughter. He tried to settle himself and then tried again. "Wicker said," and then he began to giggle. "Wicker said Mundry." and once again the containment was too much and the two of them heaved with laughter. Cobber almost silently laughing and Wicker barking out a raucous spasm, with tears running down his face. It was infectious, Sam had no idea why they were laughing but joined in a marathon laughing fit until Wicker slid off the settee and took him and Cobber into a paroxysm of hysterics, Sam was slightly perturbed he would soil his underwear. Cobber, still laughing silently, tried to stand to find the sherry bottle but he had forgotten about gravity and with a dancing side step the ground gave him a cuddle. Sam fell forward laughing and he too slid onto the floor and by doing so, found the sherry bottle. He continued laughing as he peered through its brown glass but he could see very little inside it. The sherry bottle had become just bottle. Sam rolled onto his back and felt very sleepy. He had probably nodded off when he heard Cobber say.

"Christ, it's half ten." They were in a bit of a mess but Sam couldn't take anything very seriously. "They'll all be back soon." insisted Cobber rubbing his face where it hurt from laughing. There were several minutes where the three of them tried to stand and several other minutes where they tried to do it again and bouts of laughing continued until Sam suggested that standing on your head sobered you up. Eventually, three cushions were placed by the wall, deep breaths were taken, then heads on cushions, they kicked their legs into the air and tried to stand on their heads, but if being the correct way up was difficult, the reverse was almost impossible.

"So how's it work?" stuttered Cobber.

"Don't know," replied Sam, almost making it before falling over. "It's probably the," There was a pause while he tried to remember the word 'concentration' but gave in and said. "thinking about it." Wicker had been quiet for some time now and Cobber looked over to him, rocking slightly to his heartbeat.

"You all right?" he asked.

"No, a feel bloody lousy." replied Wicker.

"It's all that standin' on yer 'ed." stuttered Sam and began laughing again.

"A feel sick." continued Wicker.

"Me too." admitted Sam, the laughing now ceased. Cobber felt slightly ill too, so they cleared the place up the best they could and Wicker suggested that he and Sam should return to Wicker's house. Cobber said he would probably go to bed.

Wicker and Sam crawled back home, sometimes literally but once they were seated, they realised that they had probably overdone it.

"Good night though." smiled Wicker.

"The best." admitted Sam, with a thumbs-up sign.

When Wicker's mother returned to the house, she was surprised that it was silent. In the living room she found two young boys, one stretched out on the floor snoring like a water buffalo and the other on the settee, in free fall position with his tongue out and saliva on his cheek.

"Ohhh, look at the little lambs, sound asleep." smiled Wickers mum. His dad wasn't so charitable.

"They look like a pair of bloody wolf cubs and what's that smell." He wondered off sniffing here and there around the room.

"It seems a shame to wake them." said the mother. The father was close to his sons face as he sniffed and stood up straight.

"Your bloody angelic son is as drunk as a monkey." he spat.

15   Boredom.

As the summer holidays draw to a close, children find it more and more difficult to amuse themselves, so they seek each other's company more frequently. When they are together, they explore other areas of entertainment that normally they would not consider but boredom is a fatal disease and if not treated quickly, it soon destroys its victim. One cure, during a certain summer, was a visit to the Tip. On his journey there Sam saw Vern on his garden.

"Are you going on the Tip?" asked Sam.

"Yeah, hold on I'll tell me Mam where I'm going." called Vern. Vern was a strange lad, Sam had known him for some years and for most of them they had been best mates but sometimes Vern was hard to get on with. He hadn't got a nickname and that made him a second-class citizen on that street. They had tried nicknames but none had stuck. Because Vern was overweight, he had suffered the usual 'Porky', 'Hog' and 'Sweat'. They had all disappeared and then up came 'Dickie' as his second name was Bird but that also faded. For a time he was known as 'Pooler', which was a reference to the Football Pools company Vernons but that also went. His father was an entertainer who worked the clubs doing a Roy Orbison act but he was not over-successful, not because he was poor, in truth he was good but unfortunately Roy Orbison was still alive. It has always been the case that impression acts are best done about dead people, never the less he continued with the act, looking like Orbinson's double and even driving large, American cars. It was no surprise then, when Vern became 'Little Orb' for a while, which was reference to his father, rather than Vern's shape. Still it did not stick. The lad with no nickname came running up the garden, saying.

"It's okay, I can go." As Sam chased after Vern, he heard from Vern's house what sounded like his mother screaming,

"You get back here now you little sod!" but he could have been mistaken, it may have been "Have a nice time son."

They called for Weep but were informed by his sister that he had left earlier. They continued on towards the Tip, past the Big Tree but could find no one. They reached the railway line and noticed someone sitting by the old guard's van, it was Loz.

"What are you doing?" asked Sam.

"Sitting." was the emotionless reply.

"I can see that but why are you sitting here alone?"

"Cos I'm bored." replied Loz without raising his gaze. He poked about in the dirt a little and then looked up at the two boys and asked.

"Where are you two going anyway?"

"Just down the line to see if we can spot anyone, Weep's out here somewhere." Sam explained.

"Even if you find him there'll be nuthin' to do." Frowned Loz.

"What about going down to Peggy's?" Sam suggested.

"Rubbish, nuthin' there either." insisted Loz, kicking away some of the stones and standing up.

"Well the quarry then?" said Sam giving a half-hearted point in that general direction.

"Nahhh, I don't want to." This time it was Vern putting the spanner in the works. Sam bent down, picked up a stick and threw it into the field with little interest in where it landed, or how far it travelled.

"May as well go home then." admitted Sam in a sulky voice. Without further conversation, the three of them continued down the line around the Tip and back towards the houses. A hundred yards or so along, they saw Weep and Mumble sat on the bank throwing stones across the line aimlessly. It seemed there was great apathy around.

"That looks interesting." said Sam as they drew close to the two lads.

"Well what are you doing that's so exciting?" groaned Weep with a deep frown. Sam had to admit that he was bored too but as he turned to look over the field in an effort to spot something to do, he noticed two figures on the Tip.

"Come on," he said "let's see who that is." pointing up at the Tip. The five of them scurried up the bank to the place where the figures were but they were nowhere to be seen. They all walked down to the other end of the Tip and there they found the two people, two girls to be precise. They were; Anne who lived near Vern and Jane, who lived a little way down the road beyond the railway crossing.

"Hello." said the girls. "Where are you going?" Sam was uneasy with girls and these two, although younger, knew exactly what being a girl meant. Sam left conversation to the others.

"Exactly nil, nuthin, nowt, sod all." replied Weep in a dull voice as he sat on the ground.

"Why not come with us?" suggested Jane.

"Oh say no, please say no." Thought Sam.

"Okay, where are you going?" asked Weep standing and dusting himself down a little.

"To Fred's, Fred has made a Ouija Board and wants to try it out today." explained Jane, turning her head a little to one side as she spoke. Sam felt sick already but they all set off towards Fred's with Sam trailing a safe thirty feet behind them.

Fred was a strange person, for starters, Fred's Mother had christened Fred with a girl's name. Linda after all, is not a fitting name for a boy, it is a

148

stupid name in fact and they couldn't go around calling one of their team Linda, so Linda became Fred. Fred was plump, with freckles and had rather a gruff voice for his age and in later years began to develop breasts but passed them off, firstly as mumps and later as a rare glandular disease. When he was a little older, he lost weight and the breasts grew and looked like breasts rather than severe glandular fever, to add insult to injury, his voice had a mind of its own and instead of breaking and becoming lower, went higher, like that of a girl. So poor old Fred was cast out as a freak and had to live out the rest of his life as a rather shapely and pretty woman. But for now Fred still looked, sounded and fought like a boy and was standing on the Backs with Barmy and Biro.

"Come on you lot if you're coming, it's all set up in the shed." called Fred in a threatening manner.

"In the shed?" thought Sam. "In the shed with two girls? Oh no!"

"Will there be room for everyone?" asked Barmy doubtfully.

"I'll stay out here." offered Sam.

"An' I'm off 'ome." shrugged Loz as he walked away.

"There'll be enough room." assured Jane as she put her hand gently on Sam's shoulder. "You can squeeze in next to me." Sam dare not even look at her and wanted to join Loz in the great escape but she was insistent and once they were inside he began to shiver. Talk about nervous? Here he was, in a dark shed with two girls, all of them delving into the occult and not twenty yards away from the house was Fred's Mother, a person that thought her son was her daughter. Fred's mother was a strange person too, she was famous for her call. At only four feet three tall, it was said that her call could be heard twelve miles away and though it was probably an exaggeration, it could certainly be heard a mile away. The call that could be heard from the Tip most nights as she called Fred home, was a long drawn out "Li------nddaaaaaaaaaaa!" The last part of the word rose sharply in pitch. If she called it when the collected mass was shoehorned into the tiny shed this close, the shed would probably explode. If Sam was going to die, he hoped it was now. He heard the words,

"Is there anybody there?"

"That's not Fred's mother's voice." Thought Sam. He checked to see if his ears were bleeding and if the shed roof was still in place. There weren't and 'it' was. Someone made a sort of muffled laugh.

"Is there anybody there?" asked the voice again. It was Barmy beginning his séance, whilst everyone's, except Sam's, finger rest on the upturned glass.

"Put your finger on it or it won't work." insisted Fred. Sam didn't want a punch in the ear, so he did as he was told but before he reached the glass Jane's hand had caught his and quickly found his finger. She smiled at him strangely and slowly placed his rigid finger on the glass. Sam felt sick again. He now *wanted* Fred's Mother to lift the shed roof off.

"Is there anybody there?" asked Barmy once more. Some of the assembled were not impressed and a few whispered comments were heard but the glass began to move and slid easily to 'Yes', to no ones surprise but Sam, who was not watching it. It returned to the centre of the table with all those little fingers still attached.

"What's your name?" asked Barmy.

"Bernard Breslaw." said someone out of the corner of their mouths and the two girls giggled.

"Shut it you muffin or I'll club yer." hissed Barmy. The glass began to move again, even with the interruptions. Making the glass move to 'yes', was simple, all fingers go to the same card but when trying to do something like names, well you can imagine. Each person there thought of a name from Colin to Atilla the Hun and not spelt correctly at that, it was obvious that this eternal struggle that became a wrestling match, would go wrong. It did, the glass fell over and rolled toward Barmy.

"The spirits are angry." he said sternly. "Someone is trying to cheat." The glass was replaced and so was Sam's finger, by Jane who smiled at him again.

"Are you still there?" asked Barmy.

"Yes." Called out Vern, Barmy landed him a clip around the ear and he squealed, which made the girls giggle once more.

"That hurt." frowned Vern.

"Well stop arsing about or I'll tell what I saw you doing last Friday." insisted Barmy with a large fist to emphasize the point. In unison the whole shed said.

"Well tell us then." but Barmy began to rant a little and many threats were dished out if he didn't get quiet. The small chinks of light, that had found their way past the hastily erected curtain, were quickly hunted down and destroyed by shuffling it about and the seance continued.

"Are you still there?" asked Barmy once more. Sam thought "Yes and I wish I wasn't." but he kept still and silent. The glass moved to 'yes' once more.

"Tell us your name." Again the glass began to shake and so did the shed. The force of the fingers once more pushed over the glass and this time it rolled and fell onto the floor and smashed. An eerie voice called out.

"Ahhh the pain." The shed shook violently and the girls screamed, Weep ran kicking open the door and everyone ran outside, either screaming or shouting, no one giving quarter as they all tried to exit the small doorway at the same time. Loz stood outside laughing hysterically. He had obviously returned and was clearly the source of the eerie voice and the shed vibrations. After everyone had hurled abuse at Loz, the party broke up, Sam and Vern strolled up the Backs towards the Tip Gate and watched Barmy and Loz cross the road then walk off into the Garages. Fred walked up and said,

"That's messed that up." Sam and Vern nodded in agreement, Sam happy to be out of the fatal situation.

"Let's go to my house." suggested Vern, Sam agreed and off they went. Fred went back to the shed to clear up.

Vern's house could sometimes be a hell-hole but Vern had an attic room up a ladder and in the room was a new drum kit, which Sam found a magnetism towards. As they entered Vern's house his mother cuffed him.

"You get that bloody room tidied you idle bleeder and don't bloody well bugger off when I bloody well tell you bloody well not to, you bloody little chuffer." It was clear to Sam that Vern's mother was not a social sciences teacher, though he was not going to tell her so. Once in his room, Vern offered to let Sam play his drum kit but before he had struck three beats, a voice came screaming up the stairs and up the ladder, still having enough momentum to move dust when it entered the room.

"Stop that bloody row and get that bloody room cleaned you bloody swine." it said.

"It's not me, it's Sam." called back Vern in terror.

"Well bloody well tell the little sod to bloody well stop it or he'll get a bloody clip 'round the bloody ear."

"Thanks." said Sam to Vern, as he dismounted the kit making sure he made no sound. "I'm going home." he added.

They went downstairs, to find that Vern's Dad had come home, which began a stinging argument between his parents, it always did. Vern's Dad broke off the argument to speak to Sam, this seemed rather unreal to Sam, as if there were two people inside Vern's Dad, but then again, Vern's Dad was very complicated.

"Hello Sam, you off?" he asked. Sam stuttered and spluttered trying to answer, it was hardly surprising, as Sam wasn't sure who the man in front of him really was. Well he certainly looked like Mr. Orbison, which was where the confusion started but then again, Sam knew his stage name was Bob Denver, Sam's parents had taken him to see him play his guitar and sing a mix of country and western, with a dash of pop. He was actually quite good. But then again, Sam also knew that Vern's name was Bird so his dad had to be called Bob Bird.

"Er, yes Mr. Orbi.... er Mr. Denv..... er... Mr. Bird." Whoever he was, his focus was recalled back to the argument with his dear lady wife and Sam was about to head for the door. As they walked through the hall to the front door, the telephone rang. Sam stepped clear of it, they were instruments of the devil and in Vern's house it was bound to mean trouble.

Roy Orbison, Bob Denver or Bob Bird answered it in the guise of all three, still wearing the sunglasses with the unfeasible black lenses.

"Hello. .... Yes, ... No I haven't .... Oh no... really......" Sam thought this sounded serious and made his way to the door. "When did this happen............. oh right, do they know how? ... yes ...yes thanks." Roy placed the hand set back in its position on the evil machine. He looked pale and glanced around to the boys as Sam was opening the door. "That's sad, Brian Jones of the Rolling Stones is dead." he said and left the room.

As Sam walked up the street, he thought to himself.

"Fancy that, Vern's Dad knowing Brian Jones. I wonder if my dad knows John Lennon or even Boris Karlof? I bet Weep's dad knows somebody like Errol Flynn."

As Sam reached home, he went to brood on the garden but soon after, Chapper came walking down his garden path next door.

"What's up with you?" he asked Sam.

"Oh nothin' I was just wonderin' if my dad knows anyone famous. Does your dad?"

"Not unless someone famous goes in the local pub or the betting shop, why?"

"Well Vern's dad used to go to school with Brian Jones."

"Brian Jones is from down south and he's rich and famous." insisted Chapper.

"Well Vern's dad has got a big American car." Chapper raised his eyebrows and continued into his house, not sure how that particular counter-argument worked. Sam hung around outside, considering what knowing someone famous must be like. He didn't have long to wait, as Sam's dad returned home from work and Sam being Sam had some questions for him.

"Do you know John Lennon or Boris Karloff?"

"Who?" asked his father.

"You know who Boris Karloff is Dad, an' John Lennon is in the Beatles." insisted Sam with a frown.

"Why?" asked his dad as he pulled his shoes off.

"Oh I just wondered." replied Sam.

"I don't know those two but I used to give singing lessons to Frank Sinatra." he admitted, as he rubbed his feet.

"Don't be daft." laughed Sam "He's American."

"How do you know?" asked his dad. This caught Sam off guard, he hadn't expected such a line of reply, he was stating what he considered was obvious, thinking it was a good argument.

"Well, he speaks American, I've heard him on the radio." said Sam with some insistence.

"I gave him American lessons too."

"Wow!" said Sam as he walked off outside to play with this new knowledge. "My dad made Frank Sinatra rich and famous." "Hang on!" thought Sam. "Rich and famous? My dad would have been rich too." Thinking that his parents had been telling him lies all these years, Sam went back inside to ask more questions but before he could go further than raising his finger slightly skyward, his dad raised his arms and said,

"I spent it before I met your mother."

Once, long, long ago, children were left to their own devices and consequently, they found their own entertainment and pastimes. In one particular part of Derbyshire, these pastimes included building 'trolleys' or carts or playing games like 'Lerky', 'Bicycle Tiggy', 'Rallyco', Kick-Can, Bounty Hunter or Dare. All these had a strict set of rules decided upon prior to commencement but all these games were relatively passive and usually caused no problems to others, particularly adults. Unfortunately some adults do not like to see children enjoying themselves, mostly the elderly but some younger adults could be totally offensive to childhood, probably because they had completely lost their own and somehow blamed the children for it. Of course, these adults had to be put in their place, this the children did with a certain regularity. Some of these 'revenge' games were a little more adventurous, usually played later in the year, when the nights were darker but if the parental gauntlet was run and the children decided to stay out later than normal, much fun could be had during the summer holidays too. Shed Hopping, Bucket Banging and Knock and Run were just a few of these revenge games, all of which developed into 'Chicken' or Dare but sometimes things did not go too well.

"Let's play Hedge Hopping." suggested Sam for this was his favourite game. The idea was to begin at the top opening just above Sam's house and work their way down the hill using front gardens only, the pavement being used for those who did not measure up, or for a quick escape when 'found out'. This they agreed but had to wait a while for at least a modicum of darkness to fall. When it did, Sam, Weep, Breen, Tools, Vern and Norman entered the first garden at the very top opening and slowly made their way over hedges and fences, struggling over awkward walls and thicker garden borders. There was only one very difficult part, a tall chain link fence and apart from having no hiding places nearby to prevent detection from house owners and passers-by, the game was relatively easy for them all. A more difficult game was 'Shed Hopping' but when it was suggested by Weep, Norman remembered that he had to be '*in*' early and Tools developed a bad ankle.

Mumble appeared just then and joined in but Tools stayed on the Backs and 'Kept Keg', which was their way of saying keeping a lookout. Again, beginning at the top opening, they began their high level journey to the bottom opening, a distance of about 500 yards. High level, because this time they had to make their way down the back gardens without touching the ground. It was difficult and no one had ever done it all the way without getting down and walking to the next roof. The first problem was at Sam's house, for here, the continuation of the terraced coal houses was broken for a garage but with a lusty leap from a high wall all were across and scuttling over the garage and over to the next coal houses.

After a few more obstacles, there was a long, flat concrete roof, stretching thirty yards, then came a large gap where a gate had to be crossed 'tight rope' style and Sam was the first across followed by Weep and Mumble. Vern began the wobbly route but fell off half way, half whispering an oath as he hit the ground. Breen was next, slow but successful as the others waited on the other side. They then continued across another flat roof after dropping down onto a wall and a climb back up onto a garage, they reached the point where no one had ever passed. Two of them made an effort to cross the large gap by balancing on two large posts, but this would have been difficult in the daylight, never mind at night. They had to climb back up onto the roof in failure. Mumble thought he saw a way across from the lower wall but the gap was deceiving in the dark and he joined Vern on the Backs talking to himself about the attempt and getting a reply.

"Well I messed that up! *Well I messed that up*! You did. *You did*." he spoke and whispered. Sam knew there was no way across, he had tried on many occasions and he thought it a shame, as there were some great obstacles further on. They couldn't just climb down and forget that not one of them had made it, oh no. Sam had written the British Association of Shed Hoppers Rules and they stated that: 'If an obstacle could not be conquered without touching the ground, then progress further was not possible until at least one of the team has crossed successfully'. They wouldn't be able to look other Shed Hoppers in the face if they broke the Cardinal rule of Shed Hopping. The problem was, that 'The Human Fly, better known as Weep just could not accept that there wasn't a way across.

"What about going down the wall along the garden border?" he whispered.

"Naahh, tried it." answered Sam in a similar whisper. "I tried it ages ago, there ain't anythin' to climb onto except a little rabbit hutch and that's too far from the coal house roof." Weep still wouldn't have it and he sprung onto the wall that ran down the garden and climbed into a small tree. Sam watched through the gloom and considered that he wouldn't have been able to climb the small tree like Weep could but he also remembered there was only one place to go from the tree anyway. He panicked, very quietly but it was still panic. He motioned to Breen and hissed. "He's in the tree." Sam couldn't see Breen's features in the gloom but he knew he had seen what Sam was referring to, as he moved quickly onto the wall.

The attempt began well enough and it was a new route no one had tried but it soon became obvious that there was a good reason for this. From the tree, Weep saw that he could jump across to a shed and from there onto a garage at the other side of it. Weep readied himself for the effort and counted to three, then jumped; he landed hard on the small shed with some noise but was off at once to make the leap to the garage. Sam and Breen were close on his heels and saw this and tried to call out.

"Weep there's no......" it was too late, Weep was mid leap. ".... roof!" continued Sam. Weep disappeared through the black space that was supposed to be a garage roof but was really .... a black space. There was a deafening clatter, so Breen and Sam decided to jump down off the roof to see if Weep would appear from his mishap but lights were beginning to come on in downstairs rooms of the nearest houses. Just as the boys were about to make a quick exit a garage door was flung open and Weep issued from it, fleeing from the area followed by the others, they stopped for rest at the Post Office on the south side of the street.

When they had recovered, they congratulated Weep for trying and helped him clean the blood from his jeans where some offensive object or other had tried to break his fall. There was a smile on his face from the attempt and the adoration in finding the inspiration to explore other routes. Maybe it would be that the daring-do and the tenacity of Weep would make him into a famous explorer in his adult life, or then again maybe not, he would possibly find that life, like shed roofs sometimes decides to play a joke and refuse to offer any kind of support. For now though, he was pleased with his night's work but adventure was still the order of the day and so began a game of Knock and Run. Vern was to go first. The house that was chosen for him was up a short flight of steps. Carefully, Vern climbed the steps and approached the door. There was a large iron knocker, which Vern slowly raised and then brought down, with two quick raps, after which he fled towards the steps. Unfortunately, he missed the second step and flew over the rest; it was looking like gravity was high that night, as now two of them had fallen to earth. For Vern, the rest of the evening was then spent with torn jeans and cut knees but that was standard for Vern. It was Sam's turn next. The house chosen for Sam was large, with a long front garden and a sturdy but low front gate. Casually, Sam opened the gate and made his way to the front door. Again there was a knocker, Sam struck the door three times and fled but he had forgotten a golden rule of Knock and Run, which was to 'sprag' all gates open to prevent them springing shut. The top of the gate struck Sam in the base of the stomach and flung him clean over it. Winded, Sam struggled away, cursing under his breath. Yes, that damn high gravity was giving them some trouble, which was odd, for as Sam always maintained, 'If you didn't know about science then it probably didn't know about you.'

The next in line was Weep. Weep was always adventurous, even after the problems of earlier, so he was given a difficult house. The house, or bungalow as it should be described, sat besides the railway, which meant there was little cover for a clean escape. This mattered not to Weep, for he simply marched up to the door, turned and waved proudly to the others who were hiding behind a distant hedge and pressed the doorbell. It was unfortunate for Weep that at that very moment the owner of the bungalow was about to exit his home, it was also unfortunate that because of his bravado, Weep was unprepared for this to happen. It was also unfortunate that the man was off out to buy himself a sense of humour, for he clearly didn't have one, but Weep wasn't to know. The door swung quickly open before Weep had time to rest his finger from the button.

"Yeah, what do you want?" asked the man, before Weep knew what had hit him.

"Er .... nuthin'" spluttered Weep realising that this wasn't an adequate answer, seeing as he still had his finger on the button, the bell ringing in the distance. The man brusquely knocked his hand away. "I.. er... I mean .... we're doin' a survey, yes a survey at school." Weep beamed at the success of using his initiative.

"Oh yeah, a survey on what?" asked the man. Weep looked around for ideas.

"Er ...... er doorbells, people's doorbells." Weep smiled again. "I saw this one and thought, Ah they will know all about doorbells." he rang it once more but seeing the glare from the man he stuck his hands in his pockets.

"Well?" asked the man.

"Pardon?" said Weep.

"Aren't you supposed to ask questions in a survey?" enquired the man, as he crossed his arms and leaned on the door frame looking unconvinced.

"Er, yes that's right." stuttered Weep, pulling his hands back from his pockets and slapping them like a demented German Beer Festival reveller. He was thinking that he was missing a clipboard or something. "Questions, yes, er .... Do you like doorbells?" The man glared at him. "Er ... Has your doorbell ever fallen off the door frame?" Weep could see the man becoming agitated. "Err... If someone pressed your doorbell for no reason whatsoever, ... would you be annoyed?" This question caused Weep a pain around the ear probably due to being struck there by the man.

"Bugger off you little sod and don't let me catch you here again." he shouted. It was obvious to the others that they would have to extract revenge on this person and the house was christened 'Mad Man Bungalow.' Weep, who had been given his nickname Weeperina by his brother because he was always crying and weeping, returned to the bunch, rubbing his ear but instead of crying he was smiling. It seemed he was outgrowing his nickname, as examination under a street light showed the ear to be quite red.

Soon after this incident, Mid-Summers Eve was upon them. Now this particular evening was as wild as Halloween to the boys, so much so, that some of them had saved fireworks from the previous bonfire night, especially for the revelry. The problem was, that darkness comes late on that day in the year, very late and they would all have to run the gauntlet of parental attack when they got home. But then again, they did most nights in the summer. So, as the late darkness fell on the Summer Solstice, the boys gathered around the street light opposite the Post Office. Barmy, Weep and Vern were already there when Sam and Mumble arrived. There was no sign of Breen or Tools but a well-built lad called Loz, arrived shortly after Sam. First on their list of retributional attacks, was a man who lived near Sam, he had given them verbal abuse when they were carol singing the Christmas previous. Armed with a gallon of diesel, stolen from a Land Rover, they headed off to the man's back garden.

"God, it's not very dark is it?" said Loz, looking at the sky. Sam was surprised about the light too but he told himself that it always seems lighter outside than in.

"Screw your eyes up an' it will seem darker." smiled Sam, as he walked past him. Loz squinted and then realised what he was doing.

"That's not the sodding point is it?" hissed Loz, as Sam and Weep strode onto the lawn. "They will see us." added Loz. It was no use, Sam and Weep quietly and carefully poured the diesel oil onto the perfect lawn spelling out some rude words and it was obvious they had not been seen.

"Naahh, they can't see a thing. It's called night light." said Sam, unsure what the saying was exactly but he had heard something similar from his uncle. "My uncle was in the army and he told me about it." Sam and Weep dismissed the issue and took a quick look back at the lawn with a grin. The boys knew well that for a couple of days after, nothing would be evident but after a week or so, the grass dies and turns brown, revealing a simple message of greeting.

The next on their list was to be 'Clarky', old man Clark was hated by all the children on the street and by most adults too, so he was a usual target. The boys placed several fireworks, called 'Mini Rockets', on the roof of his coal bunker at the far end of his garden, which had a corrugated asbestos roof sloping upwards, towards the house. This made a perfect multi-lane launch pad with easy access from the Backs. They knew that these cheap rockets didn't store well and very few would work but if just one flew, it would be absolute bliss. The operation was carried out with the fine-tuning no army in the world can ever seem to achieve. Weep and Mumble carefully Sellotaped a heavy button on a string to the kitchen window of the house, another fine but long length of cotton was tied to the button and lead all the way down the garden to the rocket launch pad. While they did this, Sam and Loz laid out the rockets in the gullies on the corrugated bunker roof, making sure all were in perfect aim. Vern was busy making sure that the gate was tied securely shut, to prevent anyone following them after making their escape. Barmy held the box of matches. When all were clear of the garden, Weep began to pull gently on the cotton, just enough to make a light tapping noise on the window. Sam, Barmy and Vern stood with a match in each hand ready to light the rockets, it was tricky, the timing was so critical for it to work. The curtains slid back and the face from within peered out, straining to see.

"Night light, see, I told you." whispered Sam nodding towards the window in the gloom. As the curtains slid back, Weep gave another tug to be sure and the fireworks were lit. The door opened immediately and it looked as if the lighting of the rockets was a little early, so Weep pulled again on the thread but it broke and he was heard to hiss a curse. Clarky stepped outside for a better look, just as a barrage of rockets screamed down the garden and collided into his house about halfway up the wall, only to be sent off in some random direction. It was a pyrotechnic nightmare and a wonder the old man did not pass away but it seemed he was made of sterner stuff. The boys were a hundred yards away by the time the last rocket had burned its last.

Not all the boys victims were so deserving of their punishment, one such victim was singled out for committing the heinous crime of 'having a blue front door'. The real reason was in fact, the cast iron drainpipe close by, which was a great temptation to the boys. Two of them, namely Mumble and Loz, pushed newspapers, which had been brought for another lark entirely, up the spout of the cast iron drainpipe. Then they set light to the paper that was just sticking out of the pipe and stood some way off. As the fire in the pipe got hold and began to burn well, air was pulled through by the combustion, which caused a roar so loud that it could be heard in the victim's house. Out popped two middle age people, to see what the commotion was all about. At first, they could not pinpoint the great roar but the sparks and the flames that were shooting out of the top of the house convinced them that their drainpipe was somehow on fire. All the old moss and rubbish in the pipe was now ablaze and the blue paint was beginning to peel off to reveal a glowing, red patch near the bottom. One of the victims ran inside to phone for the fire brigade but the fire went out as quickly as it had begun, leaving a drainpipe that needed a coat of paint but nothing more. It was just down to the victims to wonder and examine the rest of their house for spontaneous combustion. It would make an interesting story at their next dinner party, that was for sure.

"and the heat from the sun created a pocket of warm air that set light to the inside of our drainpipe ... honest, as god is my witness ..... honestly, it really happened, didn't it Margaret?"

One target the boys chose, was better deserving. This man had thrown Weep's and Mumble's bikes in a ditch, for leaning them against his garage. He had to be taught a lesson. Sam and Vern found his dustbin and quietly carried it to his back door, whilst Loz looked for something to stand it on. He found an old bucket, which he placed upturned in front of the back door. The dustbin, one of the old style bins before the days that dustbins became outwardly mobile and grew wheels, was balanced on top of the upturned bucket. A rope was then tied to the bin handle and then fastened to the door handle. Barmy wrote out a note, which he posted through the front door letterbox and then knocked, before making his escape. The man in the house walked to the front door, opened it and looked outside, he saw no one, but there was a note on the floor.

"Who was it dear?" asked his wife.

"I don't know, they just left this note saying don't open the back door." Thirty seconds later, the man was gently trying to open his back door but he felt resistance, so he gave it a sharp tug. Some people take offence at having their dustbin and its contents strewn across their kitchen floor. He was no exception.

The last stunt of the evening was reserved for the most awful of revenge attacks. It was something they had done before and they enjoyed it so much each time they performed it, the lark became their 'piste de la resistance' - reserved for the worst criminals. The person to receive this 'special' treatment, this time, was a more recent enemy, Mad Man Bungalow. Weep and Mumble were sent off, with a 'borrowed' spade, to find a cowpat or some fresh dog excrement, whilst the others watched the house and planned the attack. It was all-important that this type of revenge game was easy to view, it made the rigorous planning worth it and so, the remaining boys looked for the best places to view from. After all, what's the point in organising some highly important sporting event, only to omit to get some tickets for yourself? Several places were found and as Weep and Mumble arrived back, they realised they were in luck, for the boys had found plenty of 'ammunition', and it was soft and very ripe. This 'Sludge' was placed into several sheets of newspaper and then, using more sheets, was wrapped into a rough parcel. This parcel was taken carefully to the bungalow by Barmy and Loz, both being very careful as they didn't want the man to appear again. Sam considered how they would explain it if they did and grinned.

"Your late night shit delivery sir." He said to himself. As he looked up, the two lads were quietly placing the parcel on the doorstep and as they bent down over it, Sam made himself comfortable but ready to run at a moments notice. Barmy had the honour of lighting the parcel with a match and as soon as it was well alight, Loz knocked at the door and rang the bell. They too then ran to find a safe hiding place. The man arrived at his door to find a small bonfire.

"Bleedin' vandals." he cursed as he stamped out the fire.

The boys returned home content with a feeling of a job well done. Sam considered other people's revenge as a career but decided he wouldn't like the 'night shift' regularly.

Sam sat alone on the far side of the Tip and looked out over the many fields bulging with ripe barley swaying slightly to the rhythm of a gentle breeze and he wondered why there were winters. He considered that life would be much better without them. The winter made it difficult and uncomfortable to go out every day and made the only option to stay indoors, stuck in your room, trying to find something to do. If it were always summer, he would be able to play forever. Summers had everything, warmth, fruit, long days, school holidays, yes there was nothing good about the winter. Except Sam's birthday, that was in October, so it was a great time for getting some gifts, even if they weren't quite as good as the ones at Christmas. Ahh, Christmas! Sam shuffled a little as he heard a Robin singing in the distance. Its warm, bouncing song very much a sound of summer but when that little bird with a big heart, changed the song just very slightly, that same song became a lament of summers past, like a violin played in a minor key. Then, that same song became the most beautiful sound in the winter months, that premier songster with the rustic chest - so much a part of Christmas cards, snow and Yuletide. Sam shuffled again and made himself comfortable, so he could lay back and dream. One of the fluffy, white clouds looked like Santa carrying his sack of presents. Sam loved Christmas. Yes, certainly winter had its place in Sam's heart too, for whoever heard of Christmas in the summer? It just wouldn't be the same. He closed his eyes and thought of the previous Christmas.

Sam opened his young eyes and stared into his bedroom. It was light, it was Christmas morning.
IT WAS CHRISTMAS!!!
Slowly, he turned his head to look out of the window to where the lee of the corner of the house turned at right angles, there he could see the guttering. In the night, high above the earth, water vapour had swirled and twisted, moving through eddies of warm and cold air until it had condensed into droplets of water and formed clouds. The droplets crashed into each other until they grew too heavy for the cloud to hold them and they fell to earth. As they fell, cold air froze them and more cold air currents frosted their edges until they became crystals before hitting the cold earth .... It had snowed!
Sam rushed over to the window to look outside. It wasn't deep but it was pure, honest to goodness snow and it had arrived on Christmas morning. Still in his pyjamas, Sam crossed the landing and descended the stairs. It was one day in the year he would rise early without any prompting.

The English dictionary says of prompting: *"Suggest, help out."* When concerned with Sam it meant; *"forcefully eject, drag out with one leg, purge with copious amounts of cold water."* Sam made a mockery of the dictionary. His parents were never in possession of great wealth, in fact, poor is what they were but Sam's Christmas was always strewn with presents. He knew in his heart they had scrimped and scraped all year for him, for as you might guess, Sam found out early that there was no Father Christmas. But then again, few children sit up all Christmas Eve with the previous year's broken toys ready to give Santa a ticking off for shoddy workmanship and sub standard materials. If Santa had existed, after meeting Sam, he would have retired, hiding himself away, a disciple to the philosophy of existentialism.

Wrapped presents were the first problem to Sam, for he wanted to open the best ones last. He studied the generous pile by the fireside. Firstly, he identified the ones he had already found some weeks previous, supposedly 'hidden' from his sight, these were first to be opened, his acting skills were second to none, his surprise was totally plausible, his joy absolute. Not bad going for a toy he had played with three weeks ago, when his parents were out. Then, he opened the ones that seemed the poorest, usually the smallest ones. An early one was the selection box, that way he would have breakfast of chocolate whilst opening his presents.

Sam's father had beaten him up, well I don't mean that he had kicked the living daylights out of him, it was just that he was up earlier than Sam, he always was. Sam wondered if he actually went to bed, he was in the kitchen, drinking one of his 164 cups of tea he had every morning. He was about to boil the kettle for number 96, when he heard Sam in the living room.

"You're up then?" he asked.

"No." replied Sam.

"Want a cup of tea?"

"Is it?" replied Sam. His father knew it would be at least an hour before anyone could, 'get in touch' with him. If you wanted an answer on Christmas morning, you would require the help of a very competent medium.

Surrounded by a wall of presents and discarded wrapping paper, Sam finally reached the last present. Once opened, it, like all the other items, was allotted its time for his attention, which took most of the day. Later, there was the ritual of Christmas dinner but Sam shrugged that off as an interruption to his chocolate feast, there were also those terrible moments when his parents wanted the 'family' to do something together, that always ended up as a failure but all in all Christmas day was always a success.

Boxing Day was very different, where Sam lived, it was considered illegal to 'stay in' on Boxing Day, thus, most of the boys went outside quite early.

163

Sam was a little late, for he had to digest his mother's instructions, giving him various ultimatums on his day's activity, this ritual out of the way, Sam was set free to find adventure. The problem was, unless you hadn't received a bicycle for Christmas you would be riding it, Sam hadn't so he wasn't. Most others had and were. The place was deserted. He stood on the Tip and looked out into the valley beyond. He hadn't noticed before but the place was quite beautiful. The shallow covering of snow cleansed and purified the land and in contrast with a rather grey sky, it looked inviting, not cold. His kingdom. He made a snowball and threw it into his kingdom but it barely managed to leave the Tip, landing in a small drift twenty yards below him. It was a large kingdom too. To the east, lay the quarry, in the south, he could see the tree tops that pointed out of the wood. To the west, lay the open valley spreading out to the park in the next village below. On the field at the base of the Tip, several rooks were picking a meagre living from the dusting of snow, out towards the railway banking, several other crows circled, barking out their guttural call, over to the right, he could just make out three rabbits looking for something to eat. He held the moment close, this was his land and he was the King.

"This will be here forever." he thought. How wrong he was, for in just a few years, the landscape would change drastically. For now though, he drank it in, remembering where all the other known places lay, Peggy's Brook, the Leaning Tree swing, Top Tree den, the Island ... hang on a minute, there was smoke rising from the Island. Who dare set camp in his kingdom without permission of the King? As Sam descended the Tip towards the smoke, a hare ran out from a large bush, Sam clapped his hands, it made the hare run faster, a much better spectacle, as the large hare bound athletically across the ground. He loved hares and he loved to see them at full tilt 'gliding' across the landscape, their legs a blur as they pumped away at high speed. Continuing, he crossed the immense field, walking in the direction of the Island. It wasn't really an island, it was about to become one though, it was an oxbow in the stream, a piece of land almost totally surrounded by water and hidden by small trees. This made it an excellent hiding place for small boys and he could hear voices as he moved closer but couldn't really see anyone as the stream was in a tiny valley below the level of the surrounding fields. He advanced, keeping as low as possible. He peered over the edge of the bank, down onto the island, to see Weep and two other boys from the next village, North Wingfield. They were school friends of Weep. Weep and one of the other boys were armed with pellet rifles and they sat around a small fire. Sam stood then called out, putting his hands up in a surrendering motion.

"Hey up." said Weep

"What you doin'?" asked Sam as he walked down to the Island.

"Nuthin' much." replied Weep. Sam sat on a large stone and warmed himself on the meagre fire and soon the other boys were on their way home.

"Not very sociable." insisted Sam.

"Nah, they're boring too." explained Weep. "They came up and wanted to go out over the fields but we 'aven't done anythin'"

"Christmas pressie was it?" asked Sam nodding to the gun.

"Yeah, it's pretty good." Weep handed the rifle to Sam, who looked it over as if he knew everything about it, which he didn't. He sighted the thing at the tree and looked at the trigger but the offer of having a shot didn't come.

"Nice." said Sam handing it back.

"Yeah, it's great, it fires darts as well." insisted Weep. Sam had a gun, it was a 2.2 but it didn't fire darts, being an, 'under-lever-loader'. He looked back over at Weep's new item, complete with telescopic sights and rubber shoulder pad. Sam's version didn't even have a fore sight, he maintained that if you needed a sight, you didn't make the grade. To a certain extent, this was true, for Sam could quite accurately shoot other people's guns but only Sam could knock a beans tin off a post at thirty paces with his 'under-leaver-loader'. It had once had a sight but it was obvious at some time, part of the barrel had been sawn off. Sam considered the weapon had been used on a 'bank job' but dismissed it, as he toyed with a newspaper headline:

"Vicious crooks hold up Yorkshire Bank with sawn off 2.2 pellet rifle."

The two boys talked for a while about the attributes of breach loading against the under lever system.

"Mine's a sawn off under-lever-loader of course." Said Sam, in a way that suggested he was sick of being asked about it.

"Can't load 'em very quick can ya'?" shrugged Weep.

"Yeah, quicker if you ask me." frowned Sam.

"No you can't, y' 'ave to pull the lever down to pump a shot of air then close it, then turn the lever to open the breach, load it, then turn it back before you aim." Weep continued before Sam could interrupt. "With mine, you just break it," Weep went through the motions to show how quick it was. "shove the pellet in, close and fire." The pellet zinged off into the trees as soon as the sight was up to his eye.

"I have a ..." there was a pause as Sam tried to think of word he had learned recently but 'technique' seemed lost to him now. "a thingy where I do it in one movement." Sam motioned some odd looking movement with his arms that was more reminiscent of peeling potatoes than loading a gun.

"Still slower though, an' another thing," continued Weep pointing a finger. "You can't put darts in 'em." Sam had no really good answer to that, it was well known that the turning chamber on that type of gun wouldn't take a dart. Sam laughed out loud.

"Why the hell would you want to fire darts?" Before Weep could tell him why, he killed that part of the argument with. "Anyway, you can if you trim off the flights."

"They're heavier too." added Weep. Sam was fed up with this. He went into one of his non-logic explanations.

"They are heavier for a reason, they have more power and have a bigger kick and the weight keeps them accurate an' not only that, they are made so that if you run out of ammo, you can use it as a weapon for hand combat, that's why they're heavy." Sam, nor Weep saw a situation where you would have to use hand to hand combat on a beans or treacle tin but the point stuck. "If you used that thing," he was now standing and pointing at Weep's gun with disdain. "in close quarter fighting, the damn thing would fall apart," Weep knew once Sam was in this mood he would never get a point forward until Sam had completed his 'piece'. "an' another thing," concluded Sam. "you can't buy a sawn off breach loader, they just don't make 'em anymore." Sam sat down again and warmed his hands on the pitiful remains of the fire. It was quiet until Weep looked down at his new gun and said;

"Well, I like these better." Sam shrugged his shoulders and stood again, they decided to leave and cease the subject of pellet guns. They urinated on the fire to extinguish it, then, Weep joined Sam at the top of the bank, hugging the weapon like a new-born baby.

The two boys tried to find adventure that day but there was none to be found. Adventure was rationed, or in recession and they departed their world and headed for the world of adults, that blurred world of double standards and erratic behaviour. Back to the world where logic means making statements such as: "Don't do that. Sit still and go and tidy your room up young man!" or "You can't go to that party, you're still a child so stop crying and act your age!" or, "Stop crying or I'll tan our arse!" As Sam entered the house where he lived, he was confronted with such incomprehensible theories.

"You're back early, what you done?" insisted Sam's mother.

"Nothing, I've been with Weep."

"Oh and up to no good, that's for sure."

"No, we sat by a f ..." Sam considered having to explain that sitting near a fire didn't mean it was a forest fire and he also decided that the subject of guns should be on a need-to-know basis. "... field near Peggy's, talking." he replied quickly.

166

"Well if you're staying here for the rest of the day, you are coming with us." insisted the oracle of logic.

"Where to?" asked Sam.

"Never you mind my lad, just get up them stairs and get washed and changed."

As Sam trudged up stairs he considered the options. It was obviously a secret where they were going, but how could he dress if he didn't know the occasion? For instance apparel for sledging and snowballing was very different to that for visiting Aunty Mary. He doubted they would be snowballing, but you can't wear your rugby kit to Aunty Mary's or your flowery shirt. Nor would Aunty Mary approve of his new swimming trunks. Come to think of it, Aunty Mary was cropping up a great deal. "Looks like being my trousers and new jumper." he said to himself.

About a week later, New Year's Eve rose its dubious head. Sam was unsure about this particular day of the year. Each one was different but drew to the same inevitable conclusion. He assumed that, for New Years Eve to be a success, you had to mix the following together:

"Take one paranoid, two bores, one rather large fat man, two half-wits and the spontaneous crier, seven drunks, five terminal gossips and one inadequate, soak them in alcohol, stuff the fat man with all the food that took ages to prepare and mix the gossips with the bores. To the paranoid, add one bottle of sherry and a jar of glazed cherries and stir in a story about divorce. Finally, make the inadequate think he is in charge and top the whole thing off with a tight 'git', who brings nothing but drinks everything, then leaves early."

Getting drunk was another mystery to Sam. "Why do they do it?" To Sam's mind they spent an hour sober, two hours drunk, ten minutes showing some part of their anatomy, thirty minutes talking rubbish, one hour hardly talking at all, two hours gospel singing down the toilet, three hours in bed having nightmares and the whole of the following day feeling as if they were thrown out of a speeding airplane, then run over by the London to Glasgow express - late again, only to be 'rogered' by a sex crazed elephant.

"To be truthful," thought Sam "out of all that, the only time they seem to be actually enjoying themselves, is about fifteen minutes of the two hours drunk". He considered it was like having a new pair of your favourite shoes and then having our best friend put them on and kick you to death with them. Sam had been 'under the influence' just once, he had felt so ill afterwards he decided he would never attempt it again.

This particular New Years Eve, they were at Sam's mother's, friends house. It was usual for Sam's dad to fall asleep and his mother to cry but this year, they left early and walked the mile back home. On the way, they met two drunks carrying a bottle each and in their spare arm ... each other.

"Appy you near!" said the first drunk.

"Naffy boo ear!" said the other, just before they both fell down.
Sam looked behind as he walked, to see the first man trying to pick the other up, saying

"C'mon you ... you ... ijut. Drunk agen, s'good job I stayed sober init?" and then he fell onto the second drunk.

"Have you ever been *that* drunk dad?" asked Sam.

"Yes once." answered his father. "Just once, I shit myself." Then he added. "In a taxi."

"Yes, I was so embarrassed." added Sam's mother. Sam considered years past, when he once filled his own trousers for very different reasons, but the thought of that made him shudder.

"I'm never going to drink ... EVER!" he said, intentionally omitting the word 'again'.

"Yes and pigs might fly!" added his mother as if his life was pre-planned.

"And young boys grow up to shit themselves." grinned his father.
Sam picked up a handful of snow, fashioned it into a snowball and threw it, generally aimed at the 'spirit of 'Christmas.

When Sam was younger, he had jostled with everyone else in the queue for the swimming baths. In those days, his elder cousin Chapper, took Sam every Saturday morning to the tatty swimming baths at Clay Cross. When the door to the baths finally opened, the children barged past old man Scothern, into the corrugated steel roof shack that housed the small pool. The boy's changing rooms were on the side of the pool to the left, the girl's to the right. It was a child's world, no adults were ever seen here. Sam, just like all the others, was in the pool thirty seconds after entering the building but as of yet, he could not swim. This was terrible, for all the other boys headed straight for the 'deep end', six feet deep, to lark about and dive off the boards. Sam realised that he had to learn to swim, he exited the pool, walked down the side and jumped in at the deep end. It wasn't the most elegant stroke you would ever see, but by God, he reached the other side! From then on, he never looked back, three weeks later, he could swim as well as the others. This was Sam's way, if there is something there that you want, you go and get it, even if it's surrounded by hungry wolves. A story to illustrate this happened just before a certain summer, in the depths of winter to be truly accurate.

Whilst some of the older boys were sledging down the side of the Tip, Sam sat watching, wishing he had a sledge. One of the older boys, Wilbur had a sledge that wasn't doing too well, so, after another poor effort, he brought it back up the Tip and left it lying there, completely unloved. Sam thought he should have a look at it - cast his professional eye over the vehicle. First he examined the runners, they were rusty, no wonder it wouldn't go. He began to rub down the runners with ice to get them a little shiny. Sam tried it with Wilbur looking on. It wasn't brilliant but it was definitely better.

"If it was mine I would look after it better." he thought. As Wilbur watched two sledges racing down the Tip, Sam decided to walk home.

"My God, look at that!" said Sam to himself. "I forgot to let go of that piece of rope, the one that's attached to Wilbur's sledge!" Wilbur had noticed the sledge disappear behind Sam. Sam had noticed Wilbur watching him all the way down the Tip path. If Wilbur had shouted, Sam would have run off and left the sledge but he didn't, he just watched Sam walk away with it.

"Where did you get that from?" asked Sam's dad.

"Err .. off the Tip." he answered.

"What just sat there?" asked his father.

"Yeah, just sat there and there was no one there."

"You know I don't believe you."

"Well that's up to you." admitted Sam. "but it's true, how else would I get a sledge, it's not the sort of thing you can walk away with in your pocket." His father looked at him with one eye half shut.

"Well answer me this then lad. Why would someone leave a perfectly good sledge on the Tip?"

"They must have forgotten it." smiled Sam.

"Then you ought to return it, just in case they go back for it."

"Oh no they won't ... it's been there some time." he insisted.

"Well I think you should put an advert in one of the shops. In fact, tomorrow get it done, put an advert in one of the shops." The next day, Sam armed with his advert. "Found - Sledge." sporting the wrong address. He walked two and a half miles into the next village and asked a shop keeper to display the advert for him in the window.

Sam never took chances when it came to the redistribution of wealth, he was a genius with money. Once, he delved into his moneybox to find thirteen and sixpence and thought how much nicer it would look, if it was a whole pound. He went to his mother and asked if he could have his two shillings pocket money. He then 'borrowed' one and six from his mother's 'sixpence jar' then went outside to his father, to ask for his two shillings pocket money. His father gave him the money, even though it was a little early in the week.

"Why the long face?" asked his father.

"Well." said Sam "I thought I might have had one pound this week."

"How much are you short?" asked his father.

"Well, I've got nineteen shillings." explained Sam.

"Here you are then." said his father, swapping the change for a pound note. Sam took the pound note to his mother and explained that he had borrowed one and six from her sixpence jar and could she change his pound note so he could pay her back.

"It's alright, forget it," she said, not wanting to split his pound. "but stay out of my jar in future!" So it was with Sam, thirteen and six to twenty shillings in fifteen minutes. He had lots of scams like this. Another was to steal bottles of pop from the back of the local shop, drink the pop and return the bottles for the deposit. If there was too much pop to drink, he would sell it to the other children, even charging them for the deposit on the bottles. There was also the time Mr. Johnson had just picked up his strawberries, two bags full and put them on the wall whilst he drank his cup of tea. When his back was turned, the strawberries went hurtling down the Backs in the hands of three boys, Sam saw the incident and shouted.

"I'll get 'em Mr.. Johnson!"

"Don't bother Sam, there's three of them!"

170

"It's all right, I'll get 'em!" he called, as he pursued the thieves. Sam knew exactly where the boys would go and as he entered the old garage where they hid, he said.

"You'd better run lads, he's getting the cops on yer!"

"He don't know us." said Loz.

"He does, all of you." insisted Sam.

"Come on Loz." interrupted another boy Sam didn't know. "My dad will kill me if we have the cops round."

"Look ..." said Sam "If I take the strawberries back, you could keep some of them, 'cos he won't know exactly how many there were will he?" Loz looked a little doubtfully at Sam.

"What, so you can eat all the fruit and tell them it was us?" frowned Loz.

"Never, I would never do that. Cross my heart and hope to die if I lie." Sam made the time honoured gestures. "In fact, I could tell them that you helped me get them from the other boys." Sam winked. Loz thought for a moment, then took a handful of the fruit.

"Yeah, all right." agreed Loz, as he left with his mouth full of strawberries. The other boys followed. Sam ate some of the strawberries as he made his way back to Mr. Johnson's house.

"Here you are, I caught 'em and they ran off but I think they had eaten some." he smiled.

"Did you see who they were?" asked the man.

"No, I don't think they were from around here." replied Sam shaking his head. Mr. Johnson thanked him and gave him a bag of the returned fruit. It didn't work in his favour however, for Sam's mother did not believe this doubtful story and clipped his ear for scrumping.

This was a world of irony though and Sam was well equipped for it, it wasn't so much that Sam told lots of lies, just that the truth was like a piece of new plasticine, ready to be moulded and shaped to fit the current situation. Sam was so good at 'reshaping' reality, that it became a profession for a while. His friends at school would find themselves in sticky situations, if they had not done their homework and had no good reason why, Sam would sell them an excuse or two. He also had a friend who would do other people's 'lines' for money, together they were an invaluable emergency package. Sam was sometimes asked for excuses nearer home too.

Vern awoke one morning to find his dad's garage window broken, how it had happened, no one knew but for sure, it had nothing to do with him playing football in there. Certainly not, as his father had expressly forbidden it. Nevertheless, Vern would get the blame. He called on Sam to help, Sam thought for a moment and then asked.

"Are you sure you broke it?"

"I must have done, the ball must have caught it. The first I knew was when I trod on some broken glass." Vern looked troubled and for good reason too, his parents were very strict with him and punishment was swift.

"Okay." nodded Sam with a contemplative look on his face and he showed Vern some of his wares.

"A thief broke in."

"No." said Vern "There's nothing in there to pinch and anyway, the door is never locked."

"A loud clap of thunder." offered Sam.

"No, come on." insisted Vern, "on a blazing hot July morning?"

"Particularly hot weather for this time of year?" said Sam quickly.

"Would that break glass?" asked Vern.

"It could melt it." hinted Sam.   The boys shook their heads, looking at the broken pieces of glass.

"A low flying aircraft." advised Sam.

"So low, it flew through the garage window?" frowned Vern.

"No, the noise, the loud noise." insisted Sam.

"How come it only broke one pane?" added Vern.

"Poor workmanship." added Sam. They were getting nowhere.

"How about ... a stone flew up from a car?" said Sam.

"Oh yeah .. and it shot up and over the house, rolled down the garden path, ricocheted off the coal house, flew over the rose bush between the trees and still had the speed to break the window?"

"A freak shot!" insisted Sam. They could both smell failure.

"Come on Sam, this is serious!" pleaded Vern.

"Okay but it will cost you."

"Anything!" answered Vern.   After Vern had given Sam three shillings, a copy of the Batman v Penguin DC comic and a small glider airplane, Sam began in earnest to devise an excuse. After Vern turned down typhoon, earthquake, gas explosion, anarchist and gangland revenge attack, Sam came up with one of his 'knock-on' type excuses. Firstly, they had to pick up all the broken glass from outside and place it inside the garage, break the clothes prop in half, open the upstairs window of the house, tip over the plant holders and place the garden rake near to the garage. The boys then waited for Vern's father to arrive. When he pulled up in the big black American car, that incidentally, would not fit into the garage, Vern was ready.

"Hello dad."   Vern's dad removed his black sunglasses, to see who had spoken.

"Oh hello lad." he frowned as he saw Vern.

"What a day, we nearly had a big problem this morning." insisted Vern as they walked down the path with Sam following.

"Oh aye, what's that then?" asked Vern's dad, replacing his sunglasses.

"The baby fell out of the upstairs window!" Vern looked over to Sam, who was smiling and winked conspiratorially.

"What?" cried his father, removing the glasses once more.

"It's alright, I caught him." added Vern

"Good lad!" smiled his father.

"Yeah, but I had to run to catch him and then I over balanced and tripped over the plant holders but I managed to put the baby down before I careered into the clothes prop and trod on the rake which flew up and hit the garage, breaking the window." He said in one breath and waited for a sore head.

"Don't worry about that." smiled his dad. "I broke that this morning, you must have just finished it off." Vern sighed and turned around to claim his goods back from Sam, but Sam had vanished! The strange thing was, that the baby did fall out of the window a few weeks later and with no one to catch him, luckily he escaped without so much as a cut or a bruise.

Sam wondered if saying something had happened, could make it come true. After six months of saying he had a new bike, he gave up on this theory. He also gave up on the theory that sense could be achieved from adults. They had a strange language in this part of Derbyshire, which made little or no sense to young boys. Sam's grandma would call anything that looked odd, 'A Buff Orpington'. He later found out that a Buff Orpington was a kind of hen. No paradox there! His mother would call any girl or woman she disliked. 'Sally bloody turn up.' When Sam received a slap around his head, it was called ' a flea in your ear' though it felt like a rhinoceros in your ear! Half-way was known as 'nowt nor summat' and somewhere long forgotten became, 'Timbucktoo'. Gran had a language all of her own and unknown to Sam, she also had a fondness of nicknames. A few years previous, there was one old woman who lived on the same street as Sam's gran, who, ……. Well, let us say, she had an unfortunate countenance. Of course it wasn't her fault but Sam's gran privately called her by the name of "Annie Shovelface". Sam had heard the name in quiet conversation and indeed had seen the woman in person from a distance, carrying her meagre shopping bag on the way back from the local shop. Sam hadn't really seen her at very close quarters, until one particular day, their paths crossed. Sam was quite taken aback, as she did have a rather wrinkled and weather-beaten face and probably looked much older than her years but Sam was convinced she must have been at least 180 years old, if she was a day. It was a very unlovely face indeed. Sam must have stared for a little too long, as the old woman looked down directly at him and smiled, though the smiling face looked to Sam as if a large crater had opened in a ploughed field.

"Hey up me duck, thar' must be Phoebie's grandson then?" She said placing her shopping bag on the floor. Sam looked back towards his gran's house and tried to recall his gran's name.

"Yes." he nodded to the woman remembering that was in deed her name.

"By gum, thas' growin' up quick lad, it's owny five minutes since tha' were int' pram." she warbled. Sam blushed slightly, he was never comfortable with this kind of conversation. "Thar's gunna' be a handsome chap when tha' grows up." she continued.

"I don't know about that." laughed Sam, even more embarrassed.

"Oh well, a' better get back and put me copper on. Send me regards to thee gran will tha'?" and she picked up her shopping to continue on her way. Sam watched her move off.

"Bye then m' duck." she concluded.

"Bye Mrs. Shovelface." Said Sam. After all, he couldn't have said anything else. He thought it was her name, how was he supposed to know? If there were any repercussions from the conversation, Sam never knew of it.

There was a great deal to suffer as a young boy, that much was obvious but Sam coped and did his best under adverse conditions. Sam only came off second best when the opponent was much like Sam. One such person, as it happened, was an adult. He was a friend of Sam's father, Vince was his name, known as Vin to his friends. He was a lorry driver, during the six weeks summer holidays, he would occasionally take Sam to work with him and Sam loved it, for the greater part. Vin had a Singer Gazelle with 'overdrive', in its day it was a fast car. Vin was a short, stocky man who wore spectacles with lenses so thick, it looked like he had two pint glasses strapped to the front of his head. He drove like Jim Clarke the racing driver, flat out everywhere. Sam liked the speed but couldn't understand why an adult should like it, as he always thought that adults wanted to be sensible all the time.

"Doesn't it worry you driving fast?" asked Sam.

"Not really, I can't see!" he replied. Sam gripped his seat as Vin eased the overdrive in. He drove the lorry the same way. Once, near Leeds, Vin swerved and called out.

"God I nearly hit that dog!"

"That was a horse!" answered Sam. It was all an adventure, "And anyway," thought Sam, "he's only having me on."

Sam changed his train of thought when, whilst parked at Stoney Middleton quarry, Sam waited for Vin to come back from the weighbridge. As Vin returned, he climbed into the wrong lorry and drove off. Sam spent the day with another driver and in the evening, returning home, Vin admitted he had taken the wrong truck.

"I thought you had nodded off." he said smiling. Sam shook his head and smiled too.

The summer wears on and children in Sam's village never looked forward to the end of the holidays. The nearer it came, the harder it was to accept that their life would be changing back to that time of year when other people control and influence their lives. Sam dreaded the return to school, to him it was too much to bear. Not just because of school but because he knew the days would be getting shorter and that meant dark nights and less to do. The only solace that Sam could take from it, was that his birthday came later in the year, oh and Halloween, oh and Bonfire Night, oh and Christmas. Well, maybe the back end of the year wasn't so bad. There was the thought of Bonfire toffee and parkin, Christmas cake and chocolate, yes the dark nights were okay. If Sam was totally honest, Bonfire Night was about as important as anything can be to himself and his friends. It was only marginally less important than Christmas and the preparations began in late summer, which spread the festival out somewhat, with all the collecting of combustible materials and hiding away anything that may come in, ready for the big day. In the last weeks of the summer holidays and for weeks afterwards, every boy in the village would start thinking about bonfire night and the old rituals would begin; looking for good hiding places, saving money for fireworks and planning the whole event.
As Sam sat in the September sun, he considered this and began his personal plans for the great day, he took it very seriously and he thought back to the previous year's bonfire celebration, it had been a real gem.

The previous year, Sam as always, had put aside a few of the precious fireworks that he had bought with spare bits of pocket money, for a ritual called 'Hell Night', known to others as Halloween. Halloween wasn't seen as a separate event in Sam's world, it was a taster, a precursor of his favourite night of the year. The word Halloween was of course taken from the Greek and roughly translated to: "Lighting bangers where they may scare the hell out of everyone." It sounds malicious but after all, in those days, fireworks weren't dangerous, well if they were, the boys hadn't noticed. If an adult told you "Don't put fireworks in your pocket!" this translated to "I dare you to put fireworks in your pocket." It was true, they knew of no one who had been hurt by fireworks, well not much anyway. Bonfires, on the other hand, were tricky. The problem being, that in the village, the separate groups of boys all had their own bonfires, sacred, traditional sites for each gang. There could be anything up to twenty fires within half a mile radius and the fuel for each one had to be collected, hidden and more to the point, guarded. As Bonfire Night approached, wood became very scarce and nothing was sacred, there was not a stick of wood to be found anywhere. Fences went, clothes props, ladders, trellises and even coal-house doors went into these wood piles. Car tyres and linoleum were favourite items too. Eventually, the only way to build a bigger pyre than you already had was to steal it from other bonfires, that's why they had to be guarded. Nearer the day, the wood was brought out of hiding and stacked in the traditional way, by methods handed down through generations. The well-stacked bonfire was an art form. There were 'dens' too. Nearly every fire was hollow, so that a small room could be made for the owners to stand guard. If you built your bonfire too early, there was the chance that someone would steal your wood or even burn it prematurely. For all these reasons, to take on the job of organising your own fire was a weighty responsibility but nevertheless, Sam decided that particular year, that he would not attend the 'bottom opening' bonfire but he would build his own, in the tradition of his elder cousins, Chapper and Spider. They had always had a bonfire behind their house in the field but since the brothers had grown up, their local bonfire had disappeared. Sam wanted to bring it back. He did. A massive pile of wood had been collected and hidden a little way off, behind a large garage. The trouble was, that Loz, the 'bottom opening bonfire president' had found it and unbeknown to Sam, had taken most of it for their fire. In turn, Biro who was building a bonfire across the road, had pinched some of the wood from Loz's pile for his own. Sam saw some of *his* wood on Biro's pile and waited for it to be built, with nothing but revenge in mind. Four days previous to Bonfire Night, Biro and his friends began to erect their bonfire but that night, late that night, Sam and Vern visited the site armed with two milk bottles full of paraffin and a box of matches. Once a small fire was started, the two boys ran off to watch the resulting conflagration from a distance.

"It will go like Hell soon, there's some plastic on top!" grinned Sam.

"Yeah, that'll teach 'em to pinch our wood" replied Vern. The flames took hold of the brushwood and began to roar up the side of the pile and suddenly the darkness was giving way to a bright orange glow. Sam craned forward, he thought he could hear something.

"Can fires sing?" he asked.

"I dunno" replied Vern, not sure what Sam meant.

"Well" pointed out Sam. "I reckon that fire's singing." Vern listened.

"I dunno about singing, it's more like a moaning to me." he said, his face back lit by the now constant glow. There were certainly some noises coming from the bonfire as the flames leapt higher. The noise changed from short "Eya eya's" to a long drawn out "Wwwwwhoooooa!"

177

From the depths of the fire came a horrific phoenix, belching smoke, like the four o'clock milk train and wailing like a banshee.

"Bloody 'ell." sang out Vern. "It's a soddin' fire spirit." Sam wasn't sure what it was but it was horrific enough to cause his legs to start running without him actually giving them permission. The boys had reached the Tip Gate before an even faster object overtook them across the field, a little to the left and Sam, glancing over, suddenly realised what they had awoken was not a sleeping fire demon but a sleeping Biro, presumably on guard inside the bonfire.

Fortunately, Biro survived the fire but the bonfire was history, just a smouldering grey stain in the field. With his bonfire ruined, his pride scorched and his best pullover in tatters, Biro gave up with bonfires. Sam didn't, he offered the rest of his stash to the Shand brothers and threw in with them.

Ben and Breen were great organisers and their bonfire already had drawings and plans, even a programme for the evening. The bonfire gang warfare that engulfed this little Derbyshire village subsided, whilst the last pieces of combustible materials were sought and brought for the spectacle that was to become the Shand's Bonfire. Lines and score marks crisscrossed the local landscape, making furrows from hiding place to bonfire, as items were dragged onto their sites, some by trusty trolley, some on push bikes. Some even went to the trouble of covering their tracks so that the hiding place would not be discovered. Collections of fireworks were examined one more time, to see if they were complete and Sam's meagre selection had been pawed so many times, that the writing on the labels were wearing away. His Silver Shower was becoming a 'Sile Sher' and the Volcano was reduced to 'Vo'.

This was a time when anyone could buy fireworks, they were displayed on the same shelf as Fry's Cream or cakes and pastries. Hygiene was something they only had in America. Due to the inevitable 'leakage' of the fireworks, the flavour of Bonfire Night could literally become just that, for a cream donut could become a 'sulphur and potash nut', a vanilla slice may become a '3-2-1 zero slice'.

Fireworks were also experimented upon, so called 'Duds' from Halloween, would be stripped down and rebuilt and hybrids were made by adding sugar or iron filings. Sam's favourite, was taking the drive section out of a rocket, dropping it into the bottom of an empty banger case or a home made card tube, adding iron filings and copper sulphate then calling it a Roman Candle. The only difference being, that *his* 'Roman Candle' was nothing like the standard Roman Candle and when lit, it tried to bury itself into the ground, whilst giving off blue flame and white sparks, then exploded into a million pieces. Some commercial fireworks were a little tricky too. There were "Jumping Jacks", Firecrackers or whatever you

178

wish to call them. Drop two or three of these in a crowd and you could really have some fun.

There was also a family of commercial, 'flying' fireworks that actually left the ground, with names like, "Aeroplane" or "Helicopter". When ignited on the ground, they spun around at great speed until they quickly became airborne at approximately head height. A spinning, burning, screaming projectile, flying around in random fashion, all at the height of the average human head. Brilliant fun though and if the "Aeroplane" did not get you then how about the "Hovercraft?" This was very similar to the Aeroplane but flew only at groin height. Nice. If you really timed it well, you could set off "Jumping Jacks" to make everyone leap into the air to be hit in the throat by an "Aeroplane" then as you fell to earth you would be mutilated in the testicles area by a "Hovercraft!" What harmless fun fireworks could be and Sam loved every second of it. Nothing was malicious though, it's just that safety wasn't an issue then. The only fireworks warning Sam ever saw was on a firework as big as a dustbin that could only be described as a warhead, which said on the side "Do not hold". How they expect you to get it from the shop without holding it well.....

There was also a smallish orange coloured firework called "Golden Rain", strange name admittedly but written on the side was the legend "Do no swallow".

Sparklers on the other hand were for girls and grannies. Men and boys had a firework called "Olympic Torch", a firework *designed* to be held. It was a Roman Candle with a handle. If dangerous fireworks could not be bought, they had to be made. One trick was to unwind the coils of a Catherine Wheel; this made a great 'quick fuse'. This fuse was attached to a bank of three large bangers, which were then taped to a large rocket. The rocket was ingnited, it went up and it burned, automatically igniting the fuse. The rocket eventually reached its zenith and exploded, the bangers were blown from the rocket, now also lit from the fuse and gravity being what it is, the whole shooting match fell to earth. More often than not, the bangers exploded several feet from the ground in a random area. Great fun! Other pranks were to find an empty treacle tin, part-fill it with the 'soft section' of a cowpat, then a lighted banger was pushed into its contents and the lid replaced. A treacle tin is a harmless thing, even left standing close to a group of people, it's the dull 'Pock' that it makes as it explodes and the flying cow excrement that makes them annoying.

Another 'lark', was to find a piece of old copper or steel pipe, about half an inch in diameter. One end was squashed and bent over to seal it, then a rough handle was fitted, a banger was then placed down the open end, lit and then the contraption was tilted back so that the banger slid into the pipe. Banger goes off, hey presto you have a projectile firing weapon, loosely described as a 'banger gun'. Injuries were few. More likely to be burned by a hot baked potato or chestnuts from the fire. Sam had certainly heard of accidents, that was true, but he had never witness any. That wasn't for them, no, they knew what they were doing. Well, sort of.

The Shand's bonfire was to be built in the field behind their house and it was planned that the audience was to stand behind a small fence at the edge of the field, a sensible, safe distance from these 'dangerous' fireworks.
With all the plans made, the boys set about building the bonfire. Here was to be a bone of contention.

"We have built our bonfires like this for years!" insisted Ben.

"*That*, doesn't surprise me, but it's wrong." insisted Sam. "Yes, there should be three central poles but there should be other smaller ones to pack out the base"

"Rubbish!" cried out Ben "Boxes and tea chests around the base for heat"

"Yeah" added Breen "then, push paper and lino between them."

"You've never seen a bonfire then." laughed Sam. "No wonder it burns away quickly"

"It doesn't." replied Ben.

"That's not what I heard, gone by half seven last year." smirked Sam.

"Who said that?" demanded Ben. "It's a lie, we were out here well after nine."

"I bet you were cold with no fire left then." grinned Sam.

"That's bullshit." demanded Ben as he approached closer to Sam. Ben was only about a year older than Sam but when you are young, a year can make a huge difference in size and Sam considered he would have to relent and find a scapegoat.

"I'm just repeating what Vern told me." he shrugged. Luckily Vern was gong to the bottom opening bonfire so wasn't able to argue the point. It seemed to do the trick but the conversation went on like this for some time on and off, whenever the two schools of thought collided. Eventually though, the bonfire did take shape, in a mixture of both styles as it happened but tradition was an important part of who you were and your bonfire said more about you than any fashion statement. It was to have two Guys, this was a tempestuous matter for debate too. Sam was in the school of thought which said that the Guy had to be historically accurate, where as, the Shand's didn't care, as long as there was a Guy.

"It's not a Guy Fawke's hat anyway." Breen had pointed out. "It's an old cowboy hat." That didn't matter to Sam, the fact that it wore a hat was very important and anyway, it was better than the bare head that the painted football of the other guy had. So both Guy Fawkes were to perish by flame, the historical one and the contemporary one. Brothers in adversity, to the end.

On the big day, every boy made his way home from school as quickly as possible and changed into old clothes, not bothering with tea and straight off to meet friends in the fading light of the early winter evening. Everyone knew his job but only 'Bonfire Experts' were allowed to put finishing touches to the pile, this was left to Ben, though Sam considered himself no less an expert.

The twin Guy Fawkes brothers were placed on the very top and then they waited for the adults to arrive with food and fireworks. So much food, everyone brought goodies that the boys tucked into straight away.

"I told you to have some tea my lad." Said Sam's mum as she opened a biscuit tin full of parkin.

"I wouldn't be able to eat so much cake then would I?" grinned Sam as he reached into the tin. This was the only time Sam's mum would let him get away with not eating tea. She shook her head as he walked off scoffing the sticky cake.

When everyone had arrived, Ben's dad lit the base of the boy's pride and joy. Sam's dad had noticed something and asked the obvious question.

"Why has it got two Guys? There should only be one surely?"

"Who says?" asked Sam finishing the cake.

"There's no wonder you are hopeless at history, there was one Guy." insisted his father.

"Well, one is Guy Fawkes." explained Sam. "The other is Terry Fawkes."

"Who?" asked Sam's father.

"Terry, Guy's dad." smiled Sam as his father noticed the Guy was named after him.

"Is this a pocket money joke?" asked his father.

"No." replied Sam with a cheeky grin and Sam's dad left it at that, he thought it best.

It was traditional to let off a rocket as soon as the fire was lit, to announce to the world, or more locally to other bonfire parties, here lies a bonfire and it's lit, ... probably. It certainly seemed odd to the boys that though there were all types of excellent, combustible materials in a vast pile, that first tiny glimmer at the base of the tower took ages to expand into a roaring inferno. Ben and Breen's dad was well prepared though and paraffin was liberally thrown over the brush and timbers of the fire and physics did the rest. Very soon, one side of the pile was ablaze and the flames licked around the short legs of the Fawkes twins and the boys cheered as the fire shot skyward.

Sam climbed back over the fence to where the adults were and more importantly, the food. There were all manner of food items strewn across the tables where hurricane lamps provided meagre light until the bonfire cast its orange shawl over them all. Sam saw all kinds of goodies arranged there that people had provided, including his mother's parkin, with its squidgey, soft top. There were home made toffee apples brought by Ben and Breen's aunty, many types of bonfire toffee, each one with its own recipe and a broad spectrum of tastes, boiled sausages and onions freshly cooked by Breen's mum, Mrs. Webb's savoury bonfire crackers which were herb and cheese biscuits, bonfire loaf provided by Wilbur's mum, which was like malt loaf but soaked in some strange alcohol that no one could ever work out what it was, there was a punch to drink that even the boys were allowed a little of and home made mead, provided from the honey of Breen's father's bees. There were also potatoes, onions and chestnuts to go in the fire as soon as anyone could get close and marshmallows to toast as the fire died down later.

Sam picked up a toffee apple and looked around the gathering. There were quite a few people attending and the atmosphere was very friendly, as people drifted from one conversation to another, someone laughing here and there. To Sam's right, his father and Ben and Breen's dad were talking together and laughing occasionally about some humorous story that one had told the other, sipping on the punch or mead as they did. To his left, where most of the adults gathered around the tables bathed in the light from the fire, his mum was dishing out sausages to someone Sam didn't know, whilst someone else picked up some of Mrs. Shand's extra hard bonfire toffee. There was lots of noise as the fire cracked and roared and people talked and laughed. Sam felt warm, not just from the fire, there was something inside, something he couldn't quite explain. Maybe he was just so happy, either way, as he stood there surrounded by the party atmosphere on bonfire night, he knew he would never forget that evening. And he never did, it was special and the best bonfire night he would ever experience. Something pulled him from his thoughts as he whipped around to hear the last syllables of.

"We better let some fireworks off then." It was Ben and Breen's dad with a tin in his hand. The boys knew it didn't contain 'Butterscotch' for sure, it actually held some of the fireworks. As the first fireworks were let off, the boys indulged in the ritual of breathing in the acrid smoke, like demented drug addicts. After all, it had been a year since they had last smelled that pungent aroma that only comes from fireworks. Well actually, it had only been a few days ago but they couldn't really admit to their revels on 'Hell Night', the night adults called Halloween. Sam and the other boys got as close to the fireworks as they could and soon the 'sparklers' came out. Sparklers were always in abundance, so it was inevitable that the boys would have to invent a game to go with them. It was called 'Lantern'. It involved taking one sparkler each, lighting it then using it to light the way up the field in the thick darkness, trying to remember where all the cow pats were. The one to place his still crackling sparkler the farthest away was the winner but he then had the longest trip back to the bonfire, in the dark with just the mildest glow from the raging fire. Needless to say, a few of them had the slight smell of cow dung about them later in the night.

Eventually, the bonfire was fully underway, to the extent that the larger beams were ablaze and the fire became more predictable, this was when the potatoes and onions were placed around its edge, sealed in tin foil if there was any available, without, if there was not. It was also the time the fireworks display was well and truly begun. All cooed and aahhhed to the pretty colours and effects, the boys laughed and clapped at the noisy ones. Younger children cried and old people went indoors when the few bangers were let off, bangers had that effect, they sorted the serious bonfire revellers from the amateurs. Rockets, fountains, showers, wheels of colour, Sam's expression of excitement glowed between the pulse of the fire and the harsh glare of scorching black-powder, pyrotechnic light. The smell, the sound, the sight and the feel, even the taste, nothing else was like it in the universe. Sam looked over to Breen, he was holding his arm over his eyes, trying to pull some of the potatoes out of the fire, Sam ran across to help.

"Let me have a go." he said, trying to fish some out with a long stick.

"I've got a few out but I don't know if they're done or not." called Breen, trying to be heard above the crackling of the fire. Breen had brought a small bucket, so they tossed the hot spuds into it and Breen motioned towards the tables. The hot potatoes were sliced open, spoonfuls of butter were mixed into their white flesh and consumed with gusto. Sam, Ben and Breen sat on the bank by the field with more parkin and a mug of punch, thinking they were the wealthiest boys in Britain.

As the once great bonfire became a glowing heap and the last fireworks were let off, the remaining adults went indoors and the boys gathered around the fire to sit and talk. Wrapped in the last warm glow of their work, toasting the final marshmallows or finishing the last of the hot spuds, they watched the sky, as fireworks and rockets from other parties launched into the void, ready to give their 'all in one' fabulous display, before dying and falling back to earth.

183

"They must have had more fireworks than us." said Sam a little disappointed.

"Not really, they may have started later." replied Ben.

"They've no right, 7 o'clock or not at all, I say." came Sam's definite conclusion.

"Not unless they invite us." added Breen.

"It's unnatural, ought to be illegal!" insisted Sam.

"You're only jealous because we have used our fireworks and they haven't." laughed Ben.

"Yes I am!" said Sam much to Ben's surprise. "We have to wait a year now, it's not fair! I hate Guy Fawkes!"

"Why? Without him we wouldn't have a bonfire night!" asked Ben.

"He should have blown up Parliament every day, then we would be able to celebrate it everyday." explained Sam grumpily.

"Don't be daft, they killed him for it," put forward Ben, as he pointed to the fire "and he didn't blow up Parliament anyway, they found him out."

"Then why do we celebrate it then?" asked Breen.

"'Cos they managed to stop him." was his reply.

"Well that's daft, my dad often says they ought to blow up Parliament, so why celebrate the fact that they haven't?" frowned Sam as he launched a marshmallow into his mouth.

"Don't ask me, you know what parents are like." shrugged Ben. Breen turned then said.

"I think they celebrate what should have happened."

"Hey?" asked Sam.

"Well it's like....." Breen was searching for something he had heard somewhere. "wishful thinking ain't it?" he answered.

"That's it then," Sam said "if it's all to do with *wishful thinking* we should be celebrating it everyday and if Parliament is so bad maybe they *should* burn it down."

"You can't." replied Ben.

"Why?"

"Cos its where government is and we have to have that."

"Why?" Sam seemed to be questioning everything.

"Cos we do that's all!" Ben knew he was getting nowhere.

"Why?" asked Sam again.

"I don't know, it's what adults say." Grumbled Ben. Sam and Breen were not convinced, so they relaxed by the fire and finished off the final potato skins.

"God! I'm full." grinned Breen, holding his tummy.

"Yeah, it was great grub." added Ben wiping his greasy face with his sleeve.

"Great bonfire night too." Smiled Sam, stretching out on an unburned bit of linoleum.

"Do you really think so?" asked Breen.

"Yep, really good, probably one of the best ever." Said Sam closing his eyes and enjoying the moment.

"Better than yours?" grinned Ben after a moment's silence. Sam sat bolt upright and was going to start the bonfire argument all over again but he saw the smile on Ben's face, just visible in the flickering firelight.

"I said *one* of the best." Sam laughed. As he laid back down grinning, he thought about the evening. "Yes, the very best." he said to himself.

The bang that followed the thought wasn't so very loud, no, it was just in the silence of the night and as Sam was daydreaming, it just seemed like someone had tested a new bomb. Sam jumped up but he wasn't the first, Ben was yards away, making tracks for cover, just in case the Germans had invaded again. Breen was rolling about laughing.

"It was ...... a banger..... from .... earlier." He could hardly speak for laughing and was holding his full tummy. Sam understood. One of the bangers from earlier had failed to go off and rather than throw it in the fire, Breen had kept it and surreptitiously cast it in the fire as they talked. It had gone off, showering sparks everywhere, Ben had now also gathered what had happened. Sam and Ben chased Breen all over the field, in the dark they couldn't see a thing.

Eventually the fire died so much as to fail its attempt to keep them warm. They retired until next year and Sam began the short walk home. He noticed how cold it was becoming and thought how close Christmas must be. When he finally reached home, his parents were waiting, preparing to go to bed.

"Here he is," announced his father. " the boy that thinks there are two Guy Fawkes."

"I don't, I know there's only one," sang out Sam "and I know that we celebrate bonfire night through wishful thinking." Sam's dad was amazed. He didn't know what Sam was talking about but he was amazed. Sam walked over to the small fire in the hearth grate.

"It's cold out!" he shivered.

"It's going to be a cold winter." added his mother, folding up some washing. There was a silence as Sam warmed by the fire.

"What's that bloody awful smell?" asked Sam's dad "smells like cow shit!"

Sam shuffled about, then went to bed, quickly pushing his shoes well under the bed!

Times were changing in the little Hamlet of Highfields, some of Sam's friends had recently moved to other villages with their families, others, were just busy with other things, like girls. In fact, some of the older boys were crossing that very unsteady rope bridge that joined the child's world to the adults world, and deep below it, ran the river of womanhood. Serious girlfriends were becoming a trend. As Tools walked with Sam down the Backs they contemplated the matter.

"There will be no one left here soon."

"Exactly." admitted Sam. "but I suppose we'll be here forever."

"I bet we end up as the only two on this street." added Tools. He was wrong. That summer even Tools was to go, his family moved to a new house a mile or so away, onto a new estate that was built on a treasured field that was once the site of the travelling fairground. Memories and good times obliterated and covered over by bricks and concrete. Ben and Breen had been some of the first to go, a year or so previously, so had Vern and Mesty in more recent months. Spider and Socky, two of the older boys were gone, one in the army, the other married off early. It all seemed to be happening at once, it was disquieting and Sam hated it. "Girls are bad news!" he thought.

Even so, he could not help watching one girl called Kate. She was a bit younger than Sam, blonde and slim, but most of all, she had a ponytail. Sam had a 'soft spot' for a ponytail. Kate lived down the road near the Garages, which meant that Sam spent a great deal of his time in the opening near there. On one of the rare occasions that Tools came to see Sam since he had moved, they sat on a gate at the end of the opening, close to Kate's garden.

"Let's go on the Tip" suggested Tools.

"Let's stay here." insisted Sam taking a surreptitious glance down Kate's garden.

"But it's boring" added Tools.

"Well I'll fetch my ball and we'll have a game." Unfortunately, Sam's suggested game was rugby. It was his only sporting interest but to Tools, this game seemed like an excuse for a fight. The other boys thought the same too and the game usually became just another soccer match, with a ball that had a mind of its own.

"No thanks, I think I'll go for a ride." suggested Tools, Tools was a clever lad but he could not understand why Sam would not leave the Garage area.

As Tools rode off on his bike, Sam sat watching Kate's garden in the hope she would come out.

"Hey up." said a voice to the side of Sam. There stood a tousle haired, jumper and jeans, slightly oversize for the body they contained. The face was alert and cheeky and the eyes were bright, a few years younger than Sam but made of the same stuff.

"Hey up." answered Sam. "Where d' you live?" he asked.

"There." replied the lad pointing towards the houses near the opening. Sam nodded and walked towards a convenient gate by the field and sat on its top bar.

"I haven't seen you before." smiled Sam as the lad climbed up besides him.

"I don't know why, I play round here." shrugged the lad. The truth was, that age is a great divider when you are young and this lad was only just the age where he would mix with boys like Sam, who were a little older. One year's difference was a culture apart.

"What's yer' name then?" asked Sam.

"Ian." answered the lad.

"Is that it? No nickname then?" asked Sam slightly indignant.

"No, no nickname why?" asked Ian.

"I thought everybody had a nickname." shrugged Sam, even that tradition was dying out it seemed.

"What's yours then?" asked Ian with a look of interest.

"Sam." he replied as if it was obvious. Ian jumped down off the gate and asked.

"So what are you up to today?"

"Same as everyday, nowt'." replied Sam casually.

"Fancy a walk on the Tip then?" asked Ian, pointing over the road as if Sam wouldn't know where it was. Sam thought for a moment and looked back to Kate's house.

"Why not?" he smiled as he jumped down, after all, this new friend, Ian lived quite close to Kate and he probably knew her, yes, Ian may be a handy mate to have. It was obvious from the start the two of them hit it off and Ian brought out the best in Sam. As the weeks wore on Sam's friendship with Ian grew and his curiosity in Kate faded. They were a team. They had the same interests and their ideas on life were similar. They also had the same sense of humour, together they were a team, high spirited and inquisitive.

One evening, the two were returning from a wildlife safari, discussing how soon a day was over.

"Well how come then?" asked Ian "do some days go quicker than others?"

187

"They don't" answered Sam.

"They do! Yesterday went slow, today only seems to have lasted five minutes" insisted Ian.

"That's probably because yesterday you had to go out with your mother to your aunts and today you don't." answered Sam as if it was so simple. Ian frowned.

"But that's daft. Yesterday we only played from six until nine, which is three hours. Today we have played from eleven until half eight, and that's ...." there was a pause " nine hours."

"Nine and a half." added Sam.

"What about dinner?" smirked Ian.

"Well that took three quarters of an hour." answered Sam

"No it didn't, it doesn't matter anyway, all I want to know is why that is?" insisted Ian, with desperation in his voice.

"It's simple," Sam pointed out "all time is relative." He knew he had made a mistake.

"Time is relative?" commented Ian in a high-pitched voice.

"Yes relative." insisted Sam staring at Ian, "It's well known."

"What's it related to?" asked Ian. Sam thought for a moment.

"Its family I suppose." answered Sam with a modicum of sarcastic undertone.

"You don't know, do you?" grinned Ian.

"Look, it's simple." Sam paused as he grappled with a plausible explanation. "It's all to do with the theory of relativity." he liked the sound of that, so he continued. "Relativity is a theory that, when put correctly, shows that time is relative."

"Hmmm." nodded Ian with a grin.

"That means," continued Sam "that if one day time seems slow and another it seems quick, relatively speaking they are the same." Sam held his hand out as if the conclusion was obvious.

"Ever thought of taking it up as a profession?" asked Ian.

"What?" enquired Sam.

"Bullshitting!" was the wry answer. The two boys laughed and headed home. Ian's house was first port of call.

"I was just thinking that, just as we find something to do it's time to go to bed." explained Ian. Sam thought for a moment, then added.

"Get up then, early, about two o'clock when everyone's gone to bed. I do it often, it's good fun." Ian thought it sounded good too.

At two a.m. they met and wondered the lonely streets together. The whole village was theirs, they could go where they wished, when they wished but soon they became bored and returned home. They tried it several times but nothing ever happened. They decided to invite someone else to liven things up. It was to be Weep.

"Weep is always up for a night time outing, we have gone out together loads of times." Explained Sam and it seemed Ian knew Weep quite well.

Very early one Thursday morning, just before two o' clock, Sam very carefully crept past his parent's bedroom and downstairs, noting all the steps that had any kind of squeak. Dressed almost all in black, he exited the house and made his way to the opening at the bottom of the Backs. There he met Weep but Ian was a little late. Patiently they waited until at last, a dark figure could be seen across the opening.

"Let's jump him!" suggested Weep. Sam nodded and they moved along the line of the Garages to come behind the figure. The figure stopped and crouched to the floor. With all the dexterity of James Bond on a good night, the two boys closed in on the figure. When they were about six feet away, Weep motioned to Sam and the two boys leaped forward like springing cats. Honestly, the places people leave piles of bricks! Mr. Hoskin had recently taken down his coalhouse and most of the bricks had been taken away, but a few had been left. There weren't many so he put them near the wall where no one would trip over them. In his wisdom, he hadn't counted on two springing cats. Sam and Weep tripped and landed directly behind Ian.

"Ahhh!" shouted Ian as he began to run. Instinctively, the others scrambled to their feet and followed. The three ran across the opening until they reached the other wall, which they promptly vaulted. Hidden in the garden, Ian hissed.

"You daft bats, I could have had a heart attack!" Weep looked around and asked,

"Why are we hiding?" Lack of an answer convinced them there was no reason at all but as they stood and walked back to the wall, Weep pulled the other two down to the ground.

"Did you see it?" he whispered.

"See what?" asked Sam in a quiet voice. Weep kept quiet but as he leaned, crouching against the wall, he motioned in the direction of the opening with his thumb. Sam and Ian slowly raised their heads to the top of the wall not knowing what horror they may see, what dreadful apparition would meet their gaze. They scanned the opening from the Backs, which was as dark as the backside of a blackboard in a cave, to the road which was illuminated by the new sodium street lights, recently installed. It was there that they saw it, something, some kind of animal, bathed in the warm golden glow of the sodium lamp.

"It's a cat." said Ian.

"No it's legs are too short!" added Sam.

"It's a rat." concluded Weep.

"Well what the hell are we doing hiding behind a wall whispering for then?" asked Sam rather loudly. Weep pulled him back down.

"They're vicious at night. They can eat a dog at night!" added Weep.

"Don't be daft!" Ian began "a rat couldn't eat a whole sparrow, never mind a dog!"

"That's where you're wrong," whispered Weep "One attacks, then when it's fixed onto your throat, it squeaks and hundreds come running to help." The two boys were not convinced but in an attempt to protect themselves, they stumbled around the garden searching for weapons to defend themselves with. Dressed in black, like spies, they occasionally stumbled into each other, giving out a shrill squeal then abuse. Finally, when they were all armed, Weep had found an old stool and a long stick, Ian picked up a bucket and a spade and lack of anything better, caused Sam to pull up a small bush for protection.

"Armed to the teeth, Colonel Samuel Sams the commander of the crack Secret Service team, lead his men on one of the most dangerous missions he had ever undertaken. There had been a legend of the Giant Alien Rat for generations but until six months ago, no one had ever seen it. The rat had been attacking people at night and eating dogs and babies and had terrorised the whole county by whistling its thousands of helpers to come to its aid. It had to be stopped. Once the Alien Rat was destroyed all the other rats would scurry off to their lairs. Colonel Sams had been given the task of hunting down the rat and he had trained his squad especially for it. The squad made their way down the opening, the giant rat scurrying, looking for dogs and babies. As they neared the ferocious beast, it stopped running around and stood still, its flashing red eyes piercing the dark of the night."

"Its legs have dropped off." hissed Ian. Puzzled, they all peered into the darkness and sure enough, the animal had no legs.

"Is it on wheels?" offered Sam considering that it couldn't possibly be a hovering rat. No one answered. Sam poked it with the pointed end of the bush then jumped back. The animal hadn't reacted so he bent down slowly to get a better view of the static object. He very carefully picked up the object to a whispered gasp from the other two.

"It's a sodding hedgehog! A sodding hedgehog you pair of half wits!" Sam put the hedgehog back down and with his hand on his hips, shook his head in the gloom. With a touch of embarrassment the boys headed away depositing their defences in a nearby garden. The hedgehog uncurled itself and looked around in wonder at them, then continued to search for that elusive slug.

John Philip Morton had been on the beer that night. In truth, he had drunk a little too much. Early in the morning, his bladder gave up and he headed to the toilet. On his return, he glanced out of the bedroom window.

"You don't see that very often." he said to himself as he watched a stool, a bucket and a rose bush walk into the gloom beyond the street light and apparently leap over the hedge. As he walked to his bed, he realised that this was not quite normal and he returned to the window to see a hedgehog scuttle away with a large slug. He quickly woke his wife. "Mary, Mary. If I ever drink again, hit me with something heavy!"

Weep, Ian and Sam decided that coming out in the middle of the night was boring.

Sam was always fascinated with transport. Cars, lorries, buses, trains you name it - he loved it. It was clear that it would be a major part of his future life. His first memory of how brilliant transport could be, was when he was about four years old, his cousins had a 'trolley' with a large wooden frame and four pram wheels, they had utilised the pram body too and had the rear end of the coachwork complete with the folding hood that went over it. This part was attached to the rear end of their quite sizable vehicle. Sam was placed in this snug compartment as the older boys pushed the trolley all around the hamlet. It was his first experience of trolleys but it was also his first experience of independent mobility.

Sam was never lucky with transport though but his trolley was always one of the fastest in the village. The Shand brothers' version had all the James Bond optional extras, courtesy of Tools, like: Smoke Screen, a tin full of ashes that opened at the pull of a string, Tyre Puncture, a tin with tacks in that opened at the pull of a string, The Oil Slick, a tin with oil in it that - you guessed it, opened at the pull of a string. Very specialised but not fast. There was even one trolley with lights and a 'dashboard' with switches, but still, not built for speed. Sam's was but still it had limitations - it had to be pushed up a hill to run down it. Sam needed a vehicle that could go uphill as well as down.

One Christmas, Sam's parents had saved up to provide him with the perfect transport and Sam fell in love with it. It was a blue painted pedal car with working lights, in the shape of a Triumph Herald. Sam thought so much of that car, he used it long after he had out grown it and the resulting squeeze into the tiny seat caused bruising to his back, which the family doctor thought was due to a beating. It was, of course, due to Sam's insistence that the damn car didn't go fast enough and he speed pedalled so hard, that his back was black and blue. He had to have something better, or his parents would be had up for mistreating their only son.

His first bike was a 'three wheeler' tricycle with proper 'blow up' tyres and a handy little boot at the rear, to carry bits and bobs in. This bike hitched him with his epithet 'Sam', due to the artwork on the rear boot lid. The artwork depicted 'Wee Willie Winkie' with his candle. Legend has it that Sam was first called Wee Willy, which was then corrupted to Wee Willy, then Sam Chick Bubbly Gum. Heaven knows the connection there but it was so. That, being quite a mouthful was shortened to Sam Willy and then finally to Sam. There it is, unfeasible but true but then again Sam's name was relatively simple to explain, compared to some of the others.

He loved that little bike but it was plain to see it would be of little use as he grew and wanted to go further, so he began riding Breen's little two wheeler, to get used to a bicycle but it was hard work, as the tyres were flat and Tools had removed the inner tubes and replaced them with grass, then he had bound the tyres back onto the rims with bailing twine. Ugly, but it worked in a fashion, albeit a little wobbly. Sam's parents then purchased his first two wheeler bicycle, it was a small fixed-gear object that cost thirty shillings second hand and could not keep up with anything faster than a roller skate, though he covered some miles on it, albeit far behind the rest of his friends.

His first driving lesson was taken when he was about nine years old, it was on a quiet road, in a 1962 Ford Popular 100E, sitting on a small cushion, barely able to reach the pedals. His father soon considered this a mistake, as Sam was constantly wanting to drive and all subsequent 'lessons' were taken on the Backs. It was the first car his dad had owned, they had hired cars for their holidays but this was something very new. Sam loved everything about it, he had a whole back seat for his comfort but he wanted the driving seat.

His first big push-bike was a brand new Hercules with three speed Sturmey-Archer gears, which he cherished. At first it was a little large but he soon grew into it. That bike was to remain with him for quite a few years and he looked after it with a passion, never letting anyone else ride it. He had finally come of age, a citizen with proper transport, a Lord in a land where your bike was as important as a knight's charger. Not all bikes were looked after in the same manner and some were simply built up from old bits. Tools' big two wheeler, had a 'dash board' with switches for lights, which seemed to be all over the thing. Socky had a sort of racing bike with a seat that had the comfort of an Iron Maiden from medieval times. Its drop handlebars removed and some clip-ons from a motorbike fixed seemingly half way down the forks. The most bizarre machine was ridden by Erky, who had high ratio fixed gear pedals and a steering wheel from an Austin Cambridge, almost impossible to ride and if your feet ever came off the pedals, you could break an ankle trying to retrieve them. This sort of thing wasn't for Sam, his bike was brand new, not usual for Sam but he was determined to look after his trusty Hercules.

Bicycles, even adult size bicycles, are always going to be limited, that's for sure. As a boy grows older, his eyes turn to other forms of transport and some of the boys a little older than Sam, had been seen on all manner of motorised variants. Two older boys had horrible little mopeds, with ripped up seats that always seemed to be wet through and Biro had an old beaten up scooter, which he rode up and down the Tip Path. Sam encountered envy, he wanted something like that himself. He eventually found that the need to purchase some kind of motorised transport was a complete focus, something to fly down the Backs on, or down the Tip Path. His first encounter with such a vehicle, was from Loz, it was a sort of moped and Loz wanted ten shillings for it. It was a Honda 50, which came complete with no engine. Sam never found an engine for it, so he sold some parts off it for two pounds sterling and the rest of the hulk was wrecked riding it 'free wheel' down the side of the Tip. A dangerous pastime to be sure, particularly as the parts he had sold were the brakes.

A Puch Pedal moped, with a dead engine was also acquired as a joint venture between him and Tools but Tools took the bolts out of the front forks and the whole thing fell apart. Tools never explained why he had done it but Sam considered that Tools must know what he was doing, even if he didn't. The next machine he took a fancy to, was the Vespa scooter, owned by Biro, who had decided to sell. The two pounds that Biro insisted the bike was worth was not forthcoming from Sam's piggy bank though. However, Sam soon 'borrowed' the required amount from his mother and bought the scooter. He pushed it across the road and up the Backs to his house but once there, he could not get the machine to run. Closer inspection revealed there was no petrol in the tank, mainly due to the fact that there was no petrol tank. The scooter was returned, as was the two pounds from Biro, after some talk of retribution if he didn't but his mother never saw the money again. It was to be his lot that he was not to have motorised transport. After these many failed attempts, he decided to leave the acquisition of vehicles to other people who knew where to look for petrol tanks and ...... engines.

Much later, in a certain summer, Tools and Biro bought an old car, a Ford Anglia, not in too bad condition when it arrived but as soon as Tools had found a spanner or two, certain items became detached. No one really knew why Tools needed to remove items from machinery that seemed to be doing the job they were designed to do very adequately but remove them he did. Like windscreen wipers, and switches, and lights. But, there was change in the air and that could have been the reason, Sam thought. A change that would eventually spell doom for the boys' enjoyment. The railway line was being closed and dismantled. No more would great steam trains and powerful diesels rumble past the Tip and the quarry on their way to the massive collieries. No more would hundreds of coal wagons clang over the crossing at Highfields. The Tiger was to become extinct in Derbyshire. But for now, the boys saw only good in it, for where the tracks had been removed, there was left a long, flat, dirt road for their own special use, where no other vehicles ran.

194

By the time Sam first saw the old Ford Anglia, someone had broken every bit of glass in the machine. One particular day, plans were afoot to take the car down the Tip Path and onto the old railway. This was not to be missed by anyone and indeed, many were to attend the great event. As Sam arrived, Tools, Weep, Biro and Loz were already there.

"We're going to take all the seats out." said Tools, adjustable spanner already working at the bolts.

"Where's the driver going to sit?" asked Sam.

"I'm leaving that one in." laughed Tools looking back from his foetal position between the rear and front seat. Loz and Biro eventually gave him assistance and the seats were duly removed but then to Sam's discomfort, Jane and Anne arrived.

"Are you going to give us a ride then boys?" asked Anne, any 'double entandre' passing over the boys' heads.

"Yeah, if you want." agreed Biro with a large dribbling smile. Whatever could be said about Biro, he never refused anything to a pretty girl. Sam and Tools moved to the other side of the car, to be out of their way.

"Erm," began Sam in a questioning tone. " why have you taken the seats out?"

"So we can get more people in." grinned Tools slipping the spanner into his back pocket. Barmy and Vern arrived and dropped themselves onto the removed back seat, which had been casually strewn on the Backs. Biro soon entered the driver's seat and the rest of the gang piled inside seated on stuffing pulled out of the discarded seats and the car was driven down the Tip Path at a great rate of knots. Once on the railway line, it wasn't long before the more adventurous boys were climbing out of the windows, much to Biro's discomfort as he was trying to drive, and the surface was very uneven where the railway sleepers had been removed. Once they reached the quarry, the car stopped to turn around. Loz tied some rope to the rear window pillars, stood on the rear bumper and using the rope like reins, rode on the back of the car, chariot style. Sam sat on the roof to be away from the girls. They drove back down the line and then back again but as they returned, Sam had joined Loz on the rear bumper, from where they began to bounce the car. Loz being quite large, made considerable impact on the car and at times, the front went so light that the car was difficult to steer.

"Stop it! Stop it!" cried out Biro but they didn't and the car hit the bank near the quarry. Everyone was in fits of laughter, except for Biro, because the front wing had pushed into the front wheel preventing them from returning. Loz, Tools and Biro set about repairing the car, as Weep ran into the trees that edged the quarry. Sam walked over to investigate an old tool shed but it was already empty.

"Thieving gits." growled Sam. As he turned to walk back, he realised Jane had followed him.

"It's hot isn't it?" she said. Sam simply smiled nervously. She leaned on the tool shed and said. "It was cool in the car with the wind blowing, I bet it's cool in the quarry." She closed her eyes as she gripped the edge of her short skirt with both hands and fanned it as if to cool herself down, her thighs and underwear clearly visible to Sam.

"Oh Jesus." thought Sam for he had completely lost the power of speech. In her young years, she already had a reputation as Sam knew, even if he did not understand it. When his mother talked of 'The wrong sort of girl' a picture of Jane came into his mind. He wondered what the 'right sort of girl' might look like, as he had only ever seen the 'wrong sort of girl'. How was an innocent boy like Sam ever going to find 'the right sort of girl' if he had no idea what said person should look like? Jane's reputation was probably unfounded, she liked boys, she liked their company, she liked to flirt with them and she liked to be kissed by them. She knew that having something that someone else wants gives you power, she also knew that once they get what you have, the power goes. Innocent boys tend to make up what they don't understand and few understood her. To Sam this was the 'wrong sort of girl' simply because that's what everyone said 'the wrong sort of girl' was like.

"Like all girls." thought Sam. The more he considered it, he began to weigh the odds of stumbling across the 'right sort of girl'. What would she look like? He wondered again. Dressed in a long, dark, woollen frock he supposed, a thirteen or fourteen year old version of his Aunty Mavis. Yuck, the thought shook him free of his mental bond. He realised he was staring at Jane's thigh. The thing was, he kept on staring and it felt good. He looked all the way from her ankle to the top of her soft white leg.

"Are you hot?" she asked him.

"Mehh mehh nhh yeah." he eventually replied.

"Are you all right?" she enquired as she examined his tortured features. She dropped her skirt hem and came towards him. Sam's mouth opened but no words came out. "Let's go into the quarry." she said gently taking his hand. Sam thought,

"Yes, why not, there can't be any risk involved, especially with someone like me with all my special training. Yes damn it, I will." Jane squeezed his hand but Sam pulled it straight back.

"C c c c c... ca .. ca...car, gone, going, car, go ... must go. leaving, ... leave us here." he spluttered. So much for the special training. Sam quickly made his way back to where the car was, followed by Jane still trying to fathom what Sam had said.

Back at the vehicle, the repairs were nearly done, well they had nearly managed to rip the wing clean off, which probably amounted to the same thing. Sam sat on the boot of the car and Jane sat on the bank, in such a way that he could see up her skirt. He gulped and turned away. Weep returned from the trees.

"Have you done it yet?" he asked.

"Just about." came Tools' muffled reply.

"Where have you been?" asked Sam trying to forget the previous incident.

"For a crap." grinned Weep. Sam considered that Weep could always say something to make you forget your troubles.

They all, once more, piled into the car and this time, Tools was to drive but as he reversed, Weep opened the passenger door and gone was the door. After two more journeys, so was the driver's door and the boot lid. If the car had been fitted with rear doors, they too would have come adrift, as it was, the Ford Anglia was spared at least that embarrassment.

As they returned to the rear of Biro's house, the car was a wreck but they were all in high spirits, except for Biro, for the car was a shadow of its former self. Just two days later, someone slashed the tyres and the car never moved again. As they walked from the wreck that day, Sam was very aware of Jane's presence but she completely left him alone, in fact she never spoke to him again. In a strange way this bothered Sam, even if he could not explain why.

Lots of changes were taking place, not just around Sam but inside him too. For some reason, he could not remove the image of Jane by that old tool shed from his memory.

"Ah, girls, forget it - they're trouble." he thought but for some reason, simply pulling their hair had no appeal anymore, and this sick feeling in his stomach that he once thought was an allergy to girls, was becoming something else. During the last few days of the summer holidays, Sam thought more and more about girls, until it came to the point where he began to notice when they walked by.

One morning, in a certain summer, a wary eye peeped out from a crumpled heap of linen that was once a bed. The eye scanned an horizon of a new world, of new thought, as Sam leapt briskly out of bed and marched into the bathroom. Once there, without threats of torture or severance of certain limbs, Sam had a wash. Before he realised what he was doing, it was too late. Well, he may as well go the whole hog, he brushed his hair and dressed ready for his first day back at school.

"Are you all right?" asked his mother, as she reached for the thermometer.

"Yes, you don't need that." He looked down at his well-used shoes.

"I could do with some new footwear." he continued. Was it possible that these old shoes, that had run many times carrying him from certain death, shoes that had kicked Socky in the backside, shoes that had broken open Steven Marsh's's money box for him, shoes that had flown through the air and struck Weep on the head and displaced him from a tree were to be forsaken? Could it be that these old friends were to be cast aside in favour of some fancy new foot covering?

"Not until your birthday." snapped his mother. His old shoes breathed a sigh of relief to be reprieved. His old shoes, after all, had delivered him to school and back many times, usually kept his feet where they were supposed to be as he walked and generally acted as good shoes do. Still Sam was unhappy with them. Why? Was it something to do with his new found interest in girls? For sure his appearance had changed. He looked down at the shoes once more and shrugged his shoulders. Ah well, at least he wouldn't have to teach some new shoes the route through Pinkerton's orchard, or where the foot holds are on the Sycamore in the quarry, or how to tell lies about where they had been and why they had been out so late. And new shoes probably wouldn't float as well as those when they had shoe-raft races down Peggy's Brook.

He set off to school in his old trusty shoes, school which he hated with a passion, just like most children hate their greens. After school, he walked home constantly looking at his shoes and stopping to wipe them in the grass but no improvement was noticed. Once home, the shoes were flung into the cupboard and he put his plimsolls on, which were a little newer. His freedom restored, he was soon out and looking for adventure, for this was his vocation. His changed appearance did not last long, within three days, he forgot about the shoes and to a certain extent he forgot about girls because the summer was still with him and anyway, there was lots of fun to be had. It was as if all the summers of Sam's childhood had melted together and become the same one.

"Girls will have to wait." he thought to himself as he walked towards the Tip with Tools. They were on their way to two, tree dens near the quarry but as they passed the Tip, they noticed someone up there. Weep and Mumble were coming towards them.

"Who's on the Tip?" asked Sam.

"Oh it's Biro, Loz, Anne and a friend of hers." replied Weep. The two tree dens weren't going anywhere.

"Let's go on the Tip." suggested Sam. Anne's new friend was called Sally, Sam soon discovered, much to the disgust of Tools. He was also always around when a girl from Derby came visiting her grandparents. He was interested in girls, that was clear, it was also against nature, he should be scrumping or rolling truck wheels down the side of the Tip. Sam's doom was complete, he had built himself a scaffold and he was going to hang himself, Tools could only stand and watch as Sam sold his soul to the devil. He had found a new world and his life would never be his own again.

If a child is very lucky, during the school summer holidays, he or she may be taken off by their parents for a week or even two, to some resort or similar. Sam was lucky and there was a promise of a week in a caravan at Skegness. Sam liked the seaside, it was a place he always felt at home. The year previously, had been a minor disaster, Sam and his parents had travelled all the way down to Devon in their first car, a Ford Popular 100e with a 998 cc side valve engine and a three speed gearbox, capable of a staggering 52 mph on a flat road in perfect weather conditions and incapable of going up a hill of more than one in fifty. Added to which, a large container described as a 'suitcase', was lashed to the roof by a few dubious looking bits of rope, that acted like parachute and gave the already ungainly little car a slipstream coefficient of a large building, further reducing the car's top speed to 47 and a bit if travelling down hill. It was a recipe for certain hell. Twelve and a half hours travelling, most of them in darkness, locked in a tiny space no larger than a pencil case, with two other people and every other available nook and cranny in the car stuffed with various items of clothing. Driving on minor roads, stopping for a wee in every village, accompanied by Sam's mother, inevitably getting the map directions wrong and Sam asking "Are we there yet?" every four minutes and twenty five seconds. When it looked like things couldn't get any worse, the bits of rope on the suitcase ceased being bits of rope and decided they wanted to become streamers instead and wave at the other cars as they passed, this meant of course, that the suitcase took it upon itself to go on holiday on its own and fell off the roof, skidding along faster than any luge at the winter Olympics, causing mayhem and lots of swerving as it headed off into the other stream of traffic.

If nothing else, the stop had given them all time to calm down before the next wave of patience sapping dilemmas reduced them to a completely broken family unit. The decision had been taken, and no one remembered by whom, to stop and have a sleep so they would be refreshed for the rest of the journey when dawn broke. Sam, being a small boy, decided to fit that description perfectly by being so excited, that at first he complained bitterly about the delay, then went on to complain that he couldn't sleep sitting up. Arrangements were made for his father to squeeze into the rear seat, his mother to suffer much, trying to sleep in the drivers seat and Sam could get a little more comfortable in the passenger seat. He did, but being so excited and being impatient, he still couldn't sleep. He had done his best to keep his parents awake by asking stupid questions, including "Are we there yet?" but it was to no avail. His parents were so exhausted, they had fallen asleep. Sam as usual became bored quickly. He opened the door and climbed out.

"What are you doing?" asked his bleary-eyed mother in the gloom, his father hadn't even woken up.

"I need a wee." replied Sam, pointing to a nearby bush that could just be seen sat on the edge of the lay-by.

"Hurry up then." his mother hissed and she tried to adjust to a less painful position behind the steering wheel. Sam had no intention of hurrying up, he could see in the distance some lights. In our modern world, where every road seems to have stupid amounts of street lights, it may seem odd that lights could attract a small boy as if he were a moth but in Sam's young days, street lights were not all that common and most roads were bathed in thick, black, darkness at night. Sam had to investigate the source of those lights. As he strolled down the grass verge, there were no cars passing, so he struggled to see where he was treading but eventually he found his way towards those lights. It was a petrol station. Sam had never seen anything like it, this petrol station had been lit up like a Christmas tree and he could see someone inside. It seemed like a miracle of the modern age, a petrol station that was open in the middle of the night. Sam hadn't known exactly why it drew him, why its light was so comforting but he was excited by its promise and what a promise. Inside this place was a shop, where most items required by the weary traveller were for sale. He pressed his nose to the glass as a large truck rolled into the parking area, the driver jumped down and walked over. He winked at Sam, Sam smiled back and then watched the driver walk in to buy some items. Sam looked at the clock on the wall, it was two thirty, that was two thirty in the morning! Sam was dumfounded by it all. This was essentially a shop that seemingly never closed. Sam had always liked a challenge and he thrust his hand into his pocket and there he found it, some of his holiday money. He jangled it in the pocket and boldly entered the shop. There was chocolate, crisps and small individually wrapped cakes, the sort and sizes that were not available in an ordinary shop - a shop that closes at night. There were newspapers, comics, paperback books and pop. Everything the young, travelling, bored out of his mind boy, could ever wish for. There was also something Sam couldn't resist. Something for free, a small road map that anyone could have with any purchase. Sam looked at the display of goodies, it was difficult to choose which to buy. His gaze eventually fell on a larger than normal bar of Caramac, something Sam really enjoyed, he picked up the bar and then reached up for a splendid copy of a DC comic, Batman. Sam loved Batman, like Sam he walked the dark streets at night, his eyes looking for trouble. Yes, Sam saw himself just like Batman, where as, Batman walked the streets of Gotham City, Sam strolled the roads of... now exactly where was he? The free map would tell him that.

"Just these please." he said to the young man at the counter. "The map is free with these?" he added holding up the small folded map.

"Er, yes, yes it's free all right." frowned the man but as he took Sam's money he asked.

"Where are you from? There are no houses near here?"

"I know that, I'm from miles away. Do you know Chesterfield?" asked Sam tilting his head as intelligently as he could. The man seemed taken aback.

"What, Chesterfield in Derbyshire?" Sam nodded but was slightly sidetracked by the mans accent, he had never noticed before but in a different accent 'Derbyshire' sounded much more like 'Darbyshire' and not 'Durbyshire' as Sam said it. Sam drifted off in his mind wondering why that was. "Well?" asked the man. Sam looked vague for a moment then said.

"Oh, I'm not from Chesterfield." he was shaking his head. "Fairly near though, but *you* won't have heard of it." There was emphasis in the 'you' as if the boy thought the young man wouldn't understand. The man wasn't sure if this boy was playing with him or not.

"So you have just come from Chesterfield?" he asked, his frown deepened and he dropped Sam's change on the counter.

"Yeah." nodded Sam as he examined the coins, he didn't trust people from foreign parts and this area was certainly foreign. When he was sure it was proper currency of the realm, he dropped it into his pocket, making a mental note of how much he had left for the holiday. "We set off this afternoon." Then he burst out laughing. "No sorry, yesterday afternoon." and he covered his mouth as he laughed, pointing to the clock with the other hand. The man behind the counter had worked in the garage for ten months give or take a week but in all that time he had never expected such a young, careful shopper to walk in from a town that, to his knowledge was over two hundred miles away and fall in hysterics over the clock on the wall. The boy regained his composure and asked. "Do you sleep in the day then?"

"Pardon?" asked the man.

"Who looks after the shop when you are asleep?" The man shook his head.

"Just a moment, are you alone?" Sam stared at the man and then looked slowly, first to his left, then just as slowly to his right. He then looked behind himself and saw another lorry driver browsing the shop over at the far end. He looked back to the man at the counter and broke into a deep grin.

"Course I am. I bet it makes you see stuff hey?"

"What are you talking about?" asked the bemused man.

"Sleeping in the daylight." replied Sam, with a more serious look on his face. The man was really becoming confused and needed to be rid of this strange child.

"Is there anyone with you? Have you come here with anyone else?" The man spoke as if he was addressing someone who didn't understand English. Sam frowned deeply, this man ought to get more sleep, how did he ever get a job in this petrol station in the first place?

"Yeah course, my parents are in the car up the road in the lay-by." with this he tucked the comic under his arm, placed the Caramac in his pocket and walked smartly from the shop, reading the free map. Outside, he sat under a light in the forecourt on a step by the end of the shop and studied the map whilst he fumbled with the chocolate wrapper retrieved from his pocket. His now Caramac encrusted finger, traced along the A38 road until it stopped at where Sam thought he was. He finished the chocolate bar and stood to place the wrapper in the bin, as he looked out into the gloom, he saw his mother, walking in that way mothers do when you are in real trouble. A sort of forward leaning, quick stepping, arms folded tightly, kind of walk. Sam tucked the map and the comic under his arm and waited for the explosion.

"Where the bloody hell do you think you've been? I fell back to sleep and when I woke you were gone, your dad's gone off in the other direction in the pitch black looking for you." Sam just gulped. He wanted to tell her about the shop that never closes, he wanted to tell her that they were further down the road than they first thought, he wanted to tell her that he was just like Batman and loved the dark, but he didn't. A voice broke through the sticky atmosphere.

"Don't go at 'im too much missis', I've been in the shop just now listening to 'im. I've had the best laugh in years." Sam's mother didn't know what the man was talking about but it was enough to soften her tongue towards her wayward son. Sam would have to tread carefully for the rest of the journey.

They eventually arrived at their destination, the Beverley Camp, near Torquay and they immediately began to empty the car to find the tent, true it was a small car but it was also a small tent. One of those simple affairs, amusingly referred to in the brochure as; a 'three man tent' but incapable of accommodating the three men, unless they happened to be actors from the pantomime about Snow White. Still, to be fair, Sam wasn't exactly a man and Sam's mother certainly was not, so the tent manufacturers may have got off the hook in that particular case. The tent was duly erected and with the exception of a storm the following evening, the holiday was a great success, only slightly marred by the return journey that took the best part of twelve hours once more. This time, with no overnight stop. Sam enjoyed his time in Devon and the trip into Cornwall was so impressive to his young sensibilities, he returned there on many occasions in later life.

But that was the year previous, the thought of that long journey once more had put paid to another trip down south and the solution was to go nearer to home, Lincolnshire: Skegness, to be precise. They had been before on numerous occasions and this time they were to stay in a large static caravan, owned by a family friend, the same one they had been to, two years previous. It was spacious for the three of them and it allowed them to take the budgie. They had acquired the budgie a few years ago and Sam, being Sam, had decided that it just wasn't cricket keeping a bird in a small cage, so the budgie had the free run of the house in the daylight hours. Now, this would have been a suitable arrangement under normal circumstances but all things being equal, they were not quite 'normal', as they also owned a cat. It was fairly obvious that the cat and the budgie were going to come together at some point. They did, the contact point on the cat was its mouth and the contact point on the bird was the, well the whole body. The head, protruding from one side of the cats mouth, the tail the other. In the real world, the budgie would die and the cat would have to spend the night out, but this is fiction, isn't it? Well, to put some perspective on the story, you have to understand that the said budgie, although looking like an ordinary bird, seemed to break the rules, just like Sam. Having so much freedom, it struck up a strong relationship with the young Sam, to the point where it hardly ever left him, it sat on his shoulder like the ever-attentive parrot on the stereotypical pirate. To all and sundry, they looked like a small version of Red Beard and his trusty 'Pieces of Eight', except Sam didn't have a beard of any colour, a wooden leg or an eye patch or even a black spot on his hand but the analogy works with a good imagination.

The bird became so used to Sam that whenever he went out or up to his room, the bird scuttled off to its cage to twitter to its mirror, or some other inanimate object but when Sam reappeared it flung itself from the cage and flew to his shoulder. The bird could be taught things too, not just the talking thing, although his mother did teach the bird to ask visitors "Do you want a cup of tea?" to the rib tickling amusement of all concerned but Sam went further. He taught the bird to recognise sounds to a degree that he could say something like 'Mirror' and the bird would fly to the mirror. The word 'fly' would cause the budgie to leap into the air and fly around the room before returning to Sam's shoulder. And being almost permanently on his shoulder, this once nearly ended in tragedy. Sam walked out of the house on his way to school with the bird still sitting there, his mother noticed and called to him, at which Sam casually turned and walked straight back into the house. There was one time when the bird did get out, someone opened the outside door, just as a vacuum cleaner was started, the bird took fright and flew out. Sam was told by a neighbour that the bird had flown over the street and behind the houses, toward the Tip. Sam walked down the Tip path with a heavy heart but after calling the bird, he heard a reply and soon tracked him to a hawthorn tree on the path. Sam held up his arm and called to the bird, at which the bird flew to his hand and Sam trapped its feet with his thumb and secured the remarkable bird. The least remarkable thing about the budgie was his name. 'Joey'. Sam's parents never wasted effort on names for pets. The cat was called 'Puss'.

Once Joey was prized from the jaws of Puss, there was blood trickling down the bird's chest, with little hope of survival, they left the bird in the cage overnight and went to bed. The next morning, the bird had recovered and ironically, the cat left the bird alone ever after that incident.

So, with the car packed and the budgie in his cage on the back seat, Sam and his parents poured themselves into the gaps left by the mountain of luggage in the Ford Popular. Sam loved that little car, it was the first real car he had ever driven, so it was special, sat on a cushion and only just being able to reach the pedals, he had driven it just a few yards. For now though, the driving duties were left to his father and off they set to Skegness. Sam only managed to say "Are we there yet?" about fifty times, as they stopped twice for a cup of tea and the journey wasn't too long. Sam started to get giddy at Lincoln and by the time they passed the Cherry Tree café, with a home made replica of an Apollo lunar orbiter in the car park, he was in holiday mode, even though there were miles left to go. Through Wragby and a quick stop at a garage and cafe the other side of Horncastle. Next stop 'Skeg'.

They arrived at the campsite, unpacked the car into the spaces in the caravan and after the kettle was set to boil, Sam distributed some suction pad perches for the bird. Sam opened the cage and the budgie, having been to the caravan before, could remember the layout of the place and even knew where the stick-on perches would be.

The weather was pretty warm and around teatime they went for a walk and something to eat at the Linga-Longa cafe. Sam was full of the seaside spirit and looked eagerly at the bowl on the table that contained sugar cubes. He took one and ate it.

"Stop it." glared his mother.

"But they're nice." insisted Sam.

"It's just sugar, it's bad for your teeth." she frowned.

"But it doesn't taste like 'just sugar'" insisted Sam. This happened every time they were on holiday, Sam loved the sugar cubes and so did his mum, if she was honest. They left the cafe and walked up the sea lane to have a look at the sea for the first time that year. Sam loved the sea, he didn't know why, he didn't even question it. It was the way he was made somehow. He also loved the atmosphere, and the arcades and the sand and the donuts and the toffee apples and the... Let's just say that the only bit he didn't like was going home. At night, Sam's parents would find somewhere to go for a drink, preferably where there was some live music and somewhere for Sam to explore. Later they sometimes called off for a fish supper at Salts Fish and Chip shop, then back to the caravan. The following day Sam's dad lifted the bonnet of the car and assumed the posture. The posture was him, bent over one of the wings of the car, with his head buried in the engine bay.

"What does he find to do under that bloody bonnet?" asked his mother, not really ready for Sam's reply.

"Grandma says he has to wind the elastic band up every time." His mother rolled her eyes and said.

"She's probably not far off there." Sam continued.

"Aunty Mavis says he has a woman in there."

"Well if there is, she must be small and very oily." laughed his mother.

"He's trying to make it go faster." smiled Sam eagerly.

"He'd be better off walking to the moon, the only way he'll get that to go faster is by driving it off a cliff." Sam still loved the car though, he even got to drive it down the camp site when it wasn't busy. Eventually the day came when Sam would be in ecstasy, the day they went to the fair. Sam loved the fair and the one at Skegness was very good but Sam was told they weren't going there.

"Butlins?" he questioned.

"Yes," replied his mother. "We'll buy a day ticket and you can go on the fair as much as you want and we can do what we want." This sounded pretty good to Sam. An all-day fair. When Sam reached the fair, he saw that it was very big and there were some favourite rides there. His parents took him to where they were going to be and he said he would come back every hour to check with them and then he took off to start riding. He tried most of the rides and soon met a new friend called Tommy, who, like Sam, was on his own and had been left to ride the fair while his parents went to eat. After just over an hour, Sam explained that he had to go and see his parents and suggested Tommy come with him, which he did. Sam's parents met Tommy but in an attempt to be sociable and ask a little about the lad, they were inadvertently keeping the two lads from their rides. The boys soon made their way back to the fair though and began with the dodgems. After the dodgems, Sam and Tommy sat on a wall watching the Waltzer and Sam grinned as he took in the whole experience. He was in heaven, so many rides and it was all free. They jumped onto the Waltzer and larked about as the car spun really fast. As they left the ride, they both laughed and giggled at the fun they were having. Over to the left there was a ride that looked like fun, it was called the Merry Mixer and was constructed with three large arms, with three revolving smaller arms with cars on the end that seemed to pass very close to each other. Tommy jumped in one of the cars and Sam jumped into the other end so that they had plenty of room. The restraint was locked down and the ride began. Straight away, Sam could feel the pull of the ride as it picked up speed, it was throwing him sideways, into the outside end of the car. It was really fast, soon Tommy couldn't resist the centrifugal force and he came sliding down the seat and banged into Sam. They howled with laugher as Tommy tried, in vain, to return to the other side of the seat and then within the blink of an eye, Tommy was gone. Sam saw him slip under the bar and shoot past his feet, out of the car. Sam looked around but couldn't see where he was, but the music had stopped and the ride was slowing as quickly as could be done. The restraint bar was unlocked and Sam jumped out to see a crowd of people standing at the edge of the ride. Some were bent down and it was suddenly very quiet. Sam went a little closer and then he saw one of Tommy's feet showing through the gaps in the crowd. The shoe was missing and he couldn't see any movement. He suddenly felt sick and he began to run, he didn't know where to but he had to run. He realised he was crying, sobbing as he ran and then his strength gave up and he fell onto some grass. How could it be? In a fraction of a second, life had turned from heaven to hell. What was wrong with the world that it could be so? Sam was here, staring up at the sky and Tommy was dead, over there at the fair, that same magical place where Sam was born to be. What a terrible curse was this, that left someone like Sam to hate fairs? To despise them for their cruelty? Someone was speaking but Sam couldn't hear.

"Are you all right son?" asked the woman. Sam shot to his feet and ran again, here and there he saw faces, faces that looked at him, running and crying, trying to run away from what had happened. He stopped at a fountain and recognised the place. He turned and ran up some steps and there were his parents. He needed them now, more than anything. His mother knew something was terribly wrong.

"What is it? What's happened?" Sam sobbed out the story and relived it as he did. He wanted to run again but he knew he was safe now. His parents left immediately and took Sam back to the caravan, where he lay on his bed, his eyes stinging and his head hurting. All he could see was poor Tommy sliding past his feet.

Sam heard the caravan door open and voices discussing something, it sounded like his parents. It went quiet until the bedroom door opened and his mother walked in.

"I have just been down to the phone box." she began, as she sat besides him on the bed. "I rang Butlins and they told me that Tommy and his family were staying in the chalets across the road from the fair and although they took Tommy to the hospital," she put her hand on his leg and he gulped in expectation. " they let him out after check up's. He's a bit bruised and battered but he's fine." Sam sighed with relief, it had been a bit difficult for him. His mother stood and said. "You alright then?" Sam nodded. She smiled and turned to leave.

"Thanks Mam." She smiled back at him and then left. Sam sat up and looked out of the window. He watched a seagull fly over, its life in the balance every day and thought of his own future. He grabbed a comic from the dresser than lay back on the bed.

"Beach tomorrow I think."

Sam let loose with all his might and kicked the oval ball as hard as he could, after all, you could only convert a try if the ball went over the coal houses. This lad had no time for soccer, his 'bent' was a man's game, Rugby. He had just converted a try for Scotland, for he envisaged himself as much Scottish as English as his grandad was reputedly a Scot. For some reason, that only true Scotsmen and Sam know, any connection with that God forsaken, hurricane battered, wilderness of a country made men protective and patriotic. Sam's friend Ian always played England but Sam and his team, being two other friends, were drawing, five-all. Sam stirred his team into life, in the hope that Scotland could pull into the lead in the final minutes of the game. The boys game, although Rugby Union was played like Rugby league because scrums were difficult to achieve with such small numbers. Ian kicked off and Sam caught the ball, passing of to one of the Marsh's's, two brothers from the village. Rob Marsh was about to pass to his brother Steve but Ian tackled him and the ball went into the air. Tools caught it, but as Rugby wasn't Tools' best sport, he was easily tackled by the younger Steve. Steve passed long over to Sam but Weep intercepted the throw and sped towards the goal line.

"The crowd at Twickenham rose to their feet as the English number eight carried the ball, chased by the Scottish fly-half, Rob. Sam was close too, this experienced winger, whom England had begged to play for them, had refused, preferring to play for Scotland, was on the chase. Rob leapt and brought Weep to the ground. The usual turf at Twickenham had been replaced specially for this match with gravel and concrete, which was a little harsh on elbows and knees but was traditional in the area and much to the liking of the players. Sam picked up the ball and turned to run, the Scottish fans going wild, he dodged past Tools but Ian was with him, so Sam, seeing Steve on his left, passed just before hitting the ground and Steve touched down. Sam once again converted as the match ended, the capacity crowd began to leave in the knowledge that they had been thoroughly entertained by two of the closest matched teams in the world."

Twickenham faded back into the opening by the Garages. The Marsh brothers left for home, so did Tools, Weep explained he had to help his brother clean out their rabbits. Sam went to look for his ball, after every conversion, it had to be retrieved from someone's garden. He pinpointed it, it was in the garden next to Kath's, a girl he knew and once liked, until she stopped wearing her hair in a pony tail. As he stared at the ball, he noticed someone pick it up. A tall girl with dark hair and a long neck, someone Sam didn't know. She walked down the path towards Sam.

"Is this yours?"

"Yes, ... yes it is." he replied. The girl was a strange sight to Sam, slim and dark, tall with deep brown eyes and an incredibly long neck. She wasn't quite a film star but she was undeniably pretty, with a smile that could melt the sugar off Sugar Puffs. The one feature that Sam was unsure about was the fact that, although she was a little younger than Sam, she had ... well ... it was obvious... no one could deny that the girl had a pair of breasts.

"Don't you want it?" she asked.

"Pardon?" gasped Sam.

"The ball, I expect you came for it."

"Yessss ... yes ... Ta!" he took the ball but then, as she turned to leave and Sam returned to the Backs. In desperation, Sam called. "Are you a friend of Kath's?"

"Yes," she turned to reply and walked casually to the gate. " but I'm staying with my gran, she lives next door to Kath, I'm here for the summer holidays. My name's Jackie." She held out her hand, which puzzled Sam. Does she want the ball back he thought? Then it clicked, this was a handshake, like adults do. She *was* a strange girl, Sam dropped the ball and shook her hand. A passing dog ran off with the ball but Sam didn't even notice. Her hand was soft and warm, her long fingers wrapped around his. She let go and turned again to return to the house.

"Will I?" Sam paused. "Do you? ..." he paused again. She turned and smiled, Sam tried again. "I might see you around sometime."

"Yes quite possibly." she admitted. Sam walked into the opening with his ball long forgotten. Ian was in hysterics.

"You shook her hand!" Sam knew it was a very grown up thing to do but it seemed right. The truth of the matter was, behind his protestations and pathological belief that he would not grow up, he was ... or at least his body was. His mind wasn't sure, after all, growing up meant walking around with a gloomy face, watching television and constantly saying "What's the world coming to?" That wasn't for Sam. Ian was still laughing.

"Shuddup you!" demanded Sam.

"Shakin' hands, that's weird!" laughed Ian.

"Well, she held her hand out ..." Sam remembered his ball. "Where's my ball?"

"Bonzo ran off with it, he's probably buried it, he buries everything else." Indeed Bonzo was the world's tidiest dog, he had tidied all manner of objects, including model cars, a bike wheel and a shovel, which on reflection seems rather counter productive. When Bonzo found a large, 'baby' doll and began to bury it, an old woman emptying her rubbish into the dustbin saw it and feinted there on the spot.

"Mind you." pointed out Ian, as he ceased laughing, "she's got tits!" not knowing why it should be an advantage.

"Yeah I noticed that!" said Sam with a blank expression. "She's not from round here anyway."

"I know" replied Ian, she's from Derby, Kath told me." The two boys walked along the Backs. Sam realised he would have to take the bull by the horns and make a decision - to like girls, or not. Unknown to him, nature had made the decision for him. Nature was like that, armed with some money you could find yourself with good intentions going to buy a bag of plums when, 'Oh my God!' you exit the shop with a bag of sherbet lemons. Usually that was nature, fruit against sweets, .. sweets win! This however was different, there was a feeling inside telling Sam that he couldn't help liking the fairer sex.

As predicted, nature won over animal instinct and Sam felt the urge to spend a great deal of time testing the water near the back of Jackie's grannies house. Not that there was any water there.

Day after day he would find some reason or other to be around that spot, constantly trying to convince his friends that they should stay local and play 'rallyco' or 'kick can'. He was becoming tedious and predictable but when Jackie finally appeared, she was with Kath. Even Sam realised he was becoming a little too old for such games as Kick Can but even so, he was more than eager to invite the girls to play. Once the rules had been explained, they began.

The rules were simple, someone was chosen to be 'it' and they turned their back, whilst the last person to be 'it' threw an old tin can as far as they could. As soon as the can landed, the new 'it' ran and collected it, whist the others hid. The can was placed on a predetermined spot and then 'it' went out looking for the others. When 'it' found someone, they both raced to the can and the first to kick the can won. If 'it' kicked the can first, then the other person was 'it', if the other kicked the can first then 'it' had to continue finding the others. Unfortunately for Sam, he was first to be 'it'. Ian threw the can and Sam ran to retrieve it. As he placed it on the mark, he hatched a plan. If he found Jackie first, he would let her win so that next time he could hide with her. Most of the children hid in between the maze of garages that sprawled on wasteland near the opening but they created a crisscross of alleys where even a boy scout could get lost. As Sam slowly entered, his senses were listening for footsteps. Behind him, he heard the can being kicked twice, telling him two of the children had hidden elsewhere. He had to be careful, or he could end up being 'it' again. Sam, like a Red Indian tracker, slid between two asbestos garages and listened, he heard two voices, it was Billy, a new boy to the street and Ian. Sam banged on the garage side and ran towards the can, from the other end, he saw Billy and Ian emerge but he beat them, calling out Billy's name first Billy was 'it' but Sam still had to find the others. That was easy, for it didn't matter now whether they beat him. Once they were all out, Sam threw the can for Billy and ran towards the Garages. To his dismay, Jackie and Kath ran to their gate and hid behind a dustbin. Sam continued to a place he knew between a garage and the hedgerow. It was a well-worn place, no grass grew for fear of busy feet. Sam sat and waited, he heard the can but couldn't make out any names. As usual, he eventually made his way back through the Garages so that no one would know about his hiding place. As he peered into the opening, he noticed that most of the others were there, so he ran and just managed to get beaten to the can, no matter, he wasn't 'it' .... oh no, it was Jackie! Billy threw the can and Jackie ran ... Sam hid. This wasn't exactly going to plan, something had to be done. Sam ran across three garage backs and appeared opposite Ian and Weep. Sam motioned with both hands, a pushing movement and Ian grinned. With a positive shove, Ian pushed Weep into the middle of the Backs and he ran, the trouble was that he ran fast and beat Jackie to the can.

"Shit!" exclaimed Sam to himself. Then he saw his chance. At the other side of the bottom garage, he saw Kath, crouching by a bush. Sam crept up behind her and said.

"C'mon, we'll have to run for it." The two of them made their way along the Backs, close to the hedge. Sam halted in a gateway, Jackie was close behind him.

"Now!" called out Sam, it was a calculated risk that paid off. Sam beat Jackie back to the can but Kath couldn't ... Kath was 'it'. Jackie threw the can and the game began again. Jackie ran into the garages and Sam followed. The tall girl seemed to struggle to find a hiding place.

"Over here." called Sam. "I know a place." he beckoned. " but it's secret, don't let on." Jackie nodded and followed. They squeezed behind the garage into Sam's hideout and sat down.

"She won't find us here." smiled Sam. "no one knows this place." Sam looked at her, a kind of sideways glance. She was looking the other way, so he turned to have a good look at her, all the way from her shiny brown hair, down her red jumper to the bottom of her long blue jeans. She turned quickly so he looked away.

"How do we know when it's safe?" she asked.

"Oh just wait until we hear the can is kicked a few times." This was Sam's place, he wanted to keep her here as long as he could. "But what if she gets bored?" he thought. "Better move soon." Sam heard the can being kicked, so he made a move.

"Come on, we had better get closer so we can see." Sam advised. "Stick close to me." he added thinking she may go without him,

"Will you help?" she asked, as they scrambled out of the hiding hole. Jackie held out her hand, Sam took it, feeling how warm and soft it was, he helped her out and along the path. As they ran across the gap between the garages Jackie's hand was still in his, holding tightly, although Sam liked it, he had to make sure no one saw him. It just wasn't done, holding hands with girls! Sam peered around the side of the garage and saw most of the others standing by the can but he couldn't see Kath.

"C'mon, let's go, you stay this side and I'll go the other, when I run ... you run!" He had done it, broken free without having to make it obvious. They slowly crept up the Backs until Sam lunged into a sprint. They both kicked the can but so had everyone else, which meant that Kath was 'it' again. Great, ... more time with Jackie!

"I'm not doing it again!" complained Kath.

"You have to, that's the idea of the game." explained Ian.

"But everyone runs faster than me!"

"Well, stay nearer the can." someone suggested.

"No. I'm going home!" and Kath turned to leave. Sam panicked, he knew Jackie would go with her.

"I'll be it" he announced, but Kath kept on walking. Jackie looked at him and shrugged her shoulders, then followed her friend. The irony was that Rob Marsh had just arrived and the International rules of Kick Can as everyone knows, was that new comers were automatically 'it'. Ian threw the can and Rob chased it as the others ran. Sam headed for his hide, but he felt let down. As he sat in his little place, head cupped in his hands, he felt strange. Like someone had bought him a new bike without a seat, or as if he had been picked to play rugger for Scotland but he wasn't allowed to touch the ball. To the side of him, he heard a rustle of leaves, someone had found his hiding place! He instinctively picked up a large piece of wood but even if the intruder was a rabid foaming wolf, there was no room to swing the club. Around the corner came head of brown hair, followed by a familiar red jumper. He threw the stick down, Jackie's smiling face looked up at him.

"Hello, I thought I'd find you here, she's gone off in a mood, so I thought I'd rejoin the game, is that okay?" There was a pause whilst Sam's blood ran back into his ego.

"Errr ... er yeah, course, yes that's great." She sat close beside him, not so long ago, it would have been far *too* close. He considered the situation, not only did she return to the game but she had decided to find Sam and be with him.

In the days and weeks that passed, they spent a little time together, but the connection never got close. Sam was a little afraid, in his world, he was in control, this wasn't at all like that. All through that year, Sam waited for the school holidays, so that Jackie would return from Derby and his mental pot would be filled with free spirit. For some reason, probably even Sam didn't know the true reason, they drifted apart, maybe Jackie didn't see him in the same way as he saw her. Sam though about her quite a lot and would wish they were sitting together, he staring at her long neck, she smiling and talking to him.

The last time Sam saw her, which was the year after the Kick Can game, became etched into his memory. Sam had just entered the Post Office opposite the house where she used to visit, when he noticed the front door open to her grannies house. Sam stepped inside the Post Office and peeped through the shop window. It was Jackie all right, coming out of her grannies house, becoming quite the young lady but she was still slim and tall and sported that long neck. To Sam's dismay, she didn't enter the Post Office but called at the shop adjacent. Sam completed his business in the Post Office and left.

"She probably won't recognise me anyway." thought Sam. He stood looking over at the opening where they used to play, remembering with a slight smile the first time she asked about his name.

"Is Sam your real name?" asked Jackie as they sat on the gate to the field, swinging their legs.

"No." replied Sam.

"Well?"

"Well what?"

"What's your real name?" She asked. Sam told her and waited for laughter. There was nothing wrong with the name but Sam preferred nicknames. To his surprise she shrugged and said.

"It's a good name, why did you change it?"

"I didn't."

"Well who did?"

"Everyone, we all used to have nicknames round here."

"How did you get Sam?"

"It's a long story." began Sam "I used to have a three wheeled bike and it had a boot, like a car and on the boot was a picture of Wee Willie Winkie." Sam shrugged his shoulders. "So I was called Wee Willie which I wasn't much impressed with, then Loz began calling me Sam Chick Bubbly Gum and the two together made Sam Willie." Sam began to realise that the truth seemed rather strange, in fact it sounded like Sam had gone potty, but the girl still looked interested, so he completed the story.

"Sam Willie soon became shortened to Sam." he held his arms out in joy of completion.

"How come Ian hasn't got a nick name, or is his real name Raymond?"

"Hmmm Raymond." thought Sam as he considered giving Ian a new name. "No it's his real name, nicknames have sort of died out now." he eventually admitted.

"That's a shame." frowned Jackie, "what do you think my name would have been?" Sam thought for a moment, several passed through his mind. "Nice" came instantly but he erased that and thought what others may have invented. "Giraffe" was a possibility and 'Toff' because she seemed on the rich side of working class to the boys. 'Leggy' was another but Sam knew Ian would have called her 'Tits'.

"Slim" said Sam unconvincingly.

A bell dinged to Sam's left and brought him out of his day-dream. Twenty yards away, Jackie emerged from the shop and stood at the roadside. Sam's sexuality had grown in the past year and was so weighty it had out grown him and showed like a shirt tail from the back of a small boy's jumper. He watched her look up and down the road, a pretty young thing she looked too. He watched her long legs cross the road and was just about to call her name when a bus pulled up in front of him to let off an elderly passenger and when it moved, she had gone.... forever.

This was Sam's luck, the only person in the world to have his future reshaped by the inaccurate timetable of a big blue bus!

"Who's farted?" asked Sam waving his left arm about wildly. He was sitting in a rather confined space, in the pitch dark, with wet clothes and trying to eat his sandwiches by a small light from a 'worse than useless' miners lamp that was attached to his oversize safety helmet. Several other people around him could be heard to gasp in the dark and eventually movement could be heard, as those people tried, in vain, to get as far away from the expanding aroma as they could. There was nowhere to go of course, as they were over 400 feet from the surface, down a pothole in the Derbyshire Peak District. Sam had been invited by his cousin, Chapper as he didn't want to go alone and Sam was always up for an adventure, although he wasn't sure that crawling through tiny passages and over broken rock, through neck deep water into tiny little caverns was exactly adventure. There was some compensation, however. Sam had seen some tiny fish that lived in the cold cave waters, fish that were colourless and blind. He was completely captivated by them. There was some discomfort, true but up until now it had been worth it until, that is, they had stopped for a rest and a bite to eat before setting off back to the surface and someone had broken wind, just as they were eating lunch. Disgusting, and Sam wanted to drown the heathen.

"Sorry everyone, it's not someone trumping, it's Lesley over here." explained the guide, though Sam considered afterwards that the girl called Lesley must have coloured up somewhat from embarrassment, as it seemed a very long pause until the guide put in a full explanation. "She has brought a hard boiled egg for lunch and as I mentioned earlier, as there are no smells down here, anything artificial smells much stronger than it really is."

"Well, it may not be a brown wind hurricane," thought Sam to himself "but it certainly smells like baked clay." The girl hurriedly replace the egg in its box and decided to just have a drink of water.

"This is a great time to be rid of something." whispered Chapper to Sam out of the corner of his mouth and almost immediately, Sam sensed another equally pungent nasal attack but this time it was probably methane, if the slight smile on Chapper's face was anything to go by. The addition of "I have been wanting to dump that for half an hour." in another whisper confirmed what Sam had thought.

"Well, shall we get on then." suggested the guide as the new stench reached his twitching nostrils. Everyone stood as the smell was thick in the small cavern but Sam pushed Chapper aside and said.

"I'll go in front of you I think."

Sam enjoyed the trip immensely but he didn't think it would be something he would take up, it wasn't claustrophobia or anything like that but he did love the sunlight, which was very welcome as they broke the surface. He also loved the open fields and the woodland, the bird song and the colour. It was true freedom and he thought of the blind, cave fish, cursed to live in the blank darkness of the cave. They knew nothing of the world around them, living in constant conditions with no seasons or knowing what a sea breeze is like, or the heat of a July afternoon. No, Sam liked life on the surface, even if it was now chucking it down with rain. Well, after all, the British summer can be like that but at least it wasn't as bland as living underground. On the bus trip back home, Sam thought more about it, he thought back to the previous winter, the February to be precise for he had spent some time underground then too.

The winter hadn't been so bad, there had been the usual cold but come the end of January, the weather was mild enough for children to venture back outdoors, the presents of the Yule season well and truly used. As February began, Sam strode out towards the Backs, passing the trolley leaning against the outside toilet, moss beginning to grow on its white tyres. He was pushing his bike, which he mounted and rode off towards the Tip. He met Weep, also on his bike in the bottom opening and they decided upon a jaunt down to the railway line but as they crossed the road to the other opening, they saw Vern coming from the direction of the Tip on foot.

"Hey up." announced Vern and the three engaged in conversation.

"What you up to?" asked Weep.

"Not much." replied Vern. "I remembered seein' some coal on the other Backs but it's gone now, I ought to 'ave known it wouldn't stay there long." Sam squinted.

"Coal? What do you want with coal?"

"You ain't 'eard then 'ave ya?" smiled the chubby lad.

"Heard what?" frowned Sam.

"There's gonna be a miners strike." he announced.

"So what?" enquired Sam. "You bought a steam engine?" he grinned.

"No, thicko." frowned Vern directly at Sam. This was an unusual reaction for Vern, he was hardly ever confrontational. "There's money in it if there's gonna be a miners strike." Sam thought for a moment, just enough time for him to register the word money.

"You mean selling it to people who are getting low on coal?" asked Sam. Vern just nodded, in a way that confirmed he still thought Sam was stupid. "Okay," began Sam. "so how do we go about this? Break into all the coal houses and cart the stuff off in a truck?" It was obvious by his expression he was not impressed by the idea.

"No." said Vern, shaking his head. "We just wait until the coal man delivers to the houses and then we pick up all the coal that drops off the truck, there's always loads of it." Vern was smiling now. Sam turned his back on Vern and walked off with his bike.

"What's up?" asked Vern, the smile now vanished, leaving a blank expression. Sam turned back and showed he was a little angry with Vern. The truth was, he had never seen the chubby lad in this mood before.

"You called me a thicko Vern, but your brilliant plan has several problems with it." Sam held up a single index finger. "One, if there is gonna be a miners strike, then there won't be any coal deliveries," Vern looked slightly deflated as Sam held up two fingers and continued. "an' two, everybody in the village is gonna be picking up every scrap of coal and wood they can find." Sam turned again and set off on his bike. Weep shook his head and followed Sam looking back at Vern with a sneaky grin.

"He's goin' crackers." suggested Weep, as he caught up.

"He's acting weird just lately." admitted Sam as he quickened his peddling. Certainly, Sam hadn't seen as much of Vern as he usually did and the lad had been a little strange but Sam had put that down to the battles that his parents had.

"Coal, phaa." spat Weep. "What is he on about?"

"He's potty Weep, even if there is a miners strike it won't last long, so nobody is gonna go paying good money for bits of coal. It would be different if we found tons of the stuff that nobody knew about." laughed Sam. "C'mon, let's go on the Tip." Sam and Weep rode across the road, up the Tip path and sat facing the houses of the village on the top edge of the grass covered shale tip. They sat chatting for some time until they heard voices. It was Barmy with Vern and Loz.

"What are you two up too?" asked Barmy. Weep became slightly uneasy at the sight of his elder brother, as he was usually on the receiving end of Barmy's jokes. Barmy was now at the age where the simple interests of the younger boys held no fun for him and the destructive edge of adolescence took over from the gentle roguishness.

"Not much." replied Sam in the time honoured way. Loz who was also slightly older sat at Sam's side, it was he who was ultimately responsible for Sam's name.

"Vern wants to be a coal man." he laughed prodding his thumb in Vern's general direction. "So we helped him." he laughed again. Sam looked at Vern who had obviously been in contact with some coal, as he was somewhat 'blackened' around the edges.

"They threw me in me grandad's coal house." scowled Vern.

"Well you said y' were after some coal, so we showed you were there was some." laughed Barmy.

"Idiots." whispered Vern under his breath, as he dusted himself down without success.

"What did you call me?" growled Barmy. Weep was up on his feet as if he could read his brothers mood, he certainly had the practice and Sam noticed him walk away a few yards.

"Nuthin'." replied Vern but it was too late, Barmy was intent on causing some kind of trouble.

"You called me an idiot you little shit." and he pushed Vern really hard so that he fell on Sam.

"Bloody hell Vern what's the matter with you?" cried out Sam, not seeing that Vern had been pushed onto him. Vern retaliated from the frustration and lashed out at Sam. Sam jumped to his feet and struck back at Vern as he regained his footing. The two boys began to fight properly as Barmy and Loz helped spur them on.

"Knock his teeth down his throat." called out Barmy as he circled the pair. Sam was doing fine, twice he caught Vern on the chin and Vern was feeling it, tears ran down his cheeks. Sam saw this and backed off, as he began to feel sorry for the lad, he had put more weight on recently and Sam knew he was being teased for it.

"Do you give in?" asked Sam with his fists in front of him. Vern nodded but Sam could see there was still fire in his eyes, whatever was going on in Vern's head was brewing up. Barmy saw the fight was about to stop, so he decided to add some fuel to the fire and pushed Sam at Vern. Sam's adrenaline caused him to try and spin around to face Barmy but he collided with Vern, the chubby lad wrestled Sam to the floor and sat on his back. He then began to beat Sam on his shoulders and his head but Sam couldn't get him off, as every time he tried to lift himself with Vern on top, Vern simply pummelled Sam's head until he dropped his arms to protect himself.

"Get off you fat pig." screamed Sam. In for a penny, in for a pound.

"Who gives in now? You Sam?" screamed back Vern, as he struck at Sam. Sam could feel the lumps and bruises forming already and he was beaten, he knew that. He was weak now and Vern was heavy.

"Okay, I give up." cried Sam. Vern hit Sam several times before he got up.

"I'm the best fighter and don't you forget it Sam." spat Vern. Sam was furious. He was hurting though and he just wanted to go home. He stood and dusted himself down, more as a gesture than a practicality and as he did, Vern continued with his chest beating. "It's not nice is it?" he growled. "You don't like having a taste of your own medicine do ya'?" Sam looked into Vern's red-faced gaze and as calmly as he could muster, he said.

"I have never hit you Vern, I have even protected you at times." Vern's face told the story, he knew that was true and Sam had simply been the punch bag for his frustrations. Sam could feel the pain of his injuries swelling with the bumps on his head. "See ya'" he concluded and turned to pick up his bike and mounted it..

"If you come back you'll get some more." called Vern, more from bravado at being on top for once, than anything else. Sam simply peddled away slowly and then turned and said.

"Next time Vern we'll be alone and you won't have your weight to help you."

"Piss off cry baby." shouted Vern.

"It's you who's got tears on your face Vern, not me." called Sam but he didn't turn this time and didn't know if Vern had heard him. That was it, the end of a close relationship that had lasted for many years. Sam and Vern, once like a television show comedy duo. Not any more.

Two weeks later and the miner's strike had hit hard, Vern's prophecy had come true and coal was worth its weight in gold, or so Sam thought, as the adults talked of nothing else. Sam and Tools walked down the railway line, its track lifted and the banks becoming overgrown and the realm of wildlife and young boys once more.

"We've only got two bags of coal left and then we can't have any fires." explained Sam.

"They said on the news that next week the power stations are going to switch the electricity off on certain days. They are running out of coal as well." replied Tools.

"Odd ain't it? All that coal in the earth and we can't get at it." smiled Sam.

"Why odd?" asked Tools.

"Well we could make some money if we could get at it."

"Oh yeah? So what are you planning now, dig a big pit?" laughed Tools. Sam was quiet for a moment.

"Do you think it could be done?" he eventually asked.

"No." was Tools' emphatic reply. "You would have to go too deep and the walls would fall in. It's not like building a den on the Tip like we used to." Sam thought back to the dens they used to have. They had lost their appeal and the boys were out growing the old games and pastimes.

"Well I know that, but they told us at school," began Sam. "that they first dug bell shaped mines that were quite small, that way the walls don't cave in."

"So you believe what you're told then?" grinned Tools.

"No," shrugged Sam. "but I know it's true 'cos I read it, we did a project on mining in history."

"Sounds like they are getting you ready for the pit then." There was a hint of irony in Tools voice.

"At our school?" laughed Sam. "You don't know it, they want us all to become bankers, it ain't gonna' happen' though. I reckon most of us will be in prison within three years of leaving, probably still in bank jobs though, if you know what I mean." Sam laughed to himself as he considered some of his school friends. "No, this project at school showed us how coal is mined, how it sits in seams under the ground. It's all at different levels you know." Sam looked at Tools who was pretending to yawn. "Okay, it's boring." Sam stopped and looked back from where they had just come. "It's odd to think how much coal has come down this railway through the years, and now it's closed."

"So you want to open your own pit then?" asked Tools walking to where Sam stood.

"Maybe, there's money in it."

"You better start digging your bell pit then 'cos it's dark in seven hours." laughed Tools. They continued walking for a mile or so, until they turned left at the quarry and decided to take the line towards Tibshelf Road, that would bring them to a landmark, known as 'Whistling Bridge'. It was reputed that if you stamped on the steel bridge from up where the road crossed it, you would hear the sound of a train whistle. Sam had jumped up and down on it many times, once like a demented rain dancer but all he had heard was the sound of his wheezing from the exertion. As they walked into the long cutting, the bridge loomed up in the distance.

"We better head off back, it's getting pretty cold out here." shivered Tools.

"Yeah, I hope the spring shows soon, it seems ages to wait for the warmer weather." admitted Sam.

"It's gonna' be a steady summer this year." remarked Tools.

"What do you mean?" asked Sam. Tools screwed up his features in a quick scowl.

"Well there's hardly anybody left round here now." Sam looked to the ground as he walked. He didn't reply, Tools was right, most of the boys had either become too old to be counted as a child, or even a young teenager and some had moved away, never to be seen again. As they closed on the Whistling Bridge, Tools bent down.

"Hang on, got a stone in me shoe." Sam sat on the bank of the cutting and broke off a stem of some frost ravaged horsetail grass. Tools removed his shoe and then sat at the side of Sam to examine it inside.

"How come, when you take off your shoe, there is nothing in there?" he asked as he peered inside and then banged it on a small rock.

"Well it runs off as you take your shoe off." laughed Sam.

"What a stone?" frowned Tools. Sam just shrugged and then looked up at the sky. Tools examined the interior of the shoe closely and explained. "Well I think that there must be a hole in the shoe, I keep getting sodding stones in there every ten minutes, does it happen to you?" Sam didn't answer. Tools began to untie the laces ready for a full examination and then replacement on his foot. Sam glanced down the cutting looking at the brown grass of winter and the bare trees, thinking back many years, to a time when he first ventured onto the railway. It was an outing with older boys, including Chapper and Spider, his cousins, Socky and Erky. Not far from this very spot, down at the next bridge, they had all reclined on the banking, listening to Spider's Bush radio and Mary Hopkins 'Those Were the Days' had been playing. It was a new song and the boys had stop to listen to it. He remembered how hot the summer sun had been and how much fun they had all had that day. It seemed a lifetime away, sitting here in this cold cutting, wondering what to do next.

"Okay, all sorted." announced Tools. There was no reaction, so Tools looked towards Sam to see him frowning, looking towards the opposite bank of the cutting. Tools followed his gaze but saw nothing.

"What's up with you?" he asked and then replaced his shoe.

"What's that up there?" asked Sam, still frowning. He was pointing up the other bank.

"Grass, trees, earth, shale, some weeds, that's all I can see." was the bored reply. Sam stood and walked over to the other bank. Tools remained seated, he didn't think it was worth the effort for a closer examination of things that he had no interest in. Sam stood at the base of the cutting and looked up, he then climbed up to where the shale was, about twenty feet up. Sam bent down and seemed to be scraping at the ground, having to hold securely to a small bush to prevent himself sliding back down the steep slope. Tools heard Sam laugh.

"What you found?" called Tools.

"Bloody hell." he heard Sam say. Tools walked over but as he stood at the base of the slope, Sam turned and called down. "Coal, I've found coal."

"Congratulations, you're an observant person, now let's go home." Sam slid down the slope and revealed a large black lump.

"What do you think?" asked Sam with a broad grin.

"It's coal, so what? We have gas fires and I'm not an expert. You aren't going to make your fortune with a few lumps of coal anyway." He dropped the lump. Sam quickly picked it up again.

"You're right but if I am not mistaken, that coal up there," Sam turned and pointed up the slope. "is a seam that was exposed when this cutting was first cut. There could be tons of the stuff." Sam thrust the coal into his pocket.

"So what are you going to do with that?" asked Tools pointing to Sam's pocket.

"Take it home and see how it burns. Come on." Sam turned and began a brisk walk. He turned back as he continued. "If it burns well, I'm coming back here with my trolley."

The following Saturday, Sam stood on the Backs with his very surprised trolley, the vehicle had considered that it was in retirement, just waiting for time to take its toll and rot all the wood. To find itself with a useful role to play again was quite a shock. It carried some sacks, a shovel and a wrapped up cheese sandwich with a bottle of pop. Sam was waiting for his fellow prospectors, Ian and Tools. Sam had insisted on total security, this was a special mission and he didn't want prying eyes anywhere near it. Down the Backs, he saw Ian appear and wave, he seemed to be dragging something behind him, that was good, Sam had suggested the equipment they would need, spades, shovels, a pick, sacks and most of all, transport. As Ian came closer, it seemed he was towing a small four-wheeled flat wagon, the sort that was usually seen fixed behind a toy pedal-type tractor. Ian had fastened some rope to the point where it would normally be fixed to the tractor. It wasn't big but it was better than carrying the stuff.

"Mornin'" announced Ian as he arrived.

"What you got there?" asked Sam.

"It's a little trailer that I saw some time ago, I was going to make it into a trolley but I reckon the wheels are too small." frowned Ian looking at the vehicle.

"I mean on top of it." pointed Sam.

"Oh that? Well you said we needed some tools, so I brought this pick."

"Who told you it was a pick?" asked Sam sitting briefly on his trolley.

"Er, well..." Ian had a look of doubt on his face. "Er nobody told me, I just thought that I didn't know what a pick looked like and so, as I didn't know what this was and it was in the tool shed, I thought it must be a pick." explained Ian.

"Well my dear Watson, you have a strange way of putting two and two together and what you have there is a hoe, and completely useless for the job at hand." explained Sam in his best, if not convincing Holmes voice.

"Oh." exclaimed Ian.

"No hoe." smiled Sam in a rare fit of 'H' usage.

"So what do you use a," there was a brief moment as Ian conjured up one of those letters of the alphabet he never used and spoke it with a certain reverence. "*hoe* for then?"

"Hoeing of course my dear Watson, now let us be away." grinned Sam.

"Aren't we waiting for Tools?" asked Ian checking his towing rope was secure.

"Nope, he's seeing us there as he lives closer than us." explained Sam taking a quick swig of pop and then starting off with his trusty trolley. The trolley still wasn't quite ready for the outing. For some time now, trolleys had become a little, 'Olde Worlde' and due to the fact that it was still winter, the poor old trolley was not quite awake from its hibernation and though eager to serve, sort of staggered about a bit as first. Ian's little wagon though was wide awake and ready for battle, its tiny wheels making neat little tracks in the dirt on the Backs, Sam's trolley was a little embarrassed.

"Where exactly are we going, or is it still a secret?" asked Ian as they walked down the Tip path.

"Whistling Bridge." announced Sam.

"So," Ian was struggling with Sam's previous explanation. There was a pause. "So," he repeated. " there is coal at Whistling bridge?"

"Yep." was Sam's succinct answer. Now Ian was a clever lad and he knew damn well that they weren't carrying shovels and hoes so that they could tend a flower bed around Whistling Bridge.

"An' we're gonna dig it up?"

"Sort of." replied Sam. Ian looked at Sam, he had that smile that Sam always sported when an idea had really come together. Ian also looked down at Sam's trolley. There were bits of wood, nails and a large but old looking hammer, it all looked very business-like and Ian considered that Sam must know what he was doing. Probably.

It was quite a way to the cutting near the bridge and they didn't take the most direct route. The main road would take them there more quickly and easier but Sam was insistent that they take the long route. Tools was waiting, he had come on his old pushbike, a machine that was in even more shock than Sam's trolley. Typically of Tools, he had come up with some sort of invention, he had constructed a kind of 'pannier' over his bike seat that had two wooden cross beams that looked like they were made to hold small sacks. The three lads greeted each other and got down to business. They dragged the trolley up the bank of the cutting and secured it at the top, then Sam looked for where the coal was most prominent.

"We'll dig here." he announced and began explaining that most of the spoil would have to be taken up the bank and hidden, just in case anyone noticed the excavation. Sam also decided to use some of the wood as a temporary barrier to prevent the spoil and coal sliding down the bank and giving away its presence. They had soon scraped away enough coal to fill the bags they had and carefully lowered them down the slope to fill the two trolleys and Tools bike. All loaded, Tools carefully pushed his bike up onto the bridge with help from the other two and then innocently rode off to Sam's house. Sam and Ian would have to make the long journey back along the railway line. On the journey back to the coal seam the following day, Ian's little trailer gave up the ghost, as the journey over the rough ground loaded with coal had simply destroyed it, Sam's trolley was coping easily and looked quite smug as the little one gave up its fight to be useful. Ian then found an old wheel barrow but Sam was worried that a boy with a wheel barrow would cause some interest from prying eyes and so they abandoned that idea and instead made a two wheel wooden trailer to fit on the rear of the trolley and then fitted two tow ropes to the front of the vehicle. It worked a treat and a large load could be brought back from the mine. They even fetched coal after school, the dark wasn't a problem either as it was dark in the mine and night time also covered their evening perambulations from prying eyes. Several days later the coalhouse was becoming quite full and customers were found for the miracle coal. With money in their pockets the boys put vigour into their work and the mine was changing shape.

"So what are we going to do now?" asked Ian. The three of them had cut so deep into the bank that the roof was looking unsteady. They had cut a hole two feet wide by two feet tall that sloped gently back, following the seam of coal but now it went back about five feet. They had kept the entrance small so that the camouflaged door they had made concealed the entrance.

"We will have to put props in there so it doesn't fall on us." admitted Sam. That would cause a problem as they would require wood, and wood - like coal burned, so - it had been and was hard to find. It was something that Sam would have to work on, for now the hard business of cutting coal had to be undertaken. As Ian and Tools continued with the mining, Sam went to have a look for anything that could be used to shore up the roof of the mine. Tools had repaired the old trailer that Ian had provided and it was used to move the bags of coal from the 'coal face' to the entrance. The bags were then stored just inside the entrance until it was time to leave. At the weekends, if they started early, they could make two trips. The work continued over the next week and Weep was brought in to help, it meant sharing four ways but the extra coal output seemed worth it as people were paying good money for the seemingly endless stream of coal. Sam's parents were customers but were not allowed to take coal from their own coalhouse, Sam would fetch their ration for them, which was a very new development for Sam, fetching in the coal.

The back of the mine was nearly ten feet deep and it was becoming too dark to work in there, so Sam suggested they would have to either start with a new mine or dig chambers off the sides. As the latter option seemed a little dangerous, they considered a new mine, this would need more wood, which was becoming a real problem.

"What if we take the wood from the old mine, from the back and work forward?" Suggested Tools. Sam shook his head.

"If it falls in, it would be easy to spot from the bottom of the bank."

"There can't be many people come down here anyway, we haven't seen many." insisted Tools.

"I don't want people to know what we're doing, if loads of folks come to dig coal, it will force down the price of our coal and anyone will be able to come and get their own." frowned Sam. Tools could see how the whole thing could develop into chaos if too many people mined there, he agreed, they would have to think of something else. A new idea was to beg, borrow or even steal hurricane lamps so that they could start a new chamber off to the left, about five feet in, that would run along the line of the bank. One rainy day, Sam sat just inside the entrance, waiting for Weep to fill the second bag. Tools, was working in the new left tunnel that was now about three feet deep. Ian was just behind Sam passing back anything Tools could dig out.

"What was that?" said Ian.

"What was what?" asked Sam looking back.

"I thought I heard something." All of them went quiet. It was silent in the tunnel, only Sam could hear the cold rain dropping at the tunnel entrance. Sam broke the silence.

"What did it sound like?"

"Dunno." shrugged Ian. "Sort of like a crack." Sam's mind darted around for a moment. There was something he once read but he couldn't find which mental drawer he had filed the information in. In the gloom, Tools' eyes beamed back inquiringly.

"Shall we get out?" he asked.

"Yes we better had." nodded Sam. They pulled out the coal they had and covered the entrance.

"The rain will probably cave it all in." Frowned Sam, quite used to the profits they were making.

"We'll know by tomorrow." sighed Tools. The four of them walked home with their small cache of coal and waited for the inevitable.

The following day was marred by more heavy rain, so the mining team stayed at home and decided to wait until the weekend to check on the mine. That Saturday was clear and bright but very cold. Sam and his friends took their equipment and set off to the mine and much to their surprise it was still intact with just a little roof fall several feet in. They used what little wood they had been able to find and began repairs immediately. Sam crawled down to the fall and Tools passed him the wood. Ian and Weep got the bags ready and hid the transport at the top of the bank. Within the hour, coal production had begun in earnest. Sam was cutting the coal on the left tunnel with a hammer and chisel and Weep was at the end of the long tunnel working with hurricane lamps and a metal spike. Tools was pulling the sacks of coal out and Ian was stacking them neatly just inside the entrance.

"Did you see that film last night?" asked Tools to anyone who could hear.

"The one about the prisoner of war camp on the tele?" called back Weep from the gloom.

"Yeah, it made me laugh a bit."

"I didn't see it." called out Sam. " What was so funny about a prisoner of war film?" They had to stop working to hear as there were fifteen or so feet around a ninety degree bend from one coal face to the other. Tools took up the story so all could hear.

"Well, they had tried loads of ways to escape but they came up with a plan to dig a tunnel out." Tools paused for a moment, to be sure they had all heard. "But instead of one tunnel, they dug three, and only one was going to be used."

"So what was funny about that?" called out Sam.

"Well, nothin' I 'spose but they showed them in the tunnel an' it looked just like this." There was a little humour in Tools' voice. "Even down to the little trolley and the fact they were short of wood."

"Yeah but they had 'lecric lights." came Weep's voice, from the long tunnel. "Instead o' these stupid stinkin' lamps."

"So why did they have three tunnels then, surely that would take more building and need extra wood?" asked Sam as he made himself comfortable.

"So if the Germans found one tunnel, they would think that it was the only one and wouldn't go looking for another." announced Tools.

"Maybe we should do that." added Ian.

"Not bloody likely." began Tools. "We haven't got enough wood for this one never mind two others."

"We're not trying to escape Germany anyway, we're just trying to stop anyone knowing about this coal." insisted Sam.

"How much have we sold this week?" asked Ian.

"Tools has sold two full sacks to someone on his street and the stuff we have left is sold to my mother's neighbour, so we are selling everything we can mine." called Sam. Tools turned to Ian and added.

"There should be another fiver each at the end of the week." Ian whistled and Weep was heard to cheer, to the younger boys this was unheard of wealth. They were making many more times what they were getting pocket money but if they had considered the hours they were spending to get that money, they probably wouldn't have been so euphoric, but then again, they were doing it themselves. True, some people had accused them of stealing it from coalhouses but as they always explained, there was no coal in other peoples' coalhouses. The doubt stayed in peoples' minds though and when asked, the boys would not say where they got the coal, so it made people doubly suspicious. Several people had even tried to follow them as if they were just going for a walk but the boys always spotted this and split up. They could only follow one and whoever that was to be, the lad would just walk them around in circles. Weep was once the one who was followed, by a stupid man who, once seeing the boys split up, strangely decided to follow the one who didn't have a trolley - Weep. Weep walked down to Peggy's Brook and then along the brook itself. Once he reached the quarry, he entered the little drainage tunnel and waited for a while, as he doubted the man would follow into the long, low tunnel. He was correct and Weep climbed out the way he entered after a few minutes and then climbed into a nearby tree to amuse himself, watching the man looking first in one end of the tunnel, and then walking around to the other end. He was then seen to scratch his head and when Weep told Sam about it, he laughed for quite some time, remembering the plot line of an old Will Hay film called 'Oh Mister Porter' where a train seemingly entered a tunnel, only to apparently disappear within it. Sam was adamant that no one should know of the coal mine, as they would not be able to protect it once it was discovered.

The thought of the extra five pounds sent them back to a frenzy of work and the coal continued to come out but the wood had now completely run out. Sam had dug as much as he could and he crawled into the main tunnel.

"Is it my turn?" asked Tools.

"No." replied Sam wiping his sweating forehead. We can't take anymore out of there without wood, it's already crumbling away." Sam stared down the main tunnel, it seemed Weep had covered some ground and was quite a way down, his meagre light casting odd shadows on the shining coal. "How you doing down there Weep? Still got some wood left?" called Sam.

"No, I ran out ages ago." he replied.

"Come out of there then, don't wait for it to cave in." insisted Sam. There was no reply but he and Tools could see by his lamp, he was coming out. The three met at the junction of the left tunnel and took their breath.

"Well that's it then. Without any wood we can't carry on digging." sighed Sam.

"Can't we just scrape the stuff from the bank, it would be easier." asked Weep.

"No," replied Sam shaking his head. "once people see there is coal here, you won't be able to sell it 'cos everybody will help themselves."

"But if we can't dig anymore, we might as well take it from the edge 'cos we can't sell it if we can't dig it." Sam understood Weeps frustration but as he said.

"We can dig as we find more stuff to prop the roof up." They sat for a moment and contemplated any other options. It wasn't long before Ian was heard to hiss.

"Someone's coming." It happened on occasions that people passed, walking a dog or just having a stroll and every time it was the same, they stopped working and whoever was at the entrance kept a look out. If the tunnel was spotted, they pretended they were building a den. Tools and Sam probably looked a little old for such a pastime but the ruse had worked.

"Hello." called out Ian as he looked out of the entrance. Ian turned inwards and whispered. "He's seen me."

"Don't worry," whispered back Sam as he moved closer to Ian. "Just pretend it's your den as we always do." Ian climbed out of the den and sat casually on the bank.

"We built a den here mister, we always build dens." said Ian. Sam and the others couldn't quite hear what the man said back but it seemed like he had said the word coal. Sam panicked and climbed to the edge of the mine.

"Oh hello, how many of you are there in that hole?" asked the man.

"Just us." replied Sam trying to keep back into the shadows, so the man wouldn't see the dust on his face.

"I was just saying to your friend here, that looks like coal in the bank." The man was climbing up and Sam was stuck for ideas. "It is, it's coal." The man began to laugh. "Well, bugger me, you've built your den in a coal seam, fancy that. All the country is scratting around for a few lumps of coal and here you two are playing in the stuff." The man had reached just below the entrance and Sam tried to make himself as big as he could, so the man couldn't see past him. The chap tried but gave in, then, Sam noticed a change in his features, the broad smile had moved on and a look of inquisitiveness came over him. He sniffed.

"I thought so." he said trying once more to see into the hole. "You've got paraffin lamps in there, I can smell the fumes."

"It must be the smell of the coal." smiled Sam. The man raised his eyebrows and stared at Sam with a look of disbelief.

"I'm a miner son, on strike at the moment and there's two things I know more than anything. One is the smell of coal and t'other is the smell of a paraffin lamp." The man held his stare on Sam. "We use them down

229

the mine y' see." Sam stayed silent and blank faced. "An' if you need a lamp, it must be dark in there. An' if it's dark in there it must be deep." The man smiled a little. "It's not a den is it?" Sam sighed, he had done his best but they were found out. He shook his head and climbed out. The man moved up and peered inside.

"Bloody 'ell there's two more o' them in 'ere." The man stood but nearly over balanced and slipped down the bank a little, Sam and Ian helped hold him upright. Tools and Weep came out of the hole and the man squeezed his upper body into the mine. He was quite large and would not have been able to turn in there, even if he could have got in but he was in, just enough for the boys not to be able to hear what he was saying. He withdrew and knelt at the edge.

"Well chaps," he said to the boys. " you lads could dig a bloody tunnel to the moon. That's a fine piece of tunnelling, no, a fine piece of mining you have done there." Ian and Weep beamed at the praise but Tools and Sam knew the gravy train had come off the rails and tipped its load on the tablecloth. "Yes it's a fine bit of engineering, if I say so myself. Natural miners the lot of you, but you need to get that back roof shored up, it'll come down if yer don't."

"We've run out of wood, we've nuthin' to prop it up with." explained Weep still proud of his work. Sam just looked at the floor dejected.

"Mmm," cooed the man with his hand on his chin as if he was thinking something over. "You have got the process right but if I was you, instead of going back, turn left and right at the back face and then after three or four feet turn again towards the entrance."

"We have done, well on one side at least." pointed out Tools.

"But why head back?" asked Sam. The man drew a small diagram in the dirt.

"'Cos if you rip round in a square you will leave a post of coal in, which will help support the roof and you'll need less wood." The man glanced inside. "An' it would be less dangerous, y' shouldn't bloody well be in there anyway." He looked back and smiled. "You selling it then?" Sam just nodded. The man looked in and shook his head then carefully stood. "I should report you lot to the union y' know. Technically you're scabs."

"What?" asked Weep a little indignant.

"Scabs Weep, anybody working during the strike is a scab." explained Tools.

"We ain't scabs mister, we ain't in the union so we can't be." explained Sam. The man nodded and once again he smiled. He carefully made his way down the bank and when he was at the bottom, he looked up and said.

"We better make you members then, that way you'll have to stop mining." He looked back down the line and then said. "Good day." then he walked off whistling to himself.

"That's buggered that then." said Weep as he slumped to his backside.

"Hmph, it won't stop me." shrugged Sam. He picked up the coal sack, they loaded up what they had and went home.

The following day, Sam was back at the mine and as he opened up the door, inside he found wood, lots of it. It seemed the man must have brought it and pushed it inside. Weep wasn't with them that day and so the work progressed slowly but they took the advice the miner had given them and it proved to be sound. They cut far more coal without using so much wood but as the power cuts became more serious, people went to extra lengths to know where the coal was coming from that the boys seemed to be able to produce at will. The outcome was that a better 'shadow' watched where they went and as they were loading up, two older boys from just out of the village, came walking past and the game was up. The following day, there were six people on the bank mining but now without trying to hide what they were about. Sam's team kept up a steady turnover but by the end of that week, there were almost two dozen people, most of them adults digging coal out of the bank. It was obvious that it was over when, as the boys arrived one morning to continue work, three men had taken over their mine and were digging into it from the top.

"Hey that's ours." called out Sam to the men.

"Bugger off you little toadies." was the only reply they got. Sam turned as quick as he could, for he considered they might take his trolley too. The three of them walked back home dejected and gave up their mining careers. Sam and Tools returned to the bridge but by way of the road and watched the proceedings from the roadside. Everyday, more and more people arrived to take coal from the bank. Sam decided it was a great pity but to be pragmatic about it and revel in the fact that they were all a little wealthier. A few days later Sam's mother came running up to Sam on the Backs.

"You know when you said you were getting the coal from Whistling Bridge?" Sam nodded, he had explained the whole thing to his parents now the secret was out. "Well, there has been fighting and the police have been called out. It's chaos." Sam ran down the path and jumped on his bike and pedalled as fast as he could all the way up to the bridge. Sure enough, there were police vans and police cars, even the television news people. Sam pushed through the crowd and over the bridge into the field opposite the bank, from there he could see all the commotion and someone being interviewed by the television people.

"What happened?" asked Sam to another lad he didn't know.

"Some of the men set about each other 'cos they thought somebody had been nickin' their coal." Sam tutted like he had heard adults do. "It turned into a pitched battle accordin' to somebody over there and they called the police." The lad explaining didn't take his gaze from the scene in the cutting as he continued. "They had to set dogs on 'em and some 'ave been taken to prison." Sam looked down into the cutting where police and police dogs could still be seen as well as a few people showing signs of blood. There were ambulances on the bridge too. Sam's mine had all but vanished, the bank almost destroyed by random over digging. Sam walked back to the bridge as the crowd eventually cleared, he leaned on the fence at the side of the metal bridge and wondered how much money they could have made if no one had found the coal seam.

"Where's your mates?" asked a voice at the side of Sam. It was the miner who had discovered their hole.

"Dunno." shrugged Sam.

"Someone must have seen you then?" asked the man looking into the cutting, as he too leaned on the fence.

"Yeah, someone followed us but if they had done the same as us, we could have all had plenty of coal, there were loads of the stuff down there." explained Sam.

"That's greed my lad, people don't want to share, they want it all." replied the man.

"Daft though innit'? Now nobody can have it." sighed Sam.

"Yep, that's how this world works. None of them miners I might add, your miner has some integrity, a miner would have worked with his mates to cut coal for everyone."

"Except he would be a scab." smiled Sam to the man.

"Not if he didn't get paid for it, if it were for the greater good an' all that."

"Oh thanks for the wood by the way." put in Sam. "We did what you said an' it worked."

"I didn't want the whole bloody lot coming down on you." Sam noticed the man fiddling with something on his jacket lapel. "Did you make much money then?" he turned to Sam with a blank face.

"Yeah, a bit." grinned the lad and then he reached for his bike and turned it round. "Thanks anyway." repeated Sam.

"I don't suppose you'll be digging anymore coal then?" the miner asked still staring into the cutting.

"Not unless I can find another railway cutting with a seam running along it." Sam mounted the bike and found the right side pedal. The man turned and walked towards him.

232

"Don't worry, the strike will be over by next week." He held out his fist with the fingers clenched and facing down. "You can't now anyway." he said nodding towards his hand. Sam carefully placed his hand under the man's and as he opened his fist, a small metallic object fell into Sam's palm. Sam turned it in his hand, it was a small enamel badge. It had a small image of colliery headstocks and said "NUM, North Derbyshire Branch." "You're in the union now, you're a miner." Sam looked at the man and back at the badge. With a broad smile, Sam pinned the badge onto his coat and pressed down the pedal and set off home on his bike. Before he was six feet away, he turned back and called.

"Okay, no more mining, and thanks again."

"Tools is here!" insisted Sam's mother, as she polished the sideboard. Sam continued prodding the screwdriver at the remains of what was once a model locomotive. Sam had found out quite early that he had the need to take everything to bits to see how it worked but he always found that in the mean time, someone had replaced all those bits and bobs with items that wouldn't fit, so he couldn't put it back together. Neither did he find out how it worked. Sam's mother left the sideboard to open the door for Tools.

"Come in me duck, I think he's gone deaf." Tools toddled over to Sam in the front room.

"Hey up. There's caterpillars down't line"

"Yeah I know, tiger moths, hawks." Sam didn't look up from the table.

"No not butterfly and moths, ... caterpillars, ... big yellow caterpillars with engines." interrupted Tools. Sam had seen some pretty big hawk moth caterpillars but none had engines!

"What are you on about?" asked Sam, looking up from his attempt at replacing a curly bit of brass with a 'thingy' on the top.

"Down the line ... loads of 'em! Caterpillars and bulldozers" replied Tools. Now Sam knew what he meant, earth movers. Most boys called any large yellow painted earth-moving vehicle, a caterpillar due to a local company of that name supplying the machinery.

"What they doing?" asked Sam.

"I'm not sure, I think they've come to dismantle the railway, to take the banks down and that."

"Come on." nodded Sam "let's go and see." The two boys walked the half-mile or so to the railway and immediately saw the half dozen earthmovers, grinding and scraping at the railway bank. To the left, in a field besides the Tip, sat most of the other boys, watching the proceedings. Tools and Sam joined them. There was too much noise to hear what Weep was saying to them but it was obvious everyone was excited by the display. They all sat for at least an hour, watching the lush green railway embankment being eaten away by these monsters. As the soil and ash banks turned into clay and mud, the whole area became a lunar landscape, the smell of turned earth drifting towards them. The boys retired to the relative quiet of the Tip. What excitement to see these noisy dinosaurs rumbling up and down eroding away the landscape. Sam noticed a hare running from the bank and he pointed to it. Once Sam would have clapped his hands to make the hare run faster, a wonderful sight - a hare flat out but the animal had lost his home now and he was running for his life.

Day by day, more of the railway bank disappeared, until one morning, late in a certain summer, Weep and Sam noticed a bulldozer on the Tip. They ran to investigate but as they reached the top, they heard the roar of another machine coming along the other way, they were pulling down the Tip! No they couldn't be. Sam wanted to explain to them that the railway was down there, this was their Tip, *they* almost owned it.

The earth mover passed within feet of the boys but all they saw was the horrible mess where the football pitch once stood. Soon, the only things left intact were the bushes where the boys spent so much of their time. It was obvious these would also soon be gone. Slowly they walked away from the Tip.

"What can we do?" asked Weep but Sam remained silent. "It's not fair, we can't let them do it, the Tip is ours, it always has been!"

"We will have to raid, after the drivers have gone." replied Sam, not exactly sure what he meant. All the boys were mustered that could be found and later that evening, they set off towards the quarry where the vehicles parked and they did their worst. True, the next day the earth movers rolled past without a single piece of glass in their cabs, but they rolled past just the same.

A few days later, the boys tried to set fire to the machines and had their first lesson in 'flash points in combustible materials'. Diesel oil doesn't burn easily and neither does metal. They bowed to the inevitable conclusion that there was nothing they could do, their playground and their countryside would slowly be torn apart.

Eventually the Tip was levelled, the railway had gone and the general landscape looked like a flat, grey plate of cold rice pudding, the boys developed a sickness. It was called 'nowhere to play syndrome'. They would play nearer home on the streets and on the Backs, which, to the adults in the village, was a new and not altogether welcome development.

"Why don't you bugger off and play somewhere else?" was the usual greeting they received. Gladly they would 'bugger off' to the Tip, the Quarry, the Wood or the railway line if the stupid adults hadn't destroyed those lovely places that teemed with wildlife and possibilities. It soon became a war. The more the boys were moved on, the more they began to resist. It was a stealing of their liberties and they were not going to stand for it. The boys played more and more pranks on the adults, until it became difficult to think of new ones. So they used old ones, which was boring, so they stopped.

That year, as the summer grew old, Sam found that all the places they used to play were destroyed or fenced off, waiting to be ripped apart and he found the only way to get away from it all was to ride his bike, but a bike can only be ridden for so long and the problem of boredom reared its ugly head once more. To rub salt into the wounds, the earthmovers had moved on to the beautiful Wolfie, that large pond to the north. There really was nowhere to play now. As expected, at the back end of the holidays, scrumping had developed into the only exciting pastime in the village, which meant that there was hardly a piece of fruit reached its owner's mouth that year.

The war came to an impasse at the end of the summer, both sides taking casualties but neither making ground. One of the casualties that the boys received, was Tools. He was now the oldest of the team remaining, but was starting work and less was seen of him. Time had played tricks once more, Sam was now the elder of the team. Being the 'oldest boy' is a mighty weight to bear, especially in these hard times. Sam decided to confide in his two lieutenants, Weep and Ian. They strolled along the old Tip path, which was much shorter than it used to be and now didn't go anywhere except to a large industrial grade metal fence.

"Tools will be at work in the holidays now!" said Sam grimly peering through the mesh.

"Yeah. 'spose that's the last we'll see o' him." admitted Weep.

"Yeah, I don't like this growin' up stuff!" said Sam as he kicked at an innocent stone. "It's like poison, I hate it!" Ian said little, for being a little younger, he wasn't sure what they were on about, he couldn't remember the 'good old days' or the all the old mates that had long since grown up, and been abducted from the planet by an alien called marriage.

"I s'pose it'll happen to us one day?" questioned Weep. Sam glared at him, even if he did realise that he was probably next himself.

"Don't talk like that! It's not over yet, I don't want it to end yet."
Sam looked across to the place where the old Tip path reached the Big Tree, long since cut down, its stump almost covered by grass, a pitiful sight to those who remembered it as a large and imposing life form. Sam pointed to it.

"I grew up with that tree." Sam felt real sadness. Weep couldn't stand it, he turned and headed for home.

"See ya." he said.

"See ya." was the sympathetic reply. Sam and Ian turned right and walked along a new path that was once the railway line but had been ripped up and flattened, then a red shale path had been laid. The path was so featureless that small saplings had been planted along its length.

"Look, they've planted trees!" pointed Ian.

"Yeah." laughed Sam, "It will be all right here in fifty years!" Ian didn't laugh, he felt the anger in Sam. They walked on through the pitiful twigs that sprouted here and there, protected by green plastic covers. Sam leaned on the new fence that bordered the area and watched a man walking a small dog towards them.

236

"All right lads?" he said as he stopped to look over the view. Sam shrugged and said nothing. Ian thrust his hands into his pockets and stubbed the toe of his shoe into the shale.

"Cat got your tongues? Hey?" quipped the man but Sam remained silent and hoped the man would carry on. The man was visibly uncomfortable with the silence, so he talked to the dog.

"Be nice here Toby when they've finished it." he tugged lightly on the lead to let the dog know he had been engaged in conversation. Sam felt anger welling up.

"Doesn't say much your dog does he?" he said in monotones.

"He's not the only bloody one is he?" replied the man and he started to move off but Sam felt an inner presence.

"Is it the first time you have been down here then mister?" The man stopped and considered he may have got off on the wrong foot with the young lads.

"Er, no I have been down here quite a few times, more so now they are laying this nice path." He looked down at the dog and said. "It's better now in't it Toby?"

"How do you make that out then?" asked Sam, still in a flat tone.

"Well, it's," there was a slight hesitation. " it's nice that they are leaving a path, somewhere to walk y' know. Nice." he pulled the lead again as if asking the dog to comment.

"Nice." Sam shook his head and smiled, then looked at the mess that had been left.

"So, y' don't like it then?" asked the man cautiously.

"Like it?" glared Sam. His love of language and words was always used for effect but for the first time, passion and anger brought them out. "How can anyone but an imbecile *like* this wanton act of destruction." Ian was amazed, he had never heard Sam speak like this before, but Sam hadn't finished. "How anyone can sanction the wholesale destruction of this natural habitat, cut down trees, hundreds of years old, to plant pathetic little saplings, fill in ponds and quarries to leave flat farmland I really can't imagine. It's probably someone who has never been to look at this place, that sits in an office looking at a map and decides he needs to justify his boring life, so that he has a reason to live, so that he can go home and walk his stupid dog down a stupid little path, with no features and no wildlife." It wasn't just Ian who was surprised, Sam was astounded at what he could do when pressed. Even the little dog was impressed as he was pulled along by the man, telling him what, 'the trouble with young people today' was.

"Everything has to change." called back the man, as he hurried along.

"Change my arse." spat Sam quietly. Ian left it a few minutes before asking.

"Will you change? Become adult I mean."

"Everyone seems to, it's hard to believe that some people have ever been children though." He looked over to the little man and his dog then shook his head contemptuously. "I don't know, I think I might not but there's nothing to be young for anymore." He looked around at his 'Kingdom'. Sam's Kingdom.

"I won't!" said Ian. "No one can make me, so I won't!" Sam felt that Ian meant it, he smiled and said.

"Okay, we will not change and to prove it, we'll meet here in fifty years to see these trees, to see if there's somewhere to play, if there is, we'll run between them and shout and roll in the grass."

"Yeah and play Robin Hood or Cavalry and Indians or the like!"

"Come on." said Sam and the two boys ran towards home with Colt 45's shooting at each other as they ran, even though Sam felt far too old to be doing it now.

They wanted to protest, they wanted to complain, they wanted to change the situation but it was hard, for they were still children in adults eyes, second class citizens.

As the summer holidays came to a close and the school term began again, the whole war came to a head. Weep and a couple of other boys were riding their bikes down the Backs when old man Clark jumped out and pulled Weep from his bike. Weep wasn't badly hurt but the man picked up his bike and threw it over the fence.

"Oi you silly old fart!" exclaimed Weep as he stood up.

"Don't you talk to me like that, you cheeky little shit!" screamed the man as he approached Weep. Weep backed away but the old man grabbed his collar and threw him to the floor. Weep squirmed away and at a safe distance, bombarded the old man with a barrage of profanities and abuse, well practiced by his older brother, Barmy. The incident was over, but it started a battle that raged for a month, for every boy who heard of this man who believed he owned the Backs, continued to ride their bikes down them. It wasn't new, 'Clarky', was universally disliked by children and adults alike but the difference was the boys had nowhere to play now. The final attack came when Weep, Sam and Rob Marsh were casually riding down the Backs, past the house where the old man lived. The man came out and stopped them.

"Clear off you little bastards, you're not supposed to be on here!"

"It's an access road mister, anyone can use it." replied Sam, in his best 'matter of fact' voice. The man exploded and stepped towards Sam, who felt a little more than uncomfortable, like a cornered rat. Sam blurted out,

"Don't touch me you old git!" It had no effect on the man, who pulled at Sam's bike, but Sam stayed fixed to it.

"Watch him Sam, he's bloody potty!" called Weep. It drew the man's attention and he targeted Weep instead.

"Sod this!" shouted Rob as he fled. The man drew back his hand and let fly at Weep. The blow shook Weep from his bike but this time, he remained standing. Weep was growing stronger than the crying banshee Sam had first met, which now seemed an age ago. The man drew back for another blow but fear and youth joined together in Weep, he punched the man on the cheek. For a moment, the man stopped then shouted,

"Bastard!" and ran at Weep. Sam leapt from his bike and separated the two, throwing the man to the ground. The man realising he was beaten, began to rant and rave. "Bloody vandals! I fought the war for the likes of you, bloody bastards. I'll make sure you get put into a home I will, I swear it!" Sam was afraid, not from the threat but from the crossing of an invisible boundary that could have far reaching repercussions, but the adrenaline pulsed through his veins and he wallowed in victory for the time being.

"You leave the kids alone from now on or you'll get some more!" The boys climbed back onto their bikes and rode off, unsure of the situation. Sam knew this was a turning point but he didn't know quite in what way. He told his parents of the incident, which though they took it very well, they told him that he was wrong and should have just left. However, they were pleased he had told them as the man was well known for stirring up trouble. Now they were 'vandals' and 'criminals', young thugs, who beat up pensioners. No matter who was right or wrong, the damage was done and there was no turning the clock back. Sam's childhood shook free from his body and rose up like a spectral warrior and flew off to a children's Valhalla. His childhood had ended!

If society couldn't let him be a child, then he would be an adult and woe-betide the human race for that decision.

Sam's period of quiet sulking lasted only for a week but it was a week spent in his room, seeing no one. When he emerged from his hibernation, he was like an ugly caterpillar that had turned into an even uglier moth. Though he had become 'one of them' he had a low regard for adults and an even lower regard for children. Probably because they had something he had lost forever and his envy gnawed at him.

Soon after this incident and although he was still well under age, he had started frequenting the local public house at the little 'off sales' room and when finances permitted, he would happily consume an amount of

Kimberley Best Bitter brewed by Hardy and Hansons. He had never liked school of course, but he now hated it even more and trouble became his new friend. His only salvation became music and he sank himself into it. Music saved him from Armageddon, for it brought a creative side out of him that Sam didn't know he possessed. Gradually, he settled down to the idea that he was growing up and began to hate the world a little less. He once again started to talk to people under his own age and generally clawed and climbed back onto the rails of life, to get run over by the express train of love. Oh dear .... that's bad news! But that's another story.